Lecture Notes in Computer Science 1419

Edited by G. Goos, J. Hartmanis and J. van Leeuwen

Springer-Verlag Berlin Heidelberg GmbH

Giovanni Vigna (Ed.)

Mobile Agents
and Security

Springer

Series Editors

Gerhard Goos, Karlsruhe University, Germany
Juris Hartmanis, Cornell University, NY, USA
Jan van Leeuwen, Utrecht University, The Netherlands

Volume Editor

Giovanni Vigna
University of California, Computer Science Department
Santa Barbara, CA 93106-5110, USA
E-mail: vigna@cs.ucsb.edu

Cataloging-in-Publication data applied for

Die Deutsche Bibliothek - CIP-Einheitsaufnahme

Mobile agents and security / Giovanni Vigna (ed.).

(Lecture notes in computer science ; Vol. 1419)
ISBN 978-3-540-64792-8

CR Subject Classification (1991): E.3, D.4.6, C.2, I.2.11, K.6.5, K.4.4

ISSN 0302-9743

ISBN 978-3-540-64792-8   ISBN 978-3-540-68671-2 (eBook)

DOI 10.1007/978-3-540-68671-2

Originally published by Springer-Verlag Berlin Heidelberg New York in 1998

Typesetting: Camera-ready by author
SPIN 10637419   06/3142 – 5 4 3 2 1 0   Printed on acid-free paper

Preface

New paradigms can popularize old technologies. A new "standalone" paradigm, the electronic desktop, popularized the personal computer. A new "connected" paradigm, the web browser, popularized the Internet. Another new paradigm, the mobile agent, may further popularize the Internet by giving people greater access to it with less effort.

Mobile Agent Paradigm

The mobile agent paradigm integrates a network of computers in a novel way designed to simplify the development of network applications. To an application developer the computers appear to form an electronic world of places occupied by agents. Each agent or place in the electronic world has the authority of an individual or an organization in the physical world. The authority can be established, for example, cryptographically.

A mobile agent can travel from one place to another subject to the destination place's approval. The source and destination places can be in the same computer or in different computers. In either case, the agent initiates the trip by executing a "go" instruction which takes as an argument the name or address of the destination place. The next instruction in the agent's program is executed in the destination place, rather than in the source place. Thus, in a sense, the mobile agent paradigm reduces networking to a program instruction.

A mobile agent can interact programmatically with the places it visits and, if the other agents approve, with the other agents it encounters in those places. An agent typically travels to obtain a service offered by an agent in a distant place. An agent might travel from a place in a personal computer to a "theater ticketing place" in a network server. Upon arrival, the agent might purchase theater tickets by interacting with a resident "theater ticketing agent". Thus agents can be instruments of electronic commerce.

Mobile Agent Advantages

The familiar remote procedure call (RPC) paradigm uses networks to carry messages —data— that request and confirm services. A client orchestrates the work of a server with a series of requests, sent from client to server, and responses, sent from server to client. To delete from a file server all files two weeks old might require one request to list the files and their modification dates and another to delete each sufficiently old file. Software on the client decides which files to delete. Deleting n files requires $2(n + 1)$ messages.

The new mobile agent paradigm uses networks to carry objects —data and procedures— that are to be executed in the presence of service providers. A client orchestrates the work of a server by sending to the server an agent whose procedure makes all of the required requests when it's executed. Deleting the old files —no matter how many— requires moving just one agent between computers. All of the orchestration, including the analysis that decides which files are old enough to delete, is done "on-site" at the server.

One advantage of mobile agents is performance. While two computers in an RPC network require ongoing communication for ongoing interaction, two computers in a mobile agent network can interact without the network's help once it has moved an agent that embodies the desired interaction from one computer to the other. The lower the network's throughput or the higher its latency or cost, the greater the performance advantage.

Another advantage of mobile agents is automation. A user can direct an agent to carry out a long sequence of tasks and then send the agent on its way. The tasks may require the agent to travel to many servers. The user's computer need be connected to the network only long enough to allow the agent to leave and perhaps later return. Thus mobile agent networks enable users to automate tasks that today they must perform interactively.

A third advantage of mobile agents is ease of software distribution. Agents enable applications to distribute themselves among the various computers on which they must execute. If installed on a client computer, an application can expand to encompass one or more servers. If installed on a server, an application can expand to encompass any number of client computers (in order to offer a service "door to door"). Thus a mobile agent network, like a personal computer, is an open platform for application developers.

Mobile Agent Applications

Users delegate to agents extended or complicated tasks they'd rather not perform themselves. Among the special talents of agents are watching, searching, and arranging.

Watching. In an investment application, a user's agent might monitor the stock market and notify the user when a specified stock reaches a specified price. The agent travels from a client computer to a stock server where it waits for the event to occur.

Searching. In a shopping application, a user's agent might determine the lowest price at which a specified product is sold. The agent travels from a client computer to a directory server and then to the commerce servers of merchants it selects from the directory.

Arranging. In an entertainment application, a user's agent might arrange a "night on the town" involving dinner and the theater, selecting a restaurant with a specified cuisine and price range and timing the reservation to allow for travel to the theater. The agent travels from a client computer to a restaurant reservation server and a theater ticketing server.

As in the last example, mobile agents can create new services by combining existing ones. In this way particularly, mobile agent networks are open platforms for developers.

The Technical Challenge

The mobile agent paradigm has problems as well as promise. Most of the problems have to do with safety and security. The mobile agent paradigm is most platform-like and so delivers the greatest value not when my agent visits my place, but when it visits yours. Before you can allow this, you must be sure that my agent, for example, can't access information you didn't intend for it to have, can't accidentally go into an infinite loop and so squander your resources, and can't deliberately interfere with the agents of other users.

In this book, you'll hear from some of the most prominent researchers in the mobile agent field. They'll tell you what they've accomplished and what remains to be accomplished. You'll gain a good understanding of the mobile agent paradigm —especially an understanding of how the paradigm can be made safe. Perhaps you'll be inspired to take on some of the remaining work yourself. We'd welcome your help.

Sunnyvale, California   James E. White
March 1998   Chief Technology Officer
                                                  General Magic, Inc.

Table of Contents

Part IV: Active Content and Security

Introduction

Mobile code technologies are receiving a great deal of interest from both industry and academia. The ability to move computations across the nodes of a wide area network allows deployment of services and applications in a more flexible, dynamic, and customizable way with respect to the well-known client-server paradigm. Yet, the wide acceptance of the mobile code approach is hampered by the security issues that arise when executable content and associated execution state (often referred to as *agents* or *mobile computations*) are moved among different computational environments (called *places* or *sites*).

Mobile agent systems provide a computing infrastructure upon which distributed applications belonging to different and potentially untrusted users can execute concurrently. Moreover, the sites composing the infrastructure may be managed by different authorities (e.g., a university or a company) with different and possibly conflicting objectives and may communicate across untrusted communication infrastructures, e.g., the Internet. In this scenario several attacks are possible. Unauthorized people may eavesdrop network traffic to access or modify agents while the agents are in transit over the network. Agents may attack the sites supporting their execution to gain privileged or unrestricted access to resources and private information (e.g., the password file of a UNIX machine). Attacks may also try to misuse the services offered by a site to probe and exploit the vulnerabilities of other systems. The Internet worm showed the effectiveness of this approach ten years ago.

Some of these security concerns have been studied by the distributed systems community for a long time. However, mechanisms and technologies developed to secure communication and control access to resources must be adapted to take into account mobility. In addition, the mobile code approach introduces a new security issue: the protection of mobile agents from malicious sites. In fact, sites could tamper with agents' code or state in order to disclose private information, gain competitive advantage with respect to other sites, or "brainwash" agents so that they will attack other sites (or agents). This new security issue is particularly challenging since it is difficult—if not impossible—to protect an executing program from the interpreter responsible for its execution.

Research on mobile agent security has delivered a number of mechanisms that follow different approaches in addressing the aforementioned security issues. Some of these mechanisms have been embedded into mobile agent systems to provide secure platforms for network programming. This book presents a collection of invited papers from researchers that provided insights and novel ideas to secure the dangerous world of mobile agents.

Overview

The book is organized in four parts: (I) Foundations, (II) Security Mechanisms, (III) Mobile Code Systems, and (IV) Active Content and Security.

Part I contains chapters providing a discussion of security issues and theoretical work on mobile code security. The chapter by David Chess presents a comprehensive overview of the security issues involved in mobile code systems. The chapter by James Riordan and Bruce Schneier presents a cryptographic technique to generate secret keys in hostile environments. The chapter by Dennis Volpano and Geoffrey Smith describes how security influences the design of languages supporting code mobility. It is followed by a chapter by Tomas Sander and Christian Tschudin that discusses the use of encrypted function computation in mobile code systems.

Part II contains chapters describing mechanisms that address security problems associated with mobile code. The chapter by George Necula and Peter Lee describes the proof-carrying code approach, which associates a mobile agent with a formal proof of its behavior. The chapter by Fritz Hohl describes an approach to protect mobile agents against malicious sites that is based on code obfuscation. The chapter by Shimshon Berkovits, Joshua Guttman, and Vipin Swarup describes an architecture to achieve authentication and protection of mobile agents. The chapter by Giovanni Vigna describes cryptographic tracing, a mechanism to detect illegal tampering with code and state of a moving agent.

Part III contains descriptions of mobile code systems and how security mechanisms have been introduced into their architecture. The chapter by Robert Gray, George Cybenko, David Kotz, and Daniela Rus describes the security architecture of D'Agents, a multiple-language mobile agent system. The chapter by Günter Karjoth, Danny Lange, and Mitsuru Oshima describes how security issues have been tackled in the IBM Aglets system. The chapter by Li Gong and Roland Schemers describes new features to protect and sign Java objects.

Part IV describes approaches to the problem of managing executable content in the World Wide Web. The chapter by John Ousterhout, Jacob Levy, and Brent Welch describes Safe-Tcl, an extension of the Tcl language for safe interpretation of executable content coming from untrusted sources. The chapter by Flavio De Paoli, Andre Dos Santos, and Richard Kemmerer describes the vulnerabilities of existing "secure" WWW browsers.

Acknowledgments

We would like to thank the anonymous reviewers for their help and excellent reviewing. In addition, we thank Carlo Ghezzi, Arno Jacobsen, Ralph Keller, Gian Pietro Picco, Christian Tschudin, Jan Vitek, and Sharon Webb for their help in the editing of this volume.

Milano, February 1998   Giovanni Vigna

Security Issues in Mobile Code Systems

David M. Chess

High Integrity Computing Lab, IBM T. J. Watson Research Center
Hawthorne, NY, USA
chess@watson.ibm.com

Abstract. In mobile code systems, programs or processes travel from host to host in order to accomplish their goals. Such systems violate some of the assumptions that underlie most existing computer security implementations. In order to make these new systems secure, we will have to deal with a number of issues that previous systems have been able to ignore or sidestep. This paper surveys the assumptions that mobile code systems violate (including the identification of programs with persons, and other assumptions that follow from that), the new security issues that arise, and some of the ways that these issues will be addressed.

1 Introduction

In December of 1987, somewhere in Western Europe, a student wrote a program called CHRISTMA EXEC, and sent it out across the European academic computer network known as EARN. When executed, the program displayed a picture of a Christmas tree, and then sent a copy of itself to everyone in the user's electronic mail address book [1,2]. The recipients, seeing what appeared to be a benign greeting card program sent from someone that they probably knew, in many cases received and executed the program, and it continued to spread. Before measures were put into place to contain it, millions of copies of CHRISTMA EXEC had flooded the communication links within EARN, BIT-NET (the related U.S. academic computer network) and VNET (IBM's internal company computer network). Some systems were brought down entirely, and many hours were spent understanding the problem, clearing out communication links, and putting safeguards in place to prevent re-infestation.

In November of 1988, a graduate student at Cornell University wrote a program that took advantage of a number of bugs and weaknesses in Unix(tm) security to send copies of itself from system to system in the Internet (which at the time consisted of fewer than 100,000 host machines). The program spread much faster and more prolifically than even the author had apparently intended, and before it was analyzed, tracked down, and eradicated, hundreds or perhaps thousands of systems had been overwhelmed by copies of the "worm" [3].

In both of these incidents, programs overwhelmed the networks of the time simply by spawning copies of themselves in ways that the systems were not

G. Vigna (Ed.): Mobile Agents and Security
LNCS 1419, pp. 1–14, 1998. © Springer–Verlag Berlin Heidelberg 1998

prepared to deal with. Both programs functioned by arranging to be executed upon arrival (in the case of the Internet worm) or upon some simple user action (in the case of CHRISTMA). And in both cases the advice of the general security community was the same: do not allow programs to execute on arrival, and do not make it too easy for users to execute programs received across the network. IBM offered a special version of the RECEIVE command which would automatically rename incoming programs to make them not immediately executable: users would have to take an additional explicit step before executing the program. The Unix security bugs that the Internet worm exploited were carefully documented, and system administrators were urged to install updates and patches to correct them. "Don't let programs become mobile," the security community said, "It's too dangerous."

In 1993, General Magic Inc. introduced Telescript [4], a language and architecture for fully mobile programs. While Telescript itself has not been a commercial success, the ideas that it embodies (themselves anticipated by earlier ideas about active mail [5,6] and distributed programming ([7], [8], [9] and many others)) helped prepare the ground for Java [10], which by 1997 had over 100 licensees, and thousands of programmers working on at least slightly-mobile programs. The typical Java program in 1997 is mobile only in the most limited sense: it travels from a server to a client, executes, and dies. But various efforts are underway to produce more general mobile code systems using Java [11,12,13], and several other systems for mobile code are in active development [14,15,16,17].

Clearly it is no longer possible for the security community to say simply "don't do that." Mobile code systems are becoming popular and ubiquitous, and while there may still be some question as to how sound the technical reasons for that are [18], the security issues that these systems raise must now be dealt with more thoroughly.

Why do mobile code systems raise new security issues at all? They do so because they violate a number of assumptions that underlie most existing computer security measures. In the rest of this paper, we will examine those assumptions, the ways that mobile code systems violate them, and the consequences of that violation for making the systems secure.

2   Common Assumptions

2.1   Identifying Programs with Persons

The most important assumption that mobile code systems violate is:

> Whenever a program attempts some action, we can easily identify a person to whom that action can be attributed, and it is safe to assume that that person intends the action to be taken.

For all intents and purposes, that is, every program that you run may be treated as though it were an extension of yourself. For brevity, we will refer to this as the Identity Assumption, since it asserts that the intentions of the user are identical to the actions of the program. Most existing computer security systems are based on this assumption, and the best-explored areas of computer security theory also incorporate it. The most common manifestation of the Identity Assumption in implemented systems looks something like this:

> *When a program attempts some action, we can determine whether or not the action should be permitted by consulting the details of the action, and the rights that have been granted to the user running the program.*

There are exceptions to this in some implemented systems. The best-known is probably the setuid feature of many Unix-inspired operating systems [19]. In these systems, a program can be specially marked to indicate that the requests that it makes should be allowed or disallowed according to the rights granted to some other user (or pseudo-user) rather than the person actually running the program.

While this feature can be used to restrict the rights of a program, it is more often used to expand them: a program that is "setuid root" can access files and other system resources on behalf of the user running the program, even though the user himself may not be authorized to touch those resources directly. Programs that are "setuid root" are of course notorious for introducing security holes into systems [20].

For an implementation to do user-based security checks in the obvious way, the system must have some notion of the rights granted to the user running each program. That is

> *Only persons that are known to the system can execute programs on the system.*

and of course a large part of traditional computer security is involved in making sure that someone unknown to the system cannot masquerade as someone known, in order to obtain access rights.

Another simplifying assumption that is related to the Identity Assumption is

> *There is one security domain corresponding to each user; all actions within that domain can be treated the same way.*

(This use of "domain" is in the sense of [21]: a single security-relevant entity.) A particular special case of this assumption is

> *Single-user systems require no security.*

Since the same user that runs all the programs on the system also owns all the resources on the system, the Identity Assumption tells us that any action taken by a program in such a system is an authorized action; no attempted action should ever fail for security reasons, so no security is required (beyond, perhaps, determining that the person sitting at the keyboard is who we think he is; but we can do that with a padlock on the power switch).

Although the assumption sounds implausible when expressed this baldly, it is the case that most single-user workstations in use today incorporate no security whatever, aside from possibly a simple password, or a key-lock on the power switch.

2.2   Trojan Horses are Rare

Now the Identity Assumption has never been entirely valid: there have always been programs which did something other than what the person executing the program intended (in fact, most programs have at one time or another done that!). But most of these failures of identity have been due to program bugs or failures, not intentional attacks, so we have not expected security systems to deal with them.

Trojan horses, programs purposely designed to attack a system by doing something other than what the user intended, have been rare and (until recently) largely insignificant. This has been true both in the commercial marketplace (where most programs have been purchased from reliable suppliers) and in the academic and research worlds (where exchange has been largely between trusted colleagues). It is only the rarity of these attacks that has made it possible to make the Identity Assumption and still have an acceptably secure system.

The primary reason that Trojan horses have been rare is another fact, a fact which serves as an underlying assumption itself:

> *Essentially all programs are obtained from easily-identifiable and generally trusted sources.*

When the origin of a program can be easily identified, the program is unlikely to contain intentionally malicious code, since the person who put it there would be unlikely to escape detection and punishment. (Computer viruses, as well as mobile code systems, represent violations of this assumption.)

Providers of programs tend to be trustworthy, and trusted, because if they were not they could not stay in business. Essentially all programs come from institutions that are in the business of providing software for a fee, or from colleagues that we know and trust. This is a social, not a technical, aspect of computer security, but it allows a great simplification in the technical aspects of implementation, since nearly all the time we can assume that if a program is attempting an action, the user running the program intends that (or at least would not mind that) the action will be carried out.

Not only can we generally assume that the user of a program trusts the provider of the program, but at least in the commercial case we can make some assumptions the other way as well. Since a business relationship (typically customer to vendor) exists, commercial custom and law place some restraints on what the user of a program will do with it. Well-understood mechanisms of copyright law and commercial custom prevent or control massive unauthorized copying of software, and a vendor generally has at least some idea of who is using the product. Trade secret and contract law protect especially valuable programs in some circumstances, and so on.

The users of a given piece of software are restrained by law and custom from various actions against the manufacturer's interests.

In the case of business software in particular, a manufacturer's major customers are often in an ongoing relationship with the manufacturer, and their (corporate) identities more or less well-known. (In the case of research or educational software, the supplier may not *care* what the users do with it.) This assumption is again primarily non-technical, but it sets an important part of the playing-field in which software is produced and sold.

2.3   The Origin of Attacks

Given the Identity Assumption, and the assumption about origins, we can say something about the sources of most security threats:

Significant security threats come from attackers running programs with the intent of accomplishing unauthorized results.

That is, the scenarios to worry about involve attackers masquerading as someone else in order to take actions that they themselves are not permitted to take, or exploiting bugs in the security system to allow their programs to do things that violate the system's security policy. The prototypical "evil hacker" scenario [22,23] is always along these lines.

Security theory has provided us with models [24,25] that allow us to take other kinds of attacks, including Trojan horses and other failures of the Identity Assumption, into account, but of the millions of deployed computer systems in the world today, few have benefited directly from those models. Most computer security efforts have gone into systems for user authentication (passwords, physical keys, biometric authentication), and user-based access control systems. Under the traditional assumptions, once we have satisfied ourselves who the user is, and made sure that programs run by that user can do only those things that that user is allowed to do, we're done.

2.4   Programs Stay Put

Another class of assumption that mobile code systems violate, and that are only loosely related to the Identity Assumption, have to do with program movement itself.

Programs cross administrative boundaries only rarely, and only when people intentionally transmit them.

The CHRISTMA and Internet worms were able to spread because the systems on which they ran incorporated this assumption, and the worms violated it. The existing security measures placed no special limits on the ability of a program to send itself from place to place, or to make copies of itself, because that sort of attack was not considered significant (or was not considered at all).

If programs are generally assumed to be immobile, processes are even more so:

> *A given instance of a program runs entirely on one machine; processes do not cross administrative boundaries at all.*

So while it is necessary to protect processes from each other within a single multi-user system, there is no need to consider inter-machine communication channels or intermediate nodes when considering the security of a program in process. (This assumption is of course violated by any fully distributed-processing system, not only by mobile code systems.)

A related assumption is

> *A given program runs on only one particular operating system.*

If we make that assumption, we can also assume that

> *Computer security is provided by the operating system.*

This is a very reasonable-sounding assumption, and it simplifies life greatly. Since the operating system is the channel through which all resource requests must pass, it provides an obvious place to implement a reference monitor (again in the sense of [21]) to control whether or not a given request from a given program should be granted. As we will see, this is another assumption that some mobile code systems violate, with interesting consequences.

3   Mobile Code Systems

Mobile code systems in use or in development today violate all of the assumptions laid out above. Because they do so, they present a number of new challenges for the design and implementation of computer security systems. Some of the requirements of these new systems have been anticipated, partially or wholly, by existing theoretical and practical work, but because this work has not been applied to large-scale real world implementations, there are likely to be places where both theory and experience are sparse or lacking. Only actual experience with widely-deployed systems will tell us where we need most urgently to shine the light of theory.

The other papers in this collection go into detail on the specific security issues that arise in mobile code systems. In the rest of this paper, we will endeavor to paint a broad outline of the field in which these issues lie, using the security assumptions presented above (or their negations) as a sort of road map.

To begin, we will simply list the facts about mobile code systems that violate each of the assumptions above. Not all of these facts apply to all systems, of course, but each applies to some significant mobile code system that is either deployed or under serious consideration today.

> *In mobile code systems, many programs may be obtained from unknown or untrusted sources.*

The social reasons that lead us to trust a program purchased from a software vendor do not apply to a program that arrives in a piece of mail, or that runs when a user clicks on a hypertext link, or that sends itself to a distant host. Without carefully-designed infrastructure, it may be impossible to identify the author or sender of the program, and even if an individual or organization can be positively identified, we may have no way to judge how much trust it is reasonable to assign to them.

The Identity Assumption itself is therefore violated, because

> When a program attempts some action, we may be unable to identify a person to whom that action can be attributed, and it is not safe to assume that any particular person intends the action to be taken.

or in implementation terms

> When a program attempts some action, we cannot determine whether or not the action should be permitted by simply consulting the rights that have been granted to the user running the program, since the program may well not reflect the intent of that user.

This considerably complicates the issue of security in mobile code systems, since we can no longer do the obvious table-lookup to see if an action should be permitted. Even when we can identify a person to whom the program's actions should be attributed, that person may be no one we know; that is

> The person most relevant to determining the trustworthiness of a program may be someone not known to the system.

This suggests that we must either have a way of finding out things about users who are unknown to the system, or lump all unknown users together into one (presumably completely untrusted) class.

Since a user of a mobile code system may cause many different programs to be executed, and these programs may come from different sources with different levels of trust, we have

> There are potentially many security domains corresponding to each user; different actions initiated by the same user may need to be treated differently.

and in particular

> Even single-user systems require security.

Although I own all the resources on my system, I need a reference monitor in place to ensure that a tic-tac-toe game that I load from the Web cannot erase my documents, alter my spreadsheets, or order caviar on my behalf. Whole new classes of threat become important.

> Significant security threats come from authorized users running programs which take advantage of the users' rights in order to accomplish undesirable results.

As the CHRISTMA and Internet Worm examples above demonstrate, uncontrolled replication of mobile code can itself constitute an attack, even if no caviar is ordered:

> *Programs cross administrative boundaries often, and can arrange for their own transmission and reproduction.*

The fact that a program in a mobile code system can travel without explicit human action is a key consideration in mobile code security. Because programs can arrive and begin to execute on a system without the owner of that system realizing that a new program is running, it is especially important that the automatic mechanisms protecting the system be reliable; they cannot rely on the judgement of some human directly deciding to run each program.

Not only can programs travel, but (at least in some mobile code systems) processes and their data and state information can travel as well:

> *A given instance of a program may move across multiple machines; processes can cross administrative boundaries.*

This has implications for security, most obviously in protecting process state information from snooping at untrusted intermediate nodes, but also in subtler worries about possible tampering with state information by the hosts the process actually runs on.

In many mobile code systems, programs can travel between hosts that are running entirely different operating systems:

> *A mobile program may run on many different operating systems.*

If some of these operating systems have no, or inadequate, native security, we can no longer assume that the operating system will provide the reference monitors that we need:

> *Computer security may not be provided by the operating system; program receivers, language interpreters and runtime libraries must also be security-aware.*

And finally, the producers of mobile code must work under a somewhat different set of assumptions about their users:

> *The users of a given piece of software may be completely unknown to the owner of the software, and may not be restrained by law or custom from various actions against the owner's interests.*

The challenges for mobile code security systems therefore include: determining the originator of an incoming program, deciding how much to trust that originator if it is someone not directly known to the system, protecting even single-user systems against malicious programs, preventing uncontrolled replication of mobile code objects, and protecting mobile programs themselves against malicious acts, both in transit and while executing on foreign hosts.

3.1   Authentication in Mobile Code Systems

At one level, the problem of authentication in mobile code systems is very similar to the problem of authentication in distributed systems in general. We have a good deal of both theory and experience in this area; we have methods, mostly cryptography-based, of ensuring within a reasonable doubt that a given person really sent a given message, and that the message has not been altered in transit (see for instance [26]).

On the other hand, some of the known difficulties with standard authentication systems are even more serious in mobile code systems. If we use a digital signature for authentication, and that signature is based on an asymmetric cryptosystem, we must be able to reliably get the public half of the sender's key in order to verify the signature. No strong and general solutions to the key distribution problem are known. Solutions that work well in small groups of people that know each other, or in applications where authentication is only casually required, do not scale well to mobile code or electronic commerce systems where critical transactions with strangers may occur at a high rate, and require strong protection.

Once we do have an acceptable key-distribution system, and can satisfy ourselves that a given incoming program or process really is signed by a given principal, there is still the problem of determining the correct semantics of the signature. Just what, that is, does a signature mean? There are a number of different signatures that might be affixed to a traveling process, and a number of different parties that might have signed it. The original author of the program may have signed the program itself. One or more certifying agencies may have signed it, to attest to its benignity, efficiency, or that the author has paid his taxes. The original sender, the principal that launched the program into the network, may have signed the program, its initial state vector, and perhaps a list of hosts that it was expected to visit. Any hosts that the process passed through before reaching the current node may have signed a statement about what the process did while resident there, including the final state vector that the process reached.

On the other hand, all this signing and forwarding of signatures may not be worth the trouble; as well as technical infrastructure, we need to have conventions and expectations about who needs to sign what, how each principal can indicate clearly just what its signature means, and how the various sorts of signature need to be interpreted.

Other papers in this volume provide more detail on some of the work going on in this critical part of the field.

3.2   Reputation and Trust

Once we have determined just who has signed a given incoming process, and what the various signatures attached to it mean, how do we proceed? If we know something about each of the signers, we will have some basis for decision.

If one or more of the signers are strangers to us, we can lump them together with all other unknown principals.

But the class of unknown principals must of course be trusted not at all, since it presumably includes at least one malicious entity. (We could choose to trust all principals whose signatures we can verify, on the theory that if they do damage us we will at least know who to prosecute, but this hardly seems to count as a *security* policy.) It would be desirable, then, to have a way of assigning some level of trust to at least some specific principals that we currently have no knowledge of.

Some work has been done in this field [27], but not enough. Its importance can only increase as it becomes more and more common for a system to encounter parties that it has no prior opinion of, in a context where the appropriate level of trust, if only it could be determined accurately, would allow more productive interactions than the default level of trust (or distrust) between strangers.

In the terminology of [27], a service that provides information about the trustworthiness of principals does so by providing endorsements; such a service can be thought of as a reputation server. In the non-electronic world, the role of reputation server is filled by bodies such as the American Automobile Association (which rates hotels, restaurants, and so on), the Better Business Bureau, Underwriters Laboratories, and so on. While network reputation services will be vulnerable to many of the same weaknesses and abuses that their offline counterparts suffer from, some form of reputation infrastructure will be a valuable enabler for mobile code, and for electronic commerce in particular.

3.3   Secure Languages

There are (at least) three different approaches to running a program securely. If the operating system supports an appropriate security model, you can start up a process or address space or equivalent, assign it the proper attributes, and start the program running in it. Work is being done on operating system architectures to support mobile code [15], but since many mobile code systems have operating system independence as a goal, the operating system cannot always be relied upon.

If you want to be able to run incoming machine code without depending on operating system security, you can apply a security policy upon receipt, to decide whether to run the code or not, but once the code is given control, it will have full run of the system. This design seems best suited for systems in which only programs signed by the most trusted principals will be run at all, and even they will be run only on non-critical hosts.

Thirdly, you can create mobile programs in a language for some virtual machine, and execute them through an interpreter that lies above the native processor and operating system, and is in charge of enforcing security. This third approach seems to be the most promising, and is in use in a number of existing mobile code systems [4,10,14,15,17].

Designing a language that can be interpreted securely, according to a wide variety of possible security policies, and actually implementing a secure interpreter, are major challenges. Strategies include placing security restrictions on an existing interpreted language such as Tcl or Perl, and designing a new language and virtual machine from scratch, as has been done in Java and Inferno.

In [28], Wallach, Balfanz, Dean, and Felten outline a set of criteria for effective implementation of security in a mobile code system, and apply it to various alternative approaches to security in Java. Any other secure interpreter must withstand similar analysis; bugs in existing interpreters for secure languages have caused considerable press attention and user concern. Although to date we know of no significant attacks exploiting these bugs, as mobile code systems become more pervasive and are used for more critical applications, the security of both the design and the implementation will no doubt be subject to actual attacks.

3.4   Preventing Floods

Our first examples of mobile code attacks, the CHRISTMA and Internet worms, demonstrate the power of simple replication to cause serious problems in distributed systems. The problem and some partial solutions to it have been known for some time, but no perfect solution exists even when the objects being replicated are passive messages [29]; and mobile code systems introduce fresh complications.

The original Telescript model of mobile code control involved giving each mobile process a limited supply of funds (called "teleclicks"), and requiring a process to expend a certain quantity of those funds in order to accomplish various results (including, presumably, spawning new copies of itself). This puts some restrictions on replication by out-of-control programs; on the other hand it may also prevent desirable behavior, as when a process hot on the trail of some obscure information needs to access more hosts than usual in order to find the facts it is looking for.

If mobile processes can interact, and even under some circumstances alter each other, it may even be possible for a virus to spread among and between mobile programs. If I receive and execute a program from a trusted friend, and it contains a virus, the virus may (because of the trust I place in my friend) have the ability to find other programs on my system and alter them, or even create brand-new programs, and transmit the infected results to people who trust me. If the virus has access to my signing key, it may be able to convince those friends to trust the infected programs as much as I trusted the original, and continue to spread, despite the protection of digital signatures. This can occur even without systems that explicitly support mobile code, of course, but the danger is much more severe in mobile code systems because of the potential for extremely rapid spread. To prevent this sort of replication, mobile code security systems must be designed with the utmost care, and resources such as signing keys and transmission channels must be carefully protected.

3.5 The Problem of Malicious Hosts

The most obvious security problems in mobile code systems involve protecting users and hosts from attacks that arise from incoming mobile programs. But another class of problem involves attacks on the mobile programs themselves, from malicious hosts or intermediaries.

Protecting a mobile process in transit is relatively simple: the sending host should bundle up the process, its programs and state, sign the result if necessary, bundle the whole up in a secure envelope such that only the destination host will be able to read it (this depends, again, on an infrastructure that allows the required distribution of keys), and then send the bundle off into the network. There are still vulnerabilities here, to traffic analysis, stolen keys, attacks on the key-distribution infrastructure, and so forth, but at least the problems are mostly well understood.

The problem of protecting mobile code is much more severe once the process arrives at a server on which it is to execute [30]. It seems obvious that if a host is to execute a process, the process can have no secrets from that host. There is nothing to prevent a host from analyzing the program, from running an altered form of the program, from changing the program's state vector before running it, or from running it multiple times with different initial states and observing the results. While a mobile process can carry some secrets, they must be stored in a form that even the process itself cannot directly access (encrypted with a key that the process does not have, for instance), if they are to be kept secret from the hosts that execute the process.

There are some possible solutions to some of these problems. The most obvious is to keep one's secrets at home, and only send out mobile programs that carry nothing of significant value. Secure hardware [31] can provide islands of trust even within untrusted hosts, at some cost. Other solutions involve requiring mobile programs to "phone home" for certain key data items periodically, or sending duplicate programs to a number of different independently controlled hosts and comparing the results, to establish with some certainty that the result comes from a faithful execution of the program. For some classes of short-lived secret, it may be possible to dispatch a mobile program that holds the secret, with a reasonable expectation that no malicious host will be able to extract and exploit the secret before its value expires [32]. And some new cryptographic work suggests that it may be possible for a mobile program to carry a secret key indirectly, so that it is able to produce signed statements of certain kinds without directly carrying the signing key [33].

But in general mobile programs are in a very asymmetrical power relationship with the hosts that execute them, and this is likely to remain one of the larger limitations on the use of mobile programs in the open network.

4 Conclusion

The design and implementation of mobile code systems includes all the security issues that arise in traditional stationary-code systems. But because mobile code systems violate many of the assumptions that underlie traditional security measures, a host of new issues also arise, and require new thinking and new solutions to address them. In particular, the fact that it is not always easy to identify a particular mobile process with a particular known principal, and depend on the operating system's reference monitors to enforce the corresponding security policy, means that we need to expand upon and refine much of what we are used to doing in computer security.

References

1. V. McLellan, "Computer Systems Under Siege", *The New York Times*, January 17, 1988.
2. Internal IBM documents.
3. E.H. Spafford, "The Internet Worm: An Analysis," Purdue University Technical Report CSD-TR-823, November 28, 1988.
4. J.E. White, "Telescript technology: the foundation for the electronic marketplace," General Magic Inc., Mountainview, California, 1994.
5. Y. Goldberg et al., "Active Mail: A Framework for Implementing Groupware", in *Proceedings of CSCW' 92*, Toronto 1992.
6. N. Borenstein, "Email with a mind of its own: the Safe-TCL language for enabled mail," in *ULPAA'94*, Boston 1994.
7. E. Jul et al., "Fine-grained mobility in the Emerald system," *ACM Transactions on Computer Systems*, 6(1), February 1988.
8. G. Ames et al., "The Eden system: A technical review," *IEEE Transactions on Software Engineering*, 11(1), January 1985.
9. F. Douglis, "Process migration in the Sprite operating system," Technical Report UCB/CSD 87/343, University of California at Berkeley, February 1987.
10. K. Arnold and J. Gosling, *The Java Programming Language*, Addison-Wesley, 1996.
11. D.B. Lange and M. Oshima, "Programming Mobile Agents in Java with the Java Aglet API," IBM Research, 1997, *http://www.trl.ibm.co.jp/aglets/aglet-book/*.
12. General Magic's Odyssey system, at *http://www.genmagic.com/agents/*.
13. ObjectScape's Voyager system, at *http://www.objectspace.com/Voyager/*.
14. R. Gray, "Agent Tcl: A flexible and secure mobile agent system". in *Proceedings of the Fourth Annual Tcl/Tk Workshop*, Monterey, 1996.
15. S. Dorward et al., "Inferno," in *IEEE Compcon '97 Proceedings*, 1997.
16. L. Cardelli, "Obliq: A language with distributed scope," Report 122, Digital Equipment Corporation Systems Research Center, 1994.
17. H. Peine, "Ara - Agents for Remote Action" in W. R. Cockayne and M. Zyda, *Mobile Agents: Explanations and Examples*, Manning/Prentice Hall, 1997.
18. D. Chess, C. Harrison, and A. Kershenbaum, "Mobile Agents: Are They a Good Idea?" in J. Vitek and C. Tschudin (eds) *Mobile Object Systems*, Springer, 1996.
19. D.M. Ritchie and K. Thompson, "The UNIX Time-Sharing System", *Communications of the ACM*, 17(7), July 1974.
20. S. Garfinkel and G. Spafford, *Practical Unix and Internet Security*, O'Reilly & Associates, 1996.
21. B. Lampson, "Protection," in *Proceedings of the Fifth Princeton Symposium on Information Sciences and Systems*, pp. 437-443, Princeton University, March 1971. Reprinted in Operating Systems Review, 8(1), pp. 18-24, January 1974.

22. C. Stoll, *The Cuckoo's Egg: Tracking a Spy Through the Maze of Computer Espionage*. New York: Pocket Books, 1989.
23. S. Dreyfus, *Underground*, Mandarin, Australia, 1997.
24. C.E. Landwehr, "Formal models for computer security," *ACM Computing Surveys*, 13(3), pp. 247-278, September 1981.
25. B. Lampson et al., "Authentication in Distributed Systems: Theory and Practice," *ACM Transactions on Computing Systems*, 10(4), pp. 265-310, November 1992.
26. C. Kaufman, R. Perlman, and M. Speciner, *Network Security: Private Communication in a Public World*, Prentice-Hall, 1995.
27. C. Lai, G. Medvinsky, and B.C. Neuman, "Endorsements, Licensing, and Insurance for Distributed System Services", in *Proceedings of the 2nd ACM Conference on Computer and Communications Security*, 1994.
28. D. Wallach et al. "Extensible Security Architectures for Java", Technical Report 546-97, Department of Computer Science, Princeton University, 1997.
29. U. Manber, "Chain Reactions in Networks", *IEEE Computer*, October 1990.
30. J. Ordille, "When agents roam, who can you trust?", *First IEEE Conference on Emerging Technologies and Applications in Communications*, May 1996.
31. E. Palmer, "An Introduction to Citadel – a secure crypto coprocessor for workstations", in *IFIP SEC'94 Conference*, Curacao, May 1994.
32. F. Hohl, "An Approach to Solve the Problem of Malicious Hosts in Mobile Agent Systems", draft, University of Stuttgart, 1997.
33. T. Sander and C. F. Tschudin, "Towards Mobile Cryptography" TR-97-049, International Computer Science Institute, Berkeley, November 1997.

Environmental Key Generation Towards Clueless Agents

James Riordan[*1] and Bruce Schneier[2]

[1] School of Mathematics, University of Minnesota
Minneapolis, MN 55455
`riordan@math.umn.edu`
[2] Counterpane Systems
101 E Minnehaha Parkway
Minneapolis, MN 55419, USA
`schneier@counterpane.com`

Abstract. In this paper, we introduce a collection of cryptographic key constructions built from environmental data that are resistant to adversarial analysis and deceit. We expound upon their properties and discuss some possible applications; the primary envisioned use of these constructions is in the creation of mobile agents whose analysis does not reveal their exact purpose.

1 Introduction

Traditional cryptographic systems rely upon knowledge of a secret key to decipher messages. One of the weaknesses induced by this reliance stems from the static nature of the secret keys: they do not depend upon temporal, spatial, or operational conditions. By contrast, the secrecy requirements of information are often strongly linked to these conditions. This disparity is, perhaps, most easily seen and most problematic in mobile agents.

Mobile agents, by nature, function in and move through a wide variety of environments. Security properties of these environments vary greatly which creates problems when the mobile agent needs to carry security sensitive, or otherwise private, material. If the agent passes through an insecure network it may be analyzed so that any information carried by the agent becomes available to the attacker.

This information is often private in nature, and cannot easily be disguised. For example, an agent written to conduct a patent search will reveal the nature of the information desired. This information may, in turn, reveal the intentions of the requester of that patent search.

The problem is somewhat similar to the one faced by designers of smart cards which keep secrets from the card's carrier. To solve that problem, smart card

---

[*] James Riordan is now with the IBM Zurich Research Laboratory in Switzerland.

G. Vigna (Ed.): Mobile Agents and Security
LNCS 1419, pp. 15–24, 1998. © Springer–Verlag Berlin Heidelberg 1998

designers have developed a number of techniques to make the hardware either tamper-resistant or tamper-evident thereby protecting the secret. Unfortunately these techniques are not applicable to mobile agents due to the fact that software, unlike hardware, is completely and trivially observable.

To address this class of problem we introduce the notion of *environmental key generation*: keying material that is constructed from certain classes of environmental data. Using these keys, agents could receive encrypted messages that they could only decrypt if some environmental conditions were true. Agents with data or executable code encrypted using such keys could remain unaware of their purpose until some environmental condition is met.[1]

Environmental key generation is similar to the idea of ephemeral keys: keys which are randomly created at the time of use and destroyed immediately afterward. Public-key systems for encrypting telephone conversations—the STU-III [6], the AT&T TSD [1], the Station-to-Station protocol [2]—make use of this idea. The communication model is different, however. Ephemeral keys are used when two parties want to communicate securely at a specific time, even though there is no secure channel available and the parties have not previously negotiated a shared secret key. Environmental key generation can be used when the sender wishes to communicate with the receiver, such that the receiver could only receive the message if some environmental conditions are true. Environmental key generation can even be used in circumstances where the receiver is not aware of the specific environmental conditions that the sender wants his communication to depend on.

The difficulty with constructing an environmental key generation protocol is that the threat model assumes that an attacker has complete control over the environment. All information available to the program is available to the attacker, all inputs to the program are supplied by the attacker and the program state itself is completely determined by the attacker. As such, the constructions must resist direct analysis and dictionary attacks in the form of Cartesian deception (in which the attacker lies about the environment).

Ultimately, if the attacker has access to both the agent and the activation environment (the environment in which the agent can construct its keys) then he will have access to all secret information as well. This is often not a problem.

In this paper, we propose three basic approaches toward securely generating cryptographic keys from environmental observations. The first involves direct manipulation of the environment in a specific and cryptographically unspoofable manner. The second involves reliance upon a partially trusted server. The third uses the obfuscation of the nature or value of the environmental data being sought through the use of one-way functions.

---

[1] These agents might reasonable be likened to the sleeper agents of "The Manchurian Candidate" and other Cold War era spy films.

2   Clueless Agents

In the basic construction, an agent has a cipher-text message (a data set, a series of instructions, etc.) and a method for searching through the environment for the data needed to generate the decryption key. When the proper environmental information is located, the key is generated, the cipher-text is decrypted, and the resulting plain-text it acted upon. Without the environmentally supplied input, the agent cannot decrypt its own message (i.e. it is *clueless*), and can be made cryptographically resistant to analysis aimed at determining the agent's function.

Let N be an integer corresponding to an environmental observation, $\mathcal{H}$ a one way function, M the hash $\mathcal{H}$ of the observation N needed for activation, $\oplus$ the bitwise *exclusive-or* operator, *comma* the catenation operator, R a nonce, & the bitwise *and* operator, and K a key. The value M is carried by the agent.

One way functions can be used to conduct tests and construct the keys in a way that examination of the agent does not reveal the required environmental information. A number of such constructions are possible:

- if $\mathcal{H}(N) = M$ then let $K := N$
- if $\mathcal{H}(\mathcal{H}(N)) = M$ then let $K := \mathcal{H}(N)$
- if $\mathcal{H}(N_i) = M_i$ then let $K := \mathcal{H}(N_1, ..., N_i)$
- if $\mathcal{H}(N) = M$ then let $K := \mathcal{H}(R_1, N) \oplus R_2$

The constructions differ in types of data which are most naturally provided as input or in the programmer's ability to determine the output (as needed by a threshold scheme 6.2); the important feature of each is knowledge of M does not provide knowledge of K.

This general sort of construction is not uncommon. The *if* clause of the first construction is used in most static encrypted password authentication schemes (e.g. Unix). As with static password schemes, dictionary attacks present a problem. The fact that an agent may pass through or even execute in a hostile environment compounds this problem greatly (as would publishing your password file). None the less, several useful and cryptographically viable constructions are possible.

3   Basic Constructions

The very simplest clueless agents look for their activation keys on a fixed data channel. Example channels include:

- Usenet news groups. A key could be embedded in any of several places in a (possibly anonymous) posting to a particular newsgroup. It could be the hash of a particular message, or the hash of a certain part of the message.
- Web pages. Likewise, a key could be explicitly or steganographically embedded in a web page or image.
- Mail messages. The message could contain a particular string that would serve as a key, or the key could be a hash of a message.

- File systems. A key could be located in a file, the hash of the file or the hash of a particular file name.
- Local network resources. A key could be generated as the hash of a local DNS block transfer or as a result of a broadcast ping packet. Threshold schemes would be particularly valuable with schemes like this.

If, for example, the agent knows that its activation key will be posted to a particular newsgroup, it would continuously scan the newsgroup looking for a message N such that $\mathcal{H}(\mathcal{H}(N)) = M$. An attacker would know that N would be posted to the newsgroup, but would need to see the message N before he could construct the key, $(\mathcal{H}(N))$, and thus figure out the agent's purpose.

The nature of the data channel determines the utility and properties of the construction based upon that channel. This nature includes:

- Who can directly or indirectly observe the channel?
- Who can manipulate parts or the whole of the channel?
- Along what paths does the channel flow?
- How do observations of the channel vary with the observer?

This abstract notion is best explained by a few diverse examples.

3.1   Example: Blind Search

We take the data channel to be an online database containing a list of patents with an online mechanism for executing search agents. The channel does not have a particularly interesting nature but yet generates an interesting agent.

We suppose that Alice has the an idea that she would like to patent. She wishes to conduct a patent search yet does not wish to describe her idea to the owners of the database search engine. This desire can be realized through the use of a clueless agent.

To make matters concrete, we assume that Alice's idea is to build a smoke detector with a "snooze alarm" so that she can temporarily de-activate the alarm without unplugging it.[2]

She begins by computing:

1. $N := $ a random nonce
2. $K := \mathcal{H}(\text{"smoke detector with snooze alarm"})$,
3. $M := E_K(\text{"report findings to alice@weaseldyne.com"})$, and
4. $O := \mathcal{H}(N \oplus \text{"smoke detector with snooze alarm"})$.

She then writes an agent which scans through the database taking hashes of five word sequences

- **for** five word sequence (x) **in** the database **do**
- **if** $\mathcal{H}(N \oplus (x)) = O$ **then** **execute**$= D_{\mathcal{H}(x)}(M)$

---

[2] This would be a very useful item for the kitchen; smoke alarm manufacturers take note.

The agent can now search through the database for references to "smoke detector with snooze alarm" without actually carrying any information from which "smoke detector with snooze alarm" could be derived.

In this example, if the owner of the database is watching all search agents in an attempt to steal idea, he will only observe a description of Alice's idea if he *already* has a description of the idea. Methods of rendering this scheme less sensitive to different wordings are discussed in Section 6.

3.2   Example: Intrusion Detection

One of the most problematic aspects of intrusion detection is that wide scale deployment of a particular method tends to limit its effectiveness. If an attacker has detailed knowledge of the detections system installed at a particular site, he is better able to avoid its triggers. As such, it would be better to deploy an intrusion detection system whose triggers are not easily analyzable. Environmental key generation could be used to encrypt sections of the intrusion detection's executable code until such time as a particular attack is executed.

While in this case the attacker could easily stage a dictionary attack by mimicking the LAN's behavior, such a simulation would require extensive knowledge of the LAN. Acquisition of that knowledge would likely to trigger the detection system.

3.3   Example: Network-Based Operation

It is often desirable to have an agent which can only run in certain environments. The agent may be collecting auditing data on certain types of machines or certain points in the network. It may need to carry out an electronic commerce transaction, but only from within the network of a certain vendor.

An interesting, although malicious, application of this sort of construction would the creation of a *directed virus*. Such a virus could carry a special set of special instructions which could only be run in a certain environment. The novelty of this construction is that examination of the virus without explicit knowledge of the activation environment would not reveal its "special instructions".

We suppose that Alice wishes to write a virus which should carry out the instructions if it finds itself inside weaseldyne.com so that it would be infeasible to determine what the special instructions are without knowing it is keyed for weaseldyne.com. Alice finds the name of a machine on the inside of weaseldyne.com's network. She does so through some combination of examining mailing list archives, social engineering, and assumptions about naming conventions (e.g. there is often a *theme*).

We will assume that the name of the machine is pooky.weaseldyne.com. She computes:

1. $K = \mathcal{H}(\text{"pooky.weaseldyne.com"})$
2. $M = E_K(\text{"report findings to alice@competitor.com"})$

She then writes a virus which, when activated, requests local DNS information and applies $\mathcal{H}$ to each entry looking for its key.

In this example, staging a dictionary attack is already quite difficult. Methods of making it yet more difficult are discussed in section 6.

4   Time Constructions

The time-based constructions allow key generation based on the time. These constructions rely upon the presence of a minimally trusted third party to prevent a date based dictionary attack. The third party is minimally trusted in the sense that it does not need to know either of the two parties nor does it need to know the nature of the the material for which it generates keys. These protocols have three distinct stages:

1. The programmer-server interaction, where the programmer gets an encryption key from the server.
2. The programmer-agent interaction, where the programmer gives the agent the encrypted message, some data required (but not sufficient) to decrypt the cipher-text, and information as to where to go to get the additional data required to decrypt the cipher-text.
3. The agent-server interaction, where the agent gets the data needed to construct the decryption key and decrypt the cipher-text.

Note that in several cases the first or last aspects are trivial and can be satisfied by publications by the sever.

The *forward-time* constructions permit key generation only after a given time while the *backward-time* permit key generation only before it. These constructions can be nested to permit key generation only during a certain time interval.

The main weakness of these constructions is that the server could collude with an attacker to analyze the agent. This type weakness can easily be abated using the methods discussed in section 6.

4.1   Forward-Time Hash Function

The first time-based construction uses a one-way function, such as SHA-1 [7] or RIPEMD-160 [3], as its sole cryptographic primitive. Let S be a secret belonging to the server.

1. The programmer sends the target time, T^*, and a nonce, R, to the server.
2. The server sets T to the current time and returns to the programmer T and $\mathcal{H}(\mathcal{H}(S,T^*),\mathcal{H}(R,T))$.
3. The programmer sets $P = \mathcal{H}(R,T)$ and $K = \mathcal{H}(\mathcal{H}(S,T^*),\mathcal{H}(R,T))$. The programmer uses K to encrypt the message to the agent, and gives the agent a copy of P. He then lets the agent loose in the world.
4. The agent continuously requests the current time's secret from the server.

5. The server returns $S_i = \mathcal{H}(S, T_i)$. (Alternatively, the server could simply continuously broadcast S_i and the agent could simply watch the broadcast stream.)
6. The agent tries to use $K = \mathcal{H}(S_i, P)$ to decrypt its instructions. It will succeed precisely when $S_i = \mathcal{H}(S, T^*)$ which is when $T_i = T^*$.

This construction has several properties worth listing:

- The use of the current time in the construction of P prevents an analyst from using the server to stage a dictionary attack.
- The form of the daily secret could easily be made hierarchical so that the secret for one day could be used to compute previous daily secrets.
- The use of a nonce, R, reduces the feasibility of a forward time dictionary attack against the server in addition to obscuring the request date of a particular key.
- Should this construction be used maliciously so that the courts order the server to participate in a particular analysis, the server could use P to compute an individual key without giving away all keys for that day.

4.2 Forward-Time Public Key

The second time-based construction uses public-key encryption, such as RSA [8] or ElGamal [4]. For each time T_i, the server has a method of generating a public-key/private-key key pair, (D_i, E_i). The server can either store these key pairs, or regenerate them as required.

1. The programmer sends a target time T^* to the server.
2. The server returns the public key, D^*, for that time.
3. The programmer uses D^* to encrypt the message to the agent. He then lets the agent loose in the world.
4. The agent continuously requests the current time's private key from the server.
5. The server returns E_i. (Again, the server could continuously broadcast E_i).
6. The agent tries to use E_i to decrypt its instructions. It will succeed precisely when $E_i = E^*$, which is when $T_i = T^*$.

This protocol has the advantage that the programmer need not interact with the server in Steps (1) and (2). The server could simply post the D_i values for values of i stretching several years in the future, and the programmer could just choose the one he needs. In this application, the server could be put in a secure location—in orbit on a satellite, for example—and be reasonably safe from compromise.

4.3 Backward-Time Hash Function

The backward time construction also uses one-way functions as its sole cryptographic primitive. Again S is a secret belonging to the server.

1. The programmer sends the target time T^* and a nonce R to the server.
2. The server returns $\mathcal{H}(S, R, T^*)$ if and only if T^* is in the future.
3. The programmer sets K to the returned value and gives the agent a copy of R and T^*.
4. At time T, the agent sends the target time T^* and a nonce R to the server. It will receive the valid key K in return if and only if T^* is later than T.

Backward time constructions in which the target time T^* is unknown to the agent are also possible and are explained in section 6.

5   General Server Constructions

The general server construct uses one-way functions and a symmetric encryption algorithm. Again S is a secret belonging to the server.

1. The programmer sends the server a program P and the hash of a particular possible output $\mathcal{H}(N)$ of the program P.
2. The server returns $E_S(P)$ and $\mathcal{H}(S, P, \mathcal{H}(N))$.
3. The programmer sets $K = \mathcal{H}(S, P, \mathcal{H}(N))$ and uses it to encrypt the message to the agent. The programmer then gives $E_S(P)$ to the agent.
4. The agent gives $E_S(P)$ to the server.
5. The server decrypts the program $P = D_S(E_S(P))$, executes it, and sets M equal to the hash of its output. It then returns $\mathcal{H}(S, P, M)$ to the agent.
6. The agent tries to use the returned value as its key. It will succeed precisely when the output of the run program matches the programmer's original expectations.

his generic construction requires a safe execution environment, as that provided by Java in web browsers, with the additional constraint that the environment does *not* contain the secret S.

While each of the previously discussed constructs can be built using this method, they loose several of the anonymity features, and require explicit agent-server interaction.

6   Further Constructions

These basic constructions can be assembled into higher level constructions.

6.1   Reduced dictionary

One way of making dictionary attacks [5] infeasible is forcing the attacker to use much too large a dictionary. Let S be a large collection of data and $S_l \subset S$ be a much smaller subset of S determined by the execution environment. Suppose that we know $x_1, \ldots x_n \in S_l$. Due to the size disparity between S and S_l it is feasible to search through all n-tuples in S_l such that $\mathcal{H}(\cdot, \ldots, \cdot) = \mathcal{H}(x_1, \ldots, x_n)$ while the analogous search in S is not possible.

A concrete example of this is to let $\mathcal{S}$ be the *complete* collection of canonical DNS names[3] of all hosts and $\mathcal{S}_l$ be the sub-collection of names from hosts inside a domain behind a firewall. Searching through all name triples in $\mathcal{S}_l$ would be quite easy while searching through all triples in $\mathcal{S}$ would be impossible.

This construction would be useful in the virus example of Section 3.3.

6.2   Thresholding

We note that we can easily create a threshold system using the ideas of secret sharing. Suppose that $\mathcal{S}$ is a set of observations of cardinality n and that we wish to be able to construct a key K if m of them are present. We let $T(m, n)$ be a secret sharing scheme with shares $s_1, \ldots, s_n$ for share holders $1, \ldots, n$. Then for each $x_i \in \mathcal{S}$ we tell the agent that share holder i has name $\mathcal{H}(N, x_i)$ and that his share is generated by the function $\mathcal{H}(\cdot) \oplus \mathcal{H}(x_i) \oplus s_i$.

6.3   Nesting

These constructions can be nested: one environmental key can decrypt a section of the agent, which would then yield another encrypted section requiring yet another environmental key. These nestings can be used to create more complex environmental constructions:

For example:

- Forward-time + Backward-time = time interval
- Forward-time + Basic = Forward time, but only if a specific event has occurred.

Agents can slough off previous information and thus can only be analyzed at times of metamorphosis. In other words, after an agent has triggered based on an environmental condition, an attacker could not analyze the agent to determine what the condition was. Moreover, the attacker could not tell where the post-transformation agent was a product of the pre-transformation agent. This properties gives rise to many useful anonymity constructions.

7   Conclusions

As applications that allow mobile code become more prevalent, people will want to limit what an attacker can learn about themselves. The notion of clueless agents presented in this paper will have all sorts of applications: blind search engines (patents and product ideas), Manchurian mobile agents, expiration dates by backward-time constructs, intrusion detection systems which are difficult to bypass (they can watch for exploit without revealing nature of the vulnerability they are guarding), logic bombs, directed viruses (both good and bad), remote alarms, etc. The notion of a software construction that hides its true nature is a powerful one, and we expect many other applications to appear as the technology matures.

---

[3] roughly the full name a host including domain information

References

1. AT&T, Telephone Security Device 3600–User's Manual, AT&T, 1992.
2. W. Diffie, P.C. can Oorschot, and M.J. Weiner, "Authentication and Authenticated Key Exchanges," *Designs, Codes, and Cryptography*, v. 2, 1992, pp. 107–125.
3. H. Dobbertin, A. Bosselaers, and B. Preneel, "RIPEMD-160: A Strengthened Version of RIEPMD," *Fast Software Encryption, Third International Workshop*, Springer-Verlag, 1996, pp. 71–82.
4. T. ElGamal, A Public-Key Cryptosystem and a Signature Scheme Based on Discrete Logarithms, IEEE Transactions on Information Theory, IT-31 (1985) 469-472.
5. D.V. Klein, "Foiling the Cracker: A Security of, and Implications to, Password Security," *Proceedings of the USENIX UNIX Security Workshop*, Aug 1990, pp. 5–14.
6. E.D. Myers, "STU-III—Multilevel Secure Computer Interface," *Proceedings of the Tenth Annual Computer Security Applications Conference*, IEEE Computer Society Press, 1994, pp. 170–179.
7. National Institute of Standards and Technology, NIST FIPS PUB 180, "Secure Hash Standard," U.S. Department of Commerce, May 1993.
8. R. Rivest, A. Shamir, and L. Adleman, "A Method for Obtaining Digital Signatures and Public-Key Cryptosystems," *Communications of the ACM*, v. 21, n. 2, Feb 1978, pp. 120-126.

Language Issues in Mobile Program Security*

Dennis Volpano[1] and Geoffrey Smith[2]

[1] Department of Computer Science, Naval Postgraduate School
Monterey, CA 93943, USA
`volpano@cs.nps.navy.mil`
[2] School of Computer Science, Florida International University
Miami, FL 33199, USA
`smithg@cs.fiu.edu`

Abstract. Many programming languages have been developed and implemented for mobile code environments. They are typically quite expressive. But while security is an important aspect of any mobile code technology, it is often treated after the fundamental design is complete, in ad hoc ways. In the end, it is unclear what security guarantees can be made for the system. We argue that mobile programming languages should be designed around certain security properties that hold for all well-formed programs. This requires a better understanding of the relationship between programming language design and security. Appropriate security properties must be identified. Some of these properties and related issues are explored.

An assortment of languages and environments have been proposed for mobile code. Some have been designed for use in executable content and others for use in agents [15, 34]. Parallel efforts in extensible networks and operating systems have also focused attention on language design for mobility. These efforts include work on active networks [33, 38], the SPIN kernel [2, 17] and Exokernel [8]. What these efforts have in common is a need for security.

We can roughly separate security concerns in this setting into *code security* and *host security*. The former is concerned with protecting mobile code from untrusted hosts while the latter is concerned with protecting hosts from untrusted mobile code. This may seem a bit artificial since one might like to model security more symmetrically.[1] Nonetheless, it is a useful distinction for now. The code security problem seems quite intractable, given that mobile code is under the control of a host. For some proposals and a discussion, see [25, 26, 40]. In the remainder of this paper, we treat only the host security problem.

---

* This material is based upon activities supported by DARPA and the National Science Foundation under Agreement Nos. CCR-9612176 and CCR-9612345.
[1] One can imagine a model that does not distinguish mobile code from a host, treating both as mutually suspicious parties.

G. Vigna (Ed.): Mobile Agents and Security
LNCS 1419, pp. 25–43, 1998. © Springer–Verlag Berlin Heidelberg 1998

1   Host Security

Our view of the problem is that mobile code is executed on a host which must be protected from privacy and integrity violations. As far as privacy goes, the host has private data that the code may need to perform some expected task. The host wants assurance that it can trust the code not to leak the private data. This is the classical view of privacy [21, 22, 23]. As for integrity, the host has information that should not be corrupted. Integrity, in general, demands total code correctness. After all, corrupt data can simply be the result of incorrect code. There are, however, weaker forms of integrity [3].

We believe that an important characteristic of the mobile code setting is that the only observable events are those that can be observed from within a mobile program using language primitives and any host utilities. There are no meta-level observers of a mobile program's behavior such as a person observing its execution behavior online. Still, depending on the language, leaks can occur in many different ways, some being much more difficult to detect than others.

1.1   Security Architectures

A common approach to host security is to monitor the execution of mobile code. You build an interpreter (or virtual machine) and slap the hands of any code that tries to touch something sensitive. The interpreter obviously needs to know whether hand slapping is in order so it might appeal to some sort of trust framework to decide. This arrangement is often called a "security architecture". Architectures are growing quite elaborate as the demand for less hand slapping rises. An example is the security architecture of the Java Developer's Kit JDK1.2 [11]. It blends some proven concepts, such as protection domains, access control, permissions, and code signing, to allow applets more room to maneuver. Netscape's "Object Signing Architecture" takes a similar approach.

One begins to wonder how much of these security architectures is really necessary. Are they a response to a need for host security given mobile programs written in a poorly-designed mobile programming language? Perhaps they can be simplified. It would seem that this is possible if mobile code is written in a language that ensures certain security properties statically.

For example, suppose that all well-typed programs have a secure flow property and that you know a certain program, needing your personal identification number (PIN), is indeed well typed. Then that program respects the privacy of your PIN and there is no need to check at runtime whether the program has permission to read it.

Our claim is not that security architectures will no longer have a role in the future. We feel their role will simply change and be more formally justified. For example, they might carry out certain static analyses or proof checking, perhaps along the lines of proof-carrying code [27]. It should be possible, for a given language, to more clearly identify the role of the security architecture. Certain desirable properties might be provable for all well-formed programs in the language, in which case some security checks can go away.

There are many different facets of mobile language design that influence security in some way. For example, access control mechanisms (encapsulation, visibility rules, etc.) are important. We will limit our attention to some of the issues that impact host privacy and integrity. On the integrity side, we look at *type safety*. Type safety is often said to be a key ingredient for security in Java and for safe kernel extensions written in Modula-3 [2]. Today, some languages like Standard ML evolve with formal treatments of the type system and semantics developed along the way. This allows one to give formal accounts of type safety that evolve as well. Other languages, like Java, lack this sort of formal treatment. Java has grown so rapidly that one quickly loses grasp of the impact of certain features on key properties like type safety.

Then we explore the relationship between privacy and language design. There are many ways mobile code can leak secrets. We start by examining information channels in a deterministic language. We look at how they are influenced by timing, synchrony, and nontermination. Then we consider channels in a simple concurrent language with shared variables. Some of these channels arise in very subtle ways. For example, they can arise from contention among processes for shared resources, like CPU cycles.

2   Type Safety

What is type safety? Consider the following description from a Java perspective:

> The Java language itself is designed to enforce security in the form of type safety. This means the compiler ensures that methods and programs do not access memory in ways that are inappropriate (i.e. dangerous). In effect, this is the most essential part of the Java security model in that it fundamentally protects the integrity of the memory map.
>
> *Secure Computing with Java: Now and the Future,*
> *1997 JavaOne Conference.*

In Java, for example, code should not somehow be able to coerce a reference of a user-defined class to one of a system class like `SecurityManager` which the runtime system (Java Virtual Machine) consults for access permissions. Obviously, this leads to trouble.

So at the heart of type safety is a guarantee against misinterpretation of data—some sequence of bits being misinterpreted by an operation. This has long been recognized as a serious computer security problem. In a well-known report published twenty-five years ago, Anderson describes a way to penetrate a time-sharing system (HIS 635/GCOS III) based on the ability to execute a user's array contents with an assigned GOTO statement in Fortran [1]. The statement can misinterpret its target, the contents of an arbitrary integer variable, as an instruction. Today we see the same sort of problem in a different context [29].

2.1   Type Preservation

An important property related to type safety is the idea of *type preservation*. Type preservation is frequently confused with type soundness in the literature. Soundness is a statement about the progress a program's execution can make if the program is well typed. Type preservation, on the other hand, merely asserts that if a well-typed program evaluates successfully, then it produces a value of the correct type. It is usually needed to prove soundness. For instance, you may know that an expression, with some type, evaluates to a value, but the value must have a specific form in order for evaluation to proceed. Type preservation gives you that the value has the same type as the expression, and with some correct forms typing lemma, you know that only values of the form needed have that type.

The following is a typical type preservation theorem. If μ is a memory, mapping locations to values, and λ is a location typing, mapping locations to types, then type preservation is stated as follows [16]:

Theorem. (Type Preservation). If $\mu \vdash e \Rightarrow v, \mu'$, $\lambda \vdash e : \tau$, and $\mu : \lambda$, then there exists λ' such that $\lambda \subseteq \lambda'$, $\mu' : \lambda'$, and $\lambda' \vdash v : \tau$.

The first hypothesis of the theorem states that under memory μ, a closed expression e evaluates to a value v and a memory μ'. Now e may contain free locations, hence e is typed with respect to a location typing λ which must be consistent with μ, that is, $\mu : \lambda$. Evaluation of e can produce new locations that wind up in v, so v is typed with respect to an extension λ' of λ.

As one can clearly see from the theorem, whether a language exhibits this property depends on the type system and the semantics. In some cases, we might expect that the type system needs to change if the property does not hold. But the semantics itself may be to blame. For instance, consider the C program in Figure 1. When compiled and executed, *c evaluates to a signed integer quan-

```
char *c;
f() {char cc = 'a'; c = &cc;}
g() {int i = -99;}
main() {f(); g(); printf("%c",*c);}
```

Fig. 1. Dereferencing a dangling pointer

tity, yet it has type char. If a C semantics prescribes this behavior, then we cannot prove type preservation with respect to that semantics; the C language says this program is unpredictable. This is one place where type preservation and C collide.[2] A formal C semantics should be clear about the outcome of dereferencing a dangling pointer, if this is considered "normal" execution, so that type preservation can be proved. Otherwise, it should specify that execution

---

[2] Thus, perhaps, it is not surprising that the SPIN group abandoned its attempts to define a "safe subset of C", adopting Modula-3 instead [2].

gets stuck in this situation, again so that type preservation holds. In the latter case, an implementation of C would be required to detect such an erroneous execution point if that implementation were *safe*. A safe (faithful) implementation guarantees that every execution is prescribed by the semantics, so that programs cannot run in ways not accounted for by the semantics. This usually requires that an implementation do some runtime type checking unless it can be proved unnecessary by a type soundness result.

Remark. Although a lack of pointer expressiveness is in general a good thing from a safety viewpoint, manifest pointers (references) are still a substantial security risk. A runtime system might accidentally provide an application a reference to a system security object that must remain invariant. This was demonstrated in Java for JDK1.1. Its entire trust framework, based on digitally-signed code, was undermined when it was discovered that applications could obtain a reference to a code signers array.[3]

2.2   Type Soundness

Type preservation theorems usually talk about successful evaluations. Their hypotheses involve an assumption about an evaluation proceeding in some number of steps to a canonical form. But this may not adequately address a type system's intentions. An objective of a system might be to guarantee termination or to ensure that programs terminate only in specified ways (e.g. no segmentation violations).[4] What is needed is a precise account of how a well-typed program can behave when executed. In other words, we want a type soundness theorem that specifies *all* the possible behaviors that a well-typed program can exhibit.

Traditional type soundness arguments based on showing that a well-typed program does not evaluate to some special untypable value are inadequate for languages like C and Java. There are many reasons why programs written in languages like Java and C may produce runtime errors. Invalid class formats in Java and invalid pointer arithmetic in C are examples. A type soundness theorem should enumerate all the errors that cause a well-typed program to get stuck (abort) according to the semantics. *These are the errors that every safe implementation must detect.* One regards the type system as *sound* if none of these errors is an error that we expect the type system to detect. This is essentially the traditional view of type soundness as a binary property. But a key point to keep in mind is that whether a given type system is sound really depends on our expectations of the type system. Though it may be clear what we expect for languages like Standard ML, it is less clear for lower-level languages like C and assembler.

---

[3] It is interesting to consider what sort of proof would have revealed the problem. One strategy would be to try finding a P-time reduction from compromising the private key used in a digital signature to executing untrusted code. It would also establish a computational lower bound on executing untrusted code using JDK1.1.

[4] Such properties are important in situations where you need guarantees against certain faults. An example is isolating *execution* behind trust boundaries [17].

For example, we give a type system for a polymorphic dialect of C in [30, 32]. The type soundness theorem basically says that executing a well-typed program either succeeds, producing a value of the appropriate type, fails to terminate, or gets stuck because of an attempt to

- access a dead address,
- access an address with an invalid offset,
- read an uninitialized address, or
- declare an empty or negative-sized array.

The first two errors are due to pointers in the language. Now one may expect the type system to detect the first error in which case our type system is unsound. However, if one believes it is beyond the scope of a type system for C, then our type system is sound. Clearly if the list included an error such as an attempt to apply an integer to an integer, then the type system would generally be regarded as unsound.

A better way to look at type soundness is merely as a property about the executions of programs that the type system says are acceptable. This allows us to compare type systems for a language by comparing their soundness properties. Some may be weaker than others in that they require implementations to check types at run time in order to remain safe. It is also useful for determining whether a particular language is suitable for some application. Some of the errors listed in a formulation of soundness may be among those that an application cannot tolerate. Further, and perhaps most importantly, it identifies those errors that an implementation must detect in order to safely implement the semantics. For instance, a safe implementation of C should trap any attempt to dereference a dangling pointer. Most C implementations are unsafe in this regard. One expects Java implementations to be safer, but despite all the attention to typing and bytecode verification, the current situation is unfortunately not as good as one might imagine.

Consider the Java class in Figure 2.[5] The class modifies itself by putting a CONSTANT_Utf8 type tag for x in that part of the constant pool where a CONSTANT_String type tag for x is expected by the ldc (load from constant pool) instruction. Method exec gets a copy of itself in the form of a bytecode array. The class is well typed, yet it aborts with a "segmentation violation" (core dump) in JDK1.1.1, even when Java is run in "verify" mode. Verification of the modified bytecodes does fail using the verify option of the Java class disassembler javap. One would expect it to also fail for the bytecodes dynamically constructed in exec, leading to a VerifyError when class SelfRef is run. Instead we get a core dump. So the JDK1.1.1 implementation of Java is unsafe.

Perhaps making class representations available in bytecode form needs to be reconsidered. It becomes quite easy to dynamically construct classes that

---

[5] A bit of history. The class stems from an attempt to implement an active network in Java. Active programs migrate among servers that invoke their exec methods. An active program maintains state by modifying its own bytecode representation prior to being forwarded. Yes, it's a hack.

```
public class SelfRef implements ActiveProgram {

    final String x = "aaba";

    public void exec(byte[] b, MyLoader loader) throws Exception {

        if (b[13] == 0x08) {    // CONSTANT_String
            b[13] = 0x01;       // set CONSTANT_Utf8
            b[14] = 0x00;
            b[15] = 0x00;
            Class classOf = loader.defineClass(b, 0, b.length);
            ActiveProgram p = (ActiveProgram) classOf.newInstance();
            p.exec(b, loader);
        }
        else System.out.println(x);
    }
    public static void main(String[] argv) throws Exception {

        FileInputStream f = new FileInputStream("SelfRef.class");
        byte[] data = new byte[f.available()];
        int c = f.read(data);
        MyLoader loader = new MyLoader();
        new SelfRef().exec(data, loader);
    }
}
```

Fig. 2. Type mismatch leading to segmentation violation in Java

are difficult to analyze statically for security guarantees. Self-modifying code, in general, makes enforcement of protection constraints difficult, if not impossible. Channel command programs in the M.I.T. Compatible Time-Sharing System (CTSS), for instance, were years ago prohibited from being self-modifying for this reason [28].

3   Privacy in a Deterministic Language

Suppose we begin by considering a very simple deterministic programming language with just variables, integer-valued expressions, assignment, conditionals, **while** loops, and sequential composition. Programs are executed relative to a memory that maps variables to integers. If a program needs I/O, then it simply reads from or writes to some specific variables of the memory. Further, suppose that some variables of the memory are considered private while others are public. Every program is free to use all variables of the memory and also knows which variables are public and which are private.

What concerns us is whether some program, in this rather anemic language, can *always* produce, in a public variable, the contents of a private variable. There are many such programs, some more complicated than others.

For instance, one can simply assign a private variable to a public one, not a terribly clever strategy for a hacker. This is an example of an *explicit channel*. Or one might try to do it more indirectly, one bit at a time, as in Figure 3 where PIN is private, y is public, and the value of mask is a power of two. This is an

```
while (mask != 0) {
    if (PIN & mask != 0) {      \\ bitwise 'and'
        y := y | mask           \\ bitwise 'or'
    }
    mask := mask / 2
}
```

Fig. 3. Implicit channel

example of an *implicit channel*. It illustrates the kind of program we wish to reject because it does not respect the privacy of PIN. We need to formalize the security property it violates.

3.1 Privacy Properties

We give a more formal statement of the privacy property we want programs to have in this simple deterministic language:

Definition. (Termination Security). Suppose that c is a command and μ and ν are memories that agree on all public variables. If $\mu \vdash c \Rightarrow \mu'$ and $\nu \vdash c \Rightarrow \nu'$, then μ' and ν' agree on all public variables.

(The judgment $\mu \vdash c \Rightarrow \mu'$ asserts that executing command c in initial memory μ terminates successfully, yielding final memory μ'.) Intuitively, Termination Security says that we can change the contents of private variables without influencing the outcome of public variables. In other words, these changes cannot interfere with the final contents of public variables. The above program does not have this property. Any change in the private PIN will result in a different final value for the public variable y.

Is the Termination Security property an acceptable privacy property for programs in our simple deterministic language? That depends on what is observable. Consider the similar program in Figure 4. If one can repeatedly run this program

```
while (PIN & mask == 0) { }
y := y | mask
```

Fig. 4. Channel from nontermination

with a different mask, one for each bit of PIN, then assuming y is initially zero, the runs will copy PIN to y. One PIN bit is leaked to y in a single run. We assume that, after a specific period of time, if a run has not terminated then it never will, and we move on to the next bit.[6]

But although the program seems insecure, it satisfies Termination Security. Changes to PIN cannot influence the outcome of y in a single run of the program. After changing the PIN, the program may no longer terminate, but this does not violate Termination Security since it only applies to successful termination.

Consider another property:

Definition. (Offline Security). Suppose that c is a command and μ and ν are memories that agree on all public variables. If $\mu \vdash c \Rightarrow \mu'$, then there is a ν' such that $\nu \vdash c \Rightarrow \nu'$, and ν' and μ' agree on all public variables.

Notice that we have removed one of the two successful evaluation hypotheses from Termination Security. The property basically says that changing private variables cannot interfere with the final contents of public variables, nor can it interfere with whether a program terminates. We call the property Offline Security because it addresses only what one can observe about a program's behavior if it is executed offline, or in batch mode (one either sees the results of a successful execution or is notified of some timeout that was reached). The time it takes for a program to terminate is not observed. In a deterministic language, Offline Security implies Termination Security. Actually, the formulation of Offline Security is suitable for treating nondeterminism as we shall see. The program in Figure 4 does not satisfy Offline Security.

Unfortunately, there are other sources of channels. Consider the program in Figure 5. Again suppose we can repeatedly execute it with different masks.

```
if (1 / (PIN & mask)) { }
y := y | mask
```

Fig. 5. Channel from partial operation

It always terminates, sometimes abnormally from division by zero. The effect, however, will be the same, to copy PIN to y one bit at a time.

Hence if we include partial operations like division, we have a situation where a program might either get stuck (terminate abnormally) or run forever, depending on a private variable. So we need yet a stronger offline security property. Basically it needs to extend Offline Security with the condition that if c terminates abnormally under μ, then it does so under ν as well [35].

None of the preceding properties addresses any difference in the *time* required to run a program under two memories that can disagree on private variables. These differences can be used to deduce values of private variables in timing

---

[6] The task obviously becomes much easier when we enrich the language with threads and a clock. Now each bit can be examined by an asynchronously-running thread, and after some timeout we can be fairly confident that all nonzero bits have been properly set in y.

attacks on cryptographic algorithms. For example, a private key used in RSA modular exponentiation has been deduced in this fashion [20]. Differences in timing under two memories can be ruled out by requiring that executions under the two memories proceed in lock step, a form of strong bisimilarity. This property, which might be called Online Security, is the most restrictive thus far. But is it really necessary for mobile programs? That depends on what is observable.

3.2   What is Observable?

Key to judging whether any of the preceding properties is necessary is determining what is observable in the model. Whether a privacy property is suitable depends on how it treats observable events. Notice that there is an observation being exploited in the preceding examples, even within a single run, that allows one PIN bit to be leaked to y. It arises due to the synchrony of sequential composition. Termination Security does not take this kind of observation into account, which makes Offline Security a better choice. Recall that Offline Security does not account for timing differences, but does this matter with mobile code? The key question is who observes the clock?

One can imagine examples in languages like Java where a downloaded applet begins by sending a startup message back to a server on the originating machine and then ends with a finish message. Each message is timestamped by the server which observes a clock external to the applet. We can model this sort of behavior in our simple deterministic language by adding a clock in order to record "timestamps" on values output to memory. Then, clock observation is internal to mobile code. This is how UDP/TCP ports should really be modeled because a UDP or TCP server's clock is observed by a client (applet) when it sends a TCP segment or UDP message. This brings us to our *offline* assumption:

> In a mobile code setting, the only observable events are those that can be observed internally, that is, from within a mobile program using primitives of the language.

So the Online Security property may be overly restrictive for mobile programs written in our simple deterministic, sequential language.

Generally, the more a program can observe, the more opportunity there is for leaking secrets. As we have seen, opportunities can arise with the most basic primitives, for instance, synchronous operations.

4   Nondeterminism and Privacy

Now suppose we introduce nondeterminism via a simple concurrent language. It is a multi-threaded imperative language based on the $\pi o\beta\lambda$ model of concurrency [19]. As before, we have commands and their sequential composition. A *thread* is a command that belongs to a thread pool (called an object pool in $\pi o\beta\lambda$). A thread pool O maps thread identifiers to threads. Threads communicate via shared variables of a global memory. A thread pool executes in one step to a new thread pool by nondeterministically selecting a thread and executing it sequentially in one step. More precisely, thread pool transitions are governed by the following two rules:

$$\frac{O(\alpha) = c \quad (c, \mu) \overset{s}{\longrightarrow} \mu'}{(O, \mu) \overset{g}{\longrightarrow} (O - \alpha, \mu')} \qquad \frac{O(\alpha) = c \quad (c, \mu) \overset{s}{\longrightarrow} (c', \mu')}{(O, \mu) \overset{g}{\longrightarrow} (O[\alpha := c'], \mu')}$$

Thread pool transitions are denoted $\overset{g}{\longrightarrow}$ (global transitions) and sequential transitions $\overset{s}{\longrightarrow}$. The first rule treats thread completion and the second treats thread continuation. Intuitively, the first rule says that if we can pick some thread (command) α from pool O, and execute it sequentially for one step in the shared memory μ, leaving a memory μ', then the entire thread pool O can execute in one step to a pool where α is gone and the shared memory is now μ'. The second rule treats the case where α does not complete but rather is transformed into a continuation (command) c' that represents what remains of c to be executed after it executes for only one step. Note that no thread scheduling policy is specified in these rules.

With threads come new ways to cleverly leak secrets. Programs that appear harmless can contain subtle channels for transmitting secrets, even in this very basic concurrent language. To illustrate, we consider a system introduced by Fine [10]. It is analyzed in [7] where it is concluded that the system is secure in the sense that "it is not possible for a high-level subject to pass information to a low-level subject". The system consists of two private variables, A and B, whose difference is public and stored in Y. As a multi-threaded program, the system is given in Figure 6.[7] Thread α corresponds to a high-level user updating the

```
Thread α :              Thread β :
B := B - A + v;         Y := B - A
A := v
```

Fig. 6. The AB system

system with some value v that can be recovered through A. Thread β corresponds to a low-level user reading public information from the system. The threads share variables A and B. Imagine each of these threads being executed repeatedly and that v is a constant input parameter. The claim is that α cannot transmit any information to β since β always sees only B - A. But this requires that α be atomic, for suppose A and B have initial values a and b respectively. If we execute the first assignment of α followed by the assignment in β, then Y becomes B - a, which is b - a + v - a. Since Y is initially b - a, we know v - a, the difference between two successive values input by α. So β can observe a difference controlled by α. The interleaving might be frequent in a real implementation if v is large.

---

[7] We ignore a third thread for low-level writing to the system.

What kind of privacy property would rule out this sort of threaded program? First, we have to rule out any analog to the Termination Security property because it applies to deterministic programs only. Instead, suppose we ask whether the outcomes of public variables can be "preserved" under changes to private variables. So in the example above, we consider an execution that leaves Y equal to b - a + v - a, say for v > a. Now we ask whether this outcome is *possible* when v is changed to a different value, say w. No matter how we interleave, Y ends up being b - a or b - a + w - a. The outcome is no longer possible. We have then the following property [31]:

Definition. (Possibilistic NI). Suppose μ and ν are memories that agree on all public variables and that $(O, \mu) \xrightarrow{g}^* (\{\}, \mu')$. Then there is a ν' such that $(O, \nu) \xrightarrow{g}^* (\{\}, \nu')$ and ν' and μ' agree on all public variables.

It is a kind of noninterference (NI) property that closely resembles Sutherland's notion of Nondeducibility on inputs [39]. Also notice the similarity between this property and Offline Security.

The program in Figure 6 does not satisfy Possibilistic NI. Another interesting example that does not satisfy Possibilistic NI is given in [31]. It uses a main thread and two triggered threads, each with a busy-wait loop implementing a semaphore, to copy every bit of a private PIN to a public variable. In fact, the program *always* produces a copy of the PIN in a public variable whenever thread scheduling is fair (every thread is scheduled infinitely often).

Practical extensions of our simple concurrent language make it easy to construct multi-threaded programs that violate Possibilistic NI. For example, simple programs have the property until a scheduling policy, like round-robin time slicing, is introduced [31]. Adding a clock, even without threading, leads to simple programs that fail to have the property. The same is true in the presence of thread priorities and preemption. So the outlook for guaranteeing this property in practical programs written in languages like Java appears bleak.

If a multi-threaded program satisfies Possibilistic NI then changes to private variables cannot interfere with the *possibility* of public variables having a certain outcome. But the changes may interfere with the *probability* of that outcome. If so, there is a probabilistic channel. Consider, for instance, the program in Figure 7. Suppose that X stores one bit and is private, Y is public, and all threads

```
        Thread α :        Thread β :        Thread γ :
        Y := X            Y := 0            Y := 1
```

Fig. 7. A probabilistic channel

have an equal probability of being scheduled. Is the program secure? Well, it satisfies Possibilistic NI so it cannot reveal X with certainty. But it is *likely* to reveal X. Suppose X is 0. Then the probability that Y has final value 0 is 2/3. When X is 1, however, the probability that Y has final value 0 drops to 1/3. In effect, the private variable interferes with the *probability* that Y has final value 0. This kind of interference Gray calls *probabilistic interference* [12]. He describes a property called P-restrictiveness that aims to rule it out in systems. The property can be viewed as a form of probabilistic noninterference [13, 14].

5   Logics and Static Analyses for Privacy

From the discussion thus far, it would appear that a privacy property is developed independently of any logic for reasoning about it. While this has been generally true of security properties studied for computer systems, it is usually not so for programming languages. Typically one starts with an intuitive idea of secure code and gives some sort of logic to capture the notion. The next step is to make the intuition precise so that the logic can be proved sound.[8] To illustrate, we sketch a logic for reasoning about privacy below. It is actually a type system utilizing subtypes. A complete description can be found in [37] where it is proved that every well-typed deterministic program satisfies Termination Security.

We take security classes, like L (low or public) and H (high or private), as our basic types which we denote by τ. Some typing rules treat explicit channels and others implicit channels. Below is the typing rule for an assignment $x := e$:

$$\frac{\gamma \vdash x : \tau \; acc, \;\; \gamma \vdash e : \tau}{\gamma \vdash x := e : \tau \; cmd} \tag{1}$$

In order for the assignment to be well typed, it must be that

- x is a variable of type τ *acc*(eptor), meaning x is capable of storing information at security level τ, and
- expression e has type τ, meaning every variable in e has type τ.[9]

Information about x is provided by γ which maps identifiers to types. So, the rule states that in order for the assignment $x := e$ to be judged secure, x must be a variable that stores information at the same security level as e. If this is true, then the rule allows us to ascribe type τ *cmd* to the entire assignment command. The command type τ *cmd* tells us that every variable assigned to by the command (here only x) can accept information of security level τ or higher.

These command types are needed to control implicit channels like the one in Figure 3. For example, here is the typing rule for conditionals:

$$\frac{\gamma \vdash e : \tau \qquad\qquad\qquad\qquad}{\begin{array}{c}\gamma \vdash c_1 : \tau \; cmd \\ \gamma \vdash c_2 : \tau \; cmd \\ \hline \gamma \vdash \textbf{if } e \textbf{ then } c_1 \textbf{ else } c_2 : \tau \; cmd\end{array}} \tag{2}$$

---

[8] Unfortunately, it is quite common to see either the logic skipped entirely, in favor of an algorithm that implements one's intuition, or soundness not treated adequately, if at all. It is important to make intuitions about security precise.

[9] Keep in mind that unlike type preservation, an expression of type τ here does not mean one that evaluates to a value of type τ. Values (in our case integers) have no intrinsic security levels.

The idea is that c_1 and c_2 execute in a context where information about the value of e is implicitly available—when c_1 executes, the value of e was *true* and when c_2 executes, the value of e was *false*. Hence if $e : \tau$, then c_1 and c_2 must not transmit any information to variables of security level lower than τ. This is enforced by requiring c_1 and c_2 to have type τ *cmd*.

Here is the typing rule for **while** loops:

$$\frac{\gamma \vdash e : \tau \qquad}{\gamma \vdash \textbf{while } e \textbf{ do } c : \tau \ cmd} \tag{3}$$
$$\gamma \vdash c : \tau \ cmd$$

and the typing rule for sequential composition:

$$\frac{\gamma \vdash c_1 : \tau \ cmd}{\gamma \vdash c_1; c_2 : \tau \ cmd} \tag{4}$$
$$\gamma \vdash c_2 : \tau \ cmd$$

The typing rules for expressions and commands simply require all subexpressions and subcommands to be typed at the same security level. For example, we require in rule (1) that the left and right sides of an assignment be typed at the same level. A similar requirement is imposed in rule (2). Yet we do want to allow *upward* information flows, such as from public to private. But the typing rules can remain simple because upward flows can be accommodated naturally through subtyping. For example, we would have $L \subseteq H$, but not $H \subseteq L$. The subtype relation can naturally be extended with subtype inclusions among types of the form τ *cmd* and τ *acc*. The type constructors *cmd* and *acc* are *antimonotonic*, meaning that if $\tau_1 \subseteq \tau_2$, then the relation is extended with

$$\tau_2 \ cmd \subseteq \tau_1 \ cmd \ \text{ and } \ \tau_2 \ acc \subseteq \tau_1 \ acc$$

Intuitively, antimonotonicity merely reflects the fact that a reader capable of reading at one security level is capable of reading at a lower level.

Also, there are two coercions associated with variables. If $x : \tau$ *var*, then $x : \tau$ and also $x : \tau$ *acc*. That is, variables are both expressions and acceptors. So if

$$\gamma(x) = H \ var \ \text{ and } \ \gamma(y) = L \ var$$

then there is an explicit upward flow from y to x in $x := y$. The assignment can be typed in two ways. We can type the assignment with $x : H$ *acc* by coercing the type of y to H, or we can type the assignment with $y : L$ by coercing the type of x to L *acc* through the antimonotonicity of acceptor types.

Now properties of the type system can be proved. For example, there are type-theoretic analogs of the well-known simple security property and *-property (Confinement) of the Bell and LaPadula model [22, 23]:

Lemma. (Type Analog of Simple Security) If $\gamma \vdash e : \tau$, then for every variable x in expression e, $\gamma \vdash x : \tau$.

Lemma. (Type Analog of Confinement) If $\gamma \vdash c : \tau \ cmd$, then for every variable x assigned to in command c, $\gamma \vdash x : \tau \ acc$.

Intuitively, Simple Security guarantees no "read up" in expressions, whereas Confinement ensures no "write down" in commands. For example, Simple Security ensures that if an expression has type L, then it contains no variables of type $H \ var$. Likewise, Confinement guarantees that if a command has type $H \ cmd$, then it contains no assignments to variables of type $L \ var$.

With these two properties, one can now prove that every well-typed program in our simple deterministic language satisfies Termination Security [37]. The type system is not limited to privacy. One can also introduce integrity classes T (trusted) and U (untrusted), such that $T \subseteq U$. Now if a program satisfies Termination Security, then no trusted variable can be "contaminated" by untrusted variables [3].

To achieve stronger security properties, such as Offline Security it is necessary to restrict the typing of **while** loops. Intuitively, a **while** loop can transmit information not only by assigning to variables, but also by terminating or failing to terminate. This idea was exploited by the program in Figure 4. To prevent such flows, one can restrict rule (3) to the following:

$$\frac{\gamma \vdash e : L \qquad \qquad \qquad \qquad \qquad \qquad \quad (5)}{\gamma \vdash \textbf{while } e \textbf{ do } c : L \ cmd}$$
$$\gamma \vdash c : L \ cmd$$

With this stricter rule, one can show that every well-typed program satisfies Offline Security [35]. By restricting the typing of partial operations like division, it is also shown in [35] that well-typed programs satisfy a stronger offline security property that addresses aborted executions as well as nontermination. Finally, under rule (5) it can be shown that every well-typed concurrent program satisfies Possibilistic NI [31].

An advantage of the type system is that it affords type inference. Procedures are polymorphic with respect to security classes. Principal types are constrained type schemes that convey how code can be used without violating privacy [36]. Notice that type checking here is not merely an optimization in that it replaces run-time checks, as in traditional type checking. Denning's early work on program certification and the lattice model over 20 years ago [4, 5, 6] showed that one cannot rely only on run-time mechanisms to enforce secure information flow, a direction that had been pursued by Fenton [9]. Static analysis is needed to reveal implicit channels like the one in Figure 3.

There is still some question about how the type system should be deployed in a mobile code setting. Currently we are exploring its use in a code certification pipeline aimed at certifying the security of e-commerce applications written in Java. But we can also imagine the need for analyzing some lower-level intermediate language like Java virtual machine instructions. The loss of program structure at this level would likely make it more difficult to specify a simple type system for privacy.

5.1   Decidability

The type system above is decidable. A type inference algorithm is given for it in [36]. A desirable property of any logic for reasoning about privacy is that it be decidable. However, there is often tension between decidability, soundness and completeness in such logics. One is naturally unwilling to compromise soundness so that can mean having to give up completeness for decidability.

For instance, the problem of deciding whether a program, written in our simple deterministic language of Section 3, has the Termination Security property is not recursively enumerable. This means that any sound and recursively enumerable logic for reasoning about Termination Security must be incomplete. Now the question is how much have we lost by conceding incompleteness? There must be examples of code that have some desired security property, but which cannot be proved in the logic. For example, here is a snippet of code in our sequential language that satisfies Termination Security, yet is untypable in the system above if X is private and Y is public:

```
X  := Y;
Y  := X
```

Further, thread β in the program of Figure 6 is also untypable. The question of how much has been lost often depends on whether such examples arise frequently in practice. If they do, then the logic may yield too many "false positives" for it to be practical. This has been a primary criticism of information-flow checkers for some time [7].

6   Conclusion

We have explored the relationship between some aspects of language design and security issues. The issues we considered in this paper, namely type safety and privacy, are really independent of code mobility. Nonetheless, the prospect of migrating code that executes financial transactions, or extends the functionality of a network switch, makes them relevant.

So what sort of advice can we offer designers of secure languages? First, security should not be viewed as a programming language graft. The literature is filled with attempts that treat security this way. Languages have a fundamental role in secure computation and should be designed with this in mind. A designer might begin by establishing the security properties of interest for a language and then attempt to introduce functionality while preserving them. This seems more promising than treating security afterward. Also, one cannot overemphasize the need for a formal semantics. It is essential for proving soundness and basic safety properties like those in [24].

We strongly believe that secure languages should have simple, compositional logics for reasoning about the security properties of interest. Compilers should be able to incorporate decision procedures for these logics as static analyses that programmers can easily understand. For instance, the type system of Section 5 is simple and has an efficient type inference algorithm for inferring type schemes that convey how programs can be used securely.

As far as privacy properties go, one has to know what is observable, and how it can be observed. There are some known pitfalls. In a concurrent setting, beware of any ability to modulate one thread with another, for instance, through a semaphore [31]. Time-sliced thread scheduling is also problematic. It does not preserve the Possibilistic NI security property in languages like Java. Java threading and its many features make it easy to build covert timing channels. This suggests that it is unsuitable for secure e-commerce applications. The subset, Java Card 2.0, proposed for smartcards, may be better since it has no threading and supports the notion of a transaction [18]. Designing a secure concurrent language that is flexible and admits simple and accurate static analyses is the subject of current research.

References

[1] James P. Anderson. Computer security technology planning study. Technical Report ESD-TR-73-51, Electronic Systems Division, Hanscom Field, Bedford, MA, 1972.

[2] Brian Bershad, et al. Extensibility, safety and performance in the SPIN operating system. In *Proc. 15th Symposium on Operating Systems Principles*, pages 267–284, December 1995.

[3] K. Biba. Integrity considerations for secure computer systems. Technical Report ESD-TR-76-372, MITRE Corp., 1977.

[4] Dorothy Denning. *Secure Information Flow in Computer Systems*. PhD thesis, Purdue University, West Lafayette, IN, May 1975.

[5] Dorothy Denning. A lattice model of secure information flow. *Communications of the ACM*, 19(5):236–242, 1976.

[6] Dorothy Denning and Peter Denning. Certification of programs for secure information flow. *Communications of the ACM*, 20(7):504–513, 1977.

[7] Steven T. Eckmann. Eliminating formal flows in automated information flow analysis. In *Proceedings 1994 IEEE Symposium on Security and Privacy*, Oakland, CA, May 1994.

[8] D.R. Engler, et al. Exokernel: An operating system architecture for application-level resource management. In *Proc. 15th Symposium on Operating Systems Principles*, December 1995.

[9] J. Fenton. *Information Protection Systems*. PhD thesis, University of Cambridge, 1973.

[10] Todd Fine. A foundation for covert channel analysis. In *Proc. 15th National Computer Security Conference*, Baltimore, MD, October 1992.

[11] Li Gong, Marianne Mueller, Hemma Prafullchandra, and Roland Schemers. Going beyond the sandbox: An overview of the new security architecture in the Java Development Kit 1.2. In *Proceedings USENIX Symposium on Internet Technologies and Systems*, Monterey, CA, December 1997.

[12] James W. Gray, III. Probabilistic interference. In *Proceedings 1990 IEEE Symposium on Security and Privacy*, pages 170–179, Oakland, CA, May 1990.

[13] James W. Gray, III. Toward a mathematical foundation for information flow security. In *Proceedings 1991 IEEE Symposium on Security and Privacy*, pages 21–34, Oakland, CA, May 1991.

[14] James W. Gray, III and Paul F. Syverson. A logical approach to multilevel security of probabilistic systems. In *Proceedings 1992 IEEE Symposium on Security and Privacy*, pages 164–176, Oakland, CA, May 1992.

[15] David Halls, John Bates, and Jean Bacon. Flexible distributed programming using mobile code. In *Proc. 7th ACM SIGOPS European Workshop, Systems Support for Worldwide Applications*, Connemara, Ireland, September 1996.

[16] Robert Harper. A simplified account of polymorphic references. *Information Processing Letters*, 51:201–206, 1994.

[17] Wilson C. Hsieh, et al. Language support for extensible operating systems. Unpublished manuscript. Available at `www-spin.cs.washington.edu.`, 1996.

[18] *Java Card 2.0 Language Subset and Virtual Machine Specification*. Sun Microsystems, October 1997.

[19] Cliff B. Jones. Some practical problems and their influence on semantics. In *Proceedings of the 6th European Symposium on Programming*, volume 1058 of *Lecture Notes in Computer Science*, pages 1–17, April 1996.

[20] Paul Kocher. Timing attacks on implementations of Diffie-Hellman, RSA, DSS and other systems. In *Proceedings 16th Annual Crypto Conference*, August 1996.

[21] Butler W. Lampson. A note on the confinement problem. *Communications of the ACM*, 16(10):613–615, 1973.

[22] Carl E. Landwehr. Formal models for computer security. *Computing Surveys*, 13(3):247–278, 1981.

[23] Leonard J. LaPadula and D. Elliot Bell. MITRE Technical Report 2547, Volume II. *Journal of Computer Security*, 4(2,3):239–263, 1996.

[24] X. Leroy and F. Rouaix. Security properties of typed applets. In *Proceedings 25th Symposium on Principles of Programming Languages*, pages 391–403, San Diego, CA, January 1998.

[25] Catherine Meadows. Detecting attacks on mobile agents. In *Proc. 1997 Foundations for Secure Mobile Code Workshop*, pages 64–65, Monterey, CA, March 1997.

[26] Yaron Minsky, Robbert van Renesse, Fred B. Schneider, and Scott Stoller. Cryptographic support for fault-tolerant distributed computing. In *Proc. 7th ACM SIGOPS European Workshop, Systems Support for Worldwide Applications*, Connemara, Ireland, September 1996.

[27] George Necula and Peter Lee. Proof-carrying code. In *Proceedings 24th Symposium on Principles of Programming Languages*, Paris, France, 1997.

[28] J.H. Saltzer. Case studies of protection system failures. Appendix 6-A, unpublished course notes on The Protection of Information in Computer Systems., 1975.

[29] Vijay Saraswat. Java is not type-safe. Unpublished manuscript. Available at `www.research.att.com/~vj/bug.html.`, 1997.

[30] Geoffrey Smith and Dennis Volpano. Towards an ML-style polymorphic type system for C. In *Proceedings of the 6th European Symposium on Programming*, volume 1058 of *Lecture Notes in Computer Science*, pages 341–355, April 1996.

[31] Geoffrey Smith and Dennis Volpano. Secure information flow in a multi-threaded imperative language. In *Proceedings 25th Symposium on Principles of Programming Languages*, pages 355–364, San Diego, CA, January 1998.

[32] Geoffrey Smith and Dennis Volpano. A sound polymorphic type system for a dialect of C. *Science of Computer Programming*, 32(2-3), 1998.

[33] D.L. Tennenhouse, J.M. Smith, W.D. Sincoskie, D.J. Wetherall, and G.J. Minden. A survey of active network research. *IEEE Communications*, 35(1):80–86, January 1997.

[34] Tommy Thorn. Programming languages for mobile code. *Computing Surveys*, 29(3):213–239, 1997.

[35] Dennis Volpano and Geoffrey Smith. Eliminating covert flows with minimum typings. In *Proc. 10th IEEE Computer Security Foundations Workshop*, pages 156–168, June 1997.

[36] Dennis Volpano and Geoffrey Smith. A type-based approach to program security. In *Proc. Theory and Practice of Software Development*, volume 1214 of *Lecture Notes in Computer Science*, pages 607–621, April 1997.

[37] Dennis Volpano, Geoffrey Smith, and Cynthia Irvine. A sound type system for secure flow analysis. *Journal of Computer Security*, 4(2,3):167–187, 1996.

[38] David J. Wetherall and David L. Tennenhouse. The ACTIVE IP option. In *Proc. 7th ACM SIGOPS European Workshop, Systems Support for Worldwide Applications*, Connemara, Ireland, September 1996.

[39] J. Todd Wittbold and Dale M. Johnson. Information flow in nondeterministic systems. In *Proceedings 1990 IEEE Symposium on Security and Privacy*, pages 144–161, Oakland, CA, May 1990.

[40] Bennet S. Yee. A sanctuary for mobile agents. In *Proc. 1997 Foundations for Secure Mobile Code Workshop*, pages 21–27, Monterey, CA, March 1997.

Protecting Mobile Agents Against Malicious Hosts

Tomas Sander and Christian F. Tschudin

International Computer Science Institute
1947 Center Street, Berkeley, CA 94704, USA
sander,tschudin@icsi.berkeley.edu

Abstract. A key element of any mobile code based distributed system are the security mechanisms available to protect (a) the host against potentially hostile actions of a code fragment under execution and (b) the mobile code against tampering attempts by the executing host. Many techniques for the first problem (a) have been developed. The second problem (b) seems to be much harder: It is the general belief that computation privacy for mobile code cannot be provided without tamper resistant hardware. Furthermore it is doubted that an agent can keep a secret (e.g., a secret key to generate digital signatures). There is an error in reasoning in the arguments supporting these beliefs which we are going to point out.

In this paper we describe software-only approaches for providing computation privacy for mobile code in the important case that the mobile code fragment computes an algebraic circuit (a polynomial). We further describe an approach how a mobile agent can digitally sign his output securely.

1   Introduction

Can a program actively protect itself against its execution environment that tries to divert the intended execution towards a malicious goal? After a little thought this seems to be a problem impossible to solve because it leads to an infinite recourse. The assessment routine that would detect wrong execution of code or tampering of data and that would try to counter them would also be subject to diversion. For mobile code applications, more specifically for mobile software agents which are designed to run on potentially arbitrary computers, this problem is of primordial importance. Without strong guarantees on computation integrity and privacy, mobile programs would always remain vulnerable to "hijacking" and "brainwashing".

Consider for example the following scenario. A customized mobile air-fare agent is sent out with the order to visit in turn the servers of several airlines, to query their databases for finding a suitable flight and, once the best offer has been determined, to book the flight. A simple and profitable attack would be to

G. Vigna (Ed.): Mobile Agents and Security
LNCS 1419, pp. 44–60, 1998. © Springer–Verlag Berlin Heidelberg 1998

tamper the agent's state and code such that it forgets the already visited servers and erroneously selects an offering of the malicious server's airline. Another attack would be to rise prices up to some threshold used internally by the agent or, if applicable, to steal the agent's electronic money without further processing. Even more problematic would be a scenario where the mobile agent wants to book the flight and therefore it wants to digitally sign an order: here the problem is that the agent must carry the user's private key and do some computation using the key.

This simple example exposes three fundamental problems of executing mobile code in an untrusted environment:

(i) Can a mobile agent *protect itself against tampering* by a malicious host? (code and execution integrity)
(ii) Can a mobile agent *conceal the program* it wants to have executed? (code privacy)
(iii) Can a mobile agent remotely *sign a document* without disclosing the user's private key? (computing with secrets in public)

Some of the problems mentioned in the shopping agent scenario are alleviated by using state–of–the–art cryptographic algorithms and specially managed trusted servers, others disappear when tamper-resistant hardware can be relied on. But true "self–defense" of mobile agents against malicious hosts is only possible if there exists a nucleus of pure software operations for which computation integrity and privacy can be mathematically proven. The question and challenge thus is whether mobile code can *carry out cryptographic primitives* even though the code a) is executed inside untrusted computing environments and b) should run autonomously, i.e., without interactions with its originating site.

We firmly believe that in many cases fully software based *cryptographic* solutions exist for protecting mobile agents against malicious hosts. This belief contradicts the folklore saying that because a host must execute and thus is in possession of an agent's code, the agent is to the host's full mercy. In Section 2 we will first discuss the problems of cleartext programs where we also sketch an approach to effectively hide computations from a malicious host. Section 3 describes in more depth the approach of computing with encrypted functions for which we give in Section 4 first possible solutions that are based on homomorphic encryption schemes and composition techniques. A solution for the signature problem that relies on another technique is proposed in Section 5. Section 6 concludes this paper.

2   Protection of Mobile Agents from Malicious Hosts

An appealing feature of mobile agent technology is that a user can delegate a task into the net: the agent autonomously roams around, locates information, computes intermediate results, and triggers remote actions all its way long without interaction with the originator. Cryptographic solutions for securing the execution of mobile agents thus should conform to the requirement that they do not introduce interactive protocols (involving the originator of the agent). The other goal we want to reach is that the agent should be able to execute security sensitive computations even in an untrusted execution environment. Before discussing the feasibility of such solutions we briefly review other techniques that were proposed in order to alleviate the threats to mobile code.

2.1 Detection of Tampering vs. Prevention

An effective approach of securing mobile agents consists in letting them circulate in *trusted execution environments* only. Thus, by setting up a trusted network of nodes, by encrypting agents as they are sent from node to node and by authenticating the host before an agents transports itself to it (as well as authenticating the agent before it enters a host), we can make it highly unlikely that an agent encounters a malicious host. However, this severely hurts the concept of an open agent system where new servers can join the system as new needs show up. It also relies on the trust model to be effective which means that this approach can not exclude the possibility that although a host is trusted it behaves maliciously.

Detection of tampering concentrates more on the longlived interests a host may have when it joins the mobile agent network: by threatening to bar a host from further business, we restrict the security measures to detecting tampering a posteriori. Should tampering be observed one could forward this information to rating agencies that maintain records on a server's trustworthiness (social control). Alternatively one could attempt legal steps to recover possible losses and to make punitive claims. Several (cryptographic and non-cryptographic) techniques have been proposed in this direction which require the host to do some extra work in order to proof later on that it duly executed a specific mobile agent [18,15]. It would also be possible to add "dummy data items" to an agents which are offered as potential objects to tamper with: a returning agent may then be checked to see whether these items were modified or not [9]. Clearly the last approach lacks the necessary cryptographic strength that would be required to serve as a proof in a court room. In general, detection approaches are ineffective for attacks where the culprit may not be identified or does not exist anymore once a fraud is detected.

A further step towards protecting a mobile agent against malicious hosts is to *make tampering difficult* or expensive. Code obfuscation, for example, proposes to make the agent's program illegible and thus difficult to manipulate [7]. One major problem is that unless provably effective techniques can be applied here, this remains an arms race where each new masquerade technique is immediately paralleled by countermeasures (see for example the case of Java byte code obfuscators [14,5]).

Still another approach would be to *protect an application as a whole* instead of protecting the individual agents it is composed of (see e.g., [18] for a discussion of such an approach and further references). A specific task may be split into several mobile agents that collaborate with each other from different computation platforms, using secret sharing schemes. One of these platforms may be a Trusted Mobile Agent Computing Base that the originator trusts. Also if the execution platform for (some of) the collaborating agents is chosen at random the threat of a collusion attack may be unlikely.

2.2   Where Tamperproof Solutions are Required

Despite all possible attacks against mobile agents that may be countered with some of the techniques described above there still remain cases where we need *provably* secure prevention. For example, detection of tampering is inappropriate for E-money if the amount of money involved is too low to justify legal actions or law enforcement is difficult. Also remote digital signing of contracts would become virtually impossible because divulging the user's private key would deprive the user from the possibility to proof that she did not order some good. If one does not exclude these types of actions a user wants to delegate to its mobile agent, then prevention of tampering and privacy guarantees are mandatory. Therefore, in this paper we concentrate on positive solutions for the problem of providing provably strong protection to individual mobile agents against tampering and spying attacks.

2.3   A General Belief on the Vulnerability of Mobile Agents

There is a widespread belief in the mobile agent community that an entity which executes a given program has fully control over its execution, that the entity may potentially fully understand the program and therefore eventually can change it in any way it wants. Without linking the execution of a program to some trusted "safe haven" there would therefore be no way to let a mobile agent do security sensitive operations. This view has been expressed at several places in the literature. Chess et al., for example, write in [3]:

> "It is impossible to **prevent** agent tampering unless trusted (and tamper-resistant) hardware is available [...]. Without such hardware, a malicious [host] can always modify/manipulate the agent. [...] As alluded to above, it is impossible to keep an agent private unless its itinerary is known in advance."

While this belief is often restated, there are no rigorous arguments that could be used to verify this statement. However, there are some intuitive arguments that seem to strongly support this view. The following points certainly apply for a mobile agent's program:

- Cleartext data can be read and changed.
- Cleartext programs can be manipulated.
- Cleartext messages, e.g., to the originator, can be faked.

But the important point is that there is no intrinsic reason why programs have to be executed in cleartext form: In the same sense that you can communicate some ciphermessage to another party without understanding it, we would like a computer to execute a cipherprogram without understanding it. So our claim is that the folklore about the mobile agent's vulnerability is wrong because it tacitly assumes that a mobile agent consists of cleartext data and cleartext programs.

2.4   The Possibility of Executing Encrypted Programs

While later on in this paper we will give examples for how one can encrypt functions such that the executing entity will not learn anything substantial about them, we will briefly review the consequences this has.

A first and nice observation is that if we can execute encrypted programs without decrypting them, we automatically have a) code privacy and b) code integrity in the sense that specific tampering is not possible. Attacks by a malicious host would then be reduced to actions "at the surface of the mobile agent": denial of service, random modifications of the program or of its output as well as replay attacks.

However, a solution for the protection of mobile code is susceptible to new attacks that were not possible in a non-mobile program environment. Because an attacker can run the program in a fully controllable setting and arbitrarily often, he could collect sufficient data to recover essential information about the program, even if it is encrypted.

2.5   Realizing Cryptographic Primitives in Unsecured Hosts

The biggest challenge is indeed the question whether useful cryptographic primitives can be realized with mobile code. If in fact sufficiently many and powerful cryptographic services can be run even at distrusted places, we can envisage fully mobile agent based software environments that can be trusted. They can keep secrets, take care of their replication for increased redundancy, perform cryptographic protocols with other mobile agents and disclose their content if told so (after they verified themselves authorization, of course). In this paper we present in Section 5 a first cryptographic primitive that a mobile agent could implement in a secure way, namely digital signing.

3   Computing with Encrypted Functions

Instead of using the more general term 'program' as we did in the previous sections we will from now on differentiate between a *function* and the *program* that implements it. Thus, our goal is to encrypt functions such that their transformation can again be implemented as programs. The resulting program will consist of cleartext instructions that a processor or interpreter understands. What the processor will not be able to understand is the "program's function".

Closely related to our goal of computing with encrypted function (CEF) is the problem of computing with encrypted data (CED). Starting from this point we will discuss in this section the limits of the solutions proposed so far and explore some structural constraints on encrypting functions that are imposed by the desired non-interactiveness for mobile agents. We then identify an important class of such encryptable functions, namely polynomials and rational functions.

3.1 Computing with Encrypted Data

The problem of computing with encrypted data (CED) has been described by Abadi and Feigenbaum [1] in the following way:

> Bob has an algorithm to compute a function f and is willing to compute $f(x)$ for Alice. Alice wants to compute f on her private input x but does not want to reveal x to Bob. Furthermore Alice should not learn anything substantial about the algorithm of Bob for computing f.

Their proposed solution yields a highly *interactive* protocol to this problem in the model of "Boolean circuits": it allows Alice to encrypt the input data x in such a way that Bob can compute $f(x)$ for her without getting to know the cleartext x. Abadi and Feigenbaum also point to the following relation between CED and computing with encrypted functions:

> *"It is also clear from this description that the distinction between 'data' and 'circuits' is unnecessary. If [Alice] has the ability to hide a circuit, then [she] can also hide some private data, simply by hardwiring it into the circuit. Conversely, in protocols in which [Alice] has the ability to hide data, [she] can also hide a circuit through a detour: [Alice] can run the protocol, take the circuit for f to be universal circuit, and use an encoding of the circuit [she] wants to hide as an input."*

Assume that Alice wants to have her function g executed by Bob. Thus, by letting Bob's algorithm f be a universal circuit, Alice can encrypt the Boolean circuit computing g as input data for Bob's universal circuit. While it is therefore principally possible to compute with encrypted functions, Abadi and Feigenbaum's solution is interactive and requires several rounds of message exchanges between Alice and Bob. The number of communication rounds is related to the depth of a Boolean circuit which represents the universal circuit and may be quite large. Hence the needed amount of interactiveness contradicts the spirit of mobile agents which should be able to perform their computation in a mostly autonomous way.

Another also important drawback is that the reduction of CEF to CED as it is described by Abadi and Feigenbaum is infeasible. It is true that a Boolean function (circuit) $f : \mathcal{B}^n \to \mathcal{B}$ can be realized by substituting in a universal Boolean function $U : \mathcal{B}^m \to \mathcal{B}$ certain variables specifying the function f. However, for a function $U : \mathcal{B}^m \to \mathcal{B}$ that is universal for the class of boolean functions $\{f : \mathcal{B}^n \to \mathcal{B}\}$ we necessarily have that $m \geq \frac{2^n}{\log(2n+2)}$ [11]. Thus we get an exponential blowup by using universal Boolean functions which means that this principally correct approach is computationally infeasible.

So seemingly there is a difference between hiding "data" and hiding "circuits". The infeasibility of the reduction suggests that CEF may me much harder then CED. We will show for an important instance of algebraic circuits that actually the opposite might be the case because we can significantly weaken the conditions on the encryption function.

3.2   Non-interactive Computing with Encrypted Functions

With the requirements of mobile agents in mind we can now state the problem that we want to solve:

> Alice has an algorithm to compute a function f. Bob has an input x and is willing to compute $f(x)$ for her, but Alice wants Bob to learn nothing substantial about f. Moreover, Bob should not need to interact with Alice during the computation of $f(x)$.

A Protocol for "Non-interactive Computing with Encrypted Functions". For letting Alice and Bob work together in the way described before, we assume that a function f can be transformed (encrypted) to some other function $E(f)$. The encryption hides the function f and may or may not produce also encrypted output data. We let the notation $P(f)$ stand for the program that implements the function f. Figure 1 depicts a protocol in which Alice does not send to Bob the program $P(f)$ for the plain function f but the program $P(E(f))$ for the encrypted function $E(f)$. Bob only learns about the program $P(E(f))$ that he has to apply to his input x and the result of this computation that he has to return to Alice.

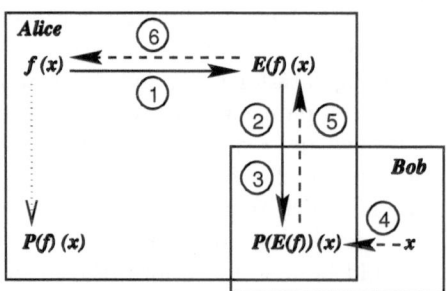

Fig. 1. Computing with encrypted functions.

The simple protocol of Figure 1 for non-interactive computing with encrypted functions looks like this:

(1) Alice encrypts f.
(2) Alice creates a program $P(E(f))$ which implements $E(f)$.
(3) Alice sends $P(E(f))$ to Bob.
(4) Bob executes $P(E(f))$ at x.
(5) Bob sends $P(E(f))(x)$ to Alice.
(6) Alice decrypts $P(E(f))(x)$ and obtains $f(x)$.

3.3 Computing with Encrypted Functions Using Composition

A simple way of achieving code privacy consists in Alice diverting the function herself. Thus, Bob is asked to compute some systematically modified function $E(f)$ whose results can be ungarbled exclusively by Alice.

Let us describe an easy example. Assume the function Alice wants to evaluate at Bob's input x on Bob's computer is a linear map A. She does not want to reveal A to Bob, so she picks at random an invertible matrix S and computes $B := SA = E(A)$. She sends B to Bob, Bob computes $y := Bx$ and sends y back to Alice. Alice computes $S^{-1}y$ and obtains the result Ax without having disclosed A to Bob.

This is an example for CEF where the encryption of a function can be realized efficiently. The encryption of matrix A also garbles the output of the computation, so Alice has to decrypt the result sent back by Bob.

The matrix example can be generalized: we encrypt a polynomial f by composing it with another function g. Assume f is a rational function (the quotient of two polynomials) and s is a rational function too such that Alice is able to invert s efficiently, then let $E(f) := s \circ f$. The security of this method is based on the difficulty of decomposing the resulting $E(f)$:

Decomposition Problem: Given a multivariate rational function h that is known to be decomposable, find s and f such that $h = s \circ f$.

Interestingly, there are already results on the hardness of decomposing rational functions. No polynomial time algorithm for decomposing multivariate rational functions is known [19]! Furthermore, ways to construct rational functions s that we use to garble f and that are easy to invert have been proposed by Shamir [13] in a different context. An in-depth analysis of such a composition approach remains to be carried out. But it shows that interesting candidates for doing CEF indeed exist.

3.4 Encrypting Polynomials and Rational Functions

The challenge is to find encryption schemes for arbitrary functions. In a first approach we identify specific function classes for which we can find encrypting transformations. An interesting class are polynomials and rational functions. At the current stage we have to leave it open whether the CEF approach is applicable to arbitrary functions – we even can not claim to have achieved a complete solution for the case of all polynomials. However, within the restricted setting of polynomials and rational functions we can prove first positive results that falsify the "general belief on mobile code vulnerability" for non trivial cases. Rational functions represent a very rich and important class of functions. By studying them we hope to find principles that apply to a much broader class of functions.

On the Relation Between General Programs, Boolean Circuits, Algebraic Circuits, and Polynomials. What are the fundamental limits for the set of functions that can be computed in encrypted form? Our goal is to map a cleartext program P to an encrypted program P_E such that Alice can recover $P(x)$ from $P_E(x)$ for some unknown input x of Bob. The encrypted program can not just be any data stream but has to be an executable program. Therefore most of the ordinary *data* encryption techniques can not be applied. Furthermore we want that the cleartext program and its encrypted form are "compatible" with each other. The mathematical analogue is the one of an algebraic structure i.e., a domain set M and a number of operations and relations on M. The mathematical analogue for "compatible transformations" are homomorphisms that are compatible with the operations and relations. Assume for example that $(G, +)$ is a group. A homomorphism $\varphi : (G, +) \to (G, +)$ is a map such that $\varphi(x + y) = \varphi(x) + \varphi(y)$. Programs are usually build out of a small set of building blocks – the instructions the programming language provides. What we need is the computational analogue to homomorphisms which respects the building blocks. Processing *data* via "homomorphic functions" has been studied e.g., in [12].

In the following section we focus on algebraic homomorphic encryption schemes i.e., maps between algebraic structures (we study rings) that are compliant with the compatibility constraint. Programs thus would be represented by algebraic circuits or polynomials. From a cryptographic viewpoint the mathematical "compatibility" requirement by using homomorphisms may be too strong. Recall that the map we use to transform a cleartext program into an encrypted program should be hard to invert for an adversary. There might not be enough (mathematical) homomorphisms available as encryption functions or they might be too easy to invert and therefore not be suited for one-way encryption functions. Consider for example the ring $\mathbb{Z}/n\mathbb{Z}$ where the only functions that are additively homomorphic are linear functions $x \to cx$ which turn out to be totally insecure. However, the required "compatibility" is considerably weaker in a computational framework than in the mathematical framework: instead of requiring for a map between groups that $\varphi(x + y) = \varphi(x) + \varphi(y)$, it is for computational purposes sufficient that $\varphi(x+y)$ can be efficiently computed from $\varphi(x)$ and $\varphi(y)$. Exponentiation in $\mathbb{Z}/p\mathbb{Z}$ is an example for such a map.

How do algebraic circuits relate to Boolean circuits? It is known that (under reasonable conditions) every algebraic circuit on finite fields can be simulated efficiently by Boolean circuits. The converse of this is wide open (cf. [16] for a discussion of these issues). Shifting from a Turing machine model to Boolean circuits is not a restriction: Every language in $\mathcal{P}$ i.e., which can be recognized by a deterministic Turing machine in polynomial time, can be recognized by uniform Boolean circuits of polynomial size [17]. So there may be programs that can not be efficiently simulated using algebraic circuits (but which are feasible for Boolean circuits). It would be very interesting to derive methods for evaluating encrypted Boolean circuits non-interactively by conceding that some information about the original circuit may be revealed. The requirement to hide *all* information (except the number of bits it requires as an input) about a Boolean circuit is too strong because it leads to the use of universal Boolean circuits which we already had identified as computationally infeasible before. But for many applications it will be enough to hide only partial information about the Boolean circuit which allows to circumvent the universal construction. In this paper we study how to evaluate polynomials $p = \sum a_{i_1 \ldots i_s} X_1^{i_1} \ldots X_s^{i_s}$ on rings $\mathbb{Z}/n\mathbb{Z}$ securely. Polynomials that can be written in this sparse representation by an expression of feasible size are a subset of the polynomials on $\mathbb{Z}/n\mathbb{Z}$ that can be computed by algebraic circuits of feasible size.

4   Homomorphic Encryption Schemes

What are the structural requirements of encryption functions that can map one function to another one? We start this investigation by looking at systems which enable to do computations on encrypted data. In the beginning of the 90s Feigenbaum and Merritt asked the following question [6]:

> Is there an encryption function E such that both $E(x + y)$ and $E(xy)$ are easy to compute from $E(x)$ and $E(y)$?

Encryption functions $E : R \rightarrow S$ for rings R and S having the property stated above are called *algebraic homomorphic encryption schemes*. Their ability to serve as encryption schemes for non-interactive computing with encrypted data and encrypted functions depends on the homomorphic properties a specific homomorphic encryption scheme (HES) has.

Definition 1. *Let R and S be rings. We call an (encryption) function $E : R \rightarrow S$*

- *additively homomorphic if there is an efficient algorithm* PLUS *to compute $E(x + y)$ from $E(x)$ and $E(y)$ that does not reveal x and y,*
- *multiplicatively homomorphic if there is an efficient algorithm* MULT *to compute $E(xy)$ from $E(x)$ and $E(y)$ that does not reveal x and y,*
- *mixed multiplicatively homomorphic if there is an efficient algorithm* MIXED-MULT *to compute $E(xy)$ from $E(x)$ and y that does not reveal x,*
- *algebraically homomorphic if it is additively and multiplicatively homomorphic.*

4.1   Homomorphic Schemes for Computing with Encrypted Data

In [6] Feigenbaum and Merritt wonder whether there exist algebraic homomorphic encryption schemes. The reason for this is the following

Proposition 1. *Algebraic homomorphic one-way trapdoor functions $E : R \rightarrow S$ allow non-interactive CED for the evaluation of polynomials (resp. algebraic circuits) $p \in R[X_1, \ldots, X_s]$.*

Proof. Assume E is algebraic (i.e., additively and multiplicatively) homomorphic and let $p = \sum a_{i_1 \ldots i_s} X_1^{i_1} \ldots X_s^{i_s}$ be the polynomial to be evaluated at some encrypted value $E(x)$. Using the following protocol, Bob computes $E(p(x))$ without knowing x.

(1) Alice computes $E(x)$ on her private input x.
(2) Alice sends the function E, the algorithms PLUS and MULT and the value $E(x)$ to Bob.
(3) Bob writes a program P that implements p in the following way:
  - each coefficient $a_{i_1 \ldots i_s}$ of p is replaced by $E(a_{i_1 \ldots i_s})$,
  - each multiplication in the evaluation of p becomes a call to MULT,
  - each addition in the evaluation of p becomes a call to PLUS.
  Using this program P, Bob computes $P(E(x))$.
(4) Bob sends $P(E(x)) = E(p(x))$ back to Alice.
(5) Alice decrypts it i.e., computes $E^{-1}(E(p(x)))$ and obtains $p(x)$.

The program P when run on the value $E(x)$ in fact returns $E(p(x))$ because $\text{PLUS}(E(a), E(b)) = E(a+b)$ and $\text{MULT}(E(a), E(b)) = E(ab)$. The algorithms for PLUS and MULT (which are dependent on E) are given to Bob e.g., in form of mobile code.

4.2 Homomorphic Schemes for Computing with Encrypted Polynomials

Along the same line as above we can also use algebraic homomorphic trapdoor functions for hiding the *function* instead of the data.

Proposition 2. *An algebraic homomorphic trapdoor one–way function $E : R \to S$ allows non-interactive CEF for polynomials (resp. algebraic circuits) $p \in R[X_1, \ldots, X_s]$.*

Proof. Similar to the case of CED we use the encryption function E to encrypt the coefficients of p. But this time it is Alice who performs the encryption: thus it is Alice who creates the program P and who sends it to Bob together with E. Sending E to Bob is necessary so he can compute $E(x)$ on his input value x before feeding it to the program P. We could imagine that E is also included in the program P as are the PLUS and MULT procedures. Bob then simply runs this fully selfcontained program P_E for the input x and returns to Alice the program's output.

Remark 1. (Limits of applicability due to information leakage) This protocol has the property that it reveals the non-zero coefficients of the cleartext polynomial p because Bob can compute $E(0)$ and compare it with the coefficients provided by Alice. Partial information about the polynomial is leaked: by comparing the coefficients of the encrypted polynomial an adversary gets to know which coefficients of the cleartext polynomial are equal and which are different.

For classes of polynomials whose coefficients belong to a small subset of R our scheme (like any deterministic public key cryptosystem) is vulnerable to low entropy attacks where an adversary computes a table of the encrypted values of the expected coefficients and then decrypts by looking up the coefficients of $E(f)$ in his table. Probabilistic encryption schemes secure against this type of attack.

However, even with probabilistic encryption schemes can not every family of polynomials be safely encrypted by our protocol. The family of RSA–encryption functions, for example, would still be vulnerable under this protocol because there is only *one* non-zero exponent to look for. As the encrypted polynomial of the RSA-function has only a polynomially bounded number of monomials an adversary might find the secret key by exhaustive search.

Unfortunately there is no secure general *algebraic* homomorphic encryption scheme known so far. So it is desirable to find other HES to perform CEF:

Proposition 3. *Let $E : R \to R$ be an additively and mixed multiplicatively homomorphic encryption scheme. Then Alice needs to publish only* PLUS, MIXED-MULT *and $E(f)$ to realize CEF for f.*

Proof. Let again $p = \sum a_{i_1 \ldots i_s} X_1^{i_1} \ldots X_s^{i_s}$

(**1**) Alice creates a program $P(X)$ that implements p in the following way:
   – each coefficient $a_{i_1 \ldots i_s}$ of p is replaced by $E(a_{i_1 \ldots i_s})$
   – the monomials of p are evaluated on the input $x_1, \ldots, x_s$ and stored in a list $L := [\ldots, x_1^{i_1} \ldots x_s^{i_s}, \ldots]$
   – the list $M := [\ldots E(a_{i_1 \ldots i_s} x_1^{i_1} \ldots x_s^{i_s}) \ldots]$ is produced by calling MIXED-MULT for L and the coefficients $E(a_{i_1 \ldots i_s})$
   – the elements of M are added up by calling PLUS.
(**2**) Alice sends the program P to Bob.
(**3**) Bob runs P on his private input $x_1, \ldots, x_s$ and obtains $P(x_1, \ldots, x_s)$
(**5**) Bob sends the result $P(x_1, \ldots, x_s) = E(p(x))$ back to Alice.
(**6**) Alice decrypts the result by applying E^{-1} and obtains $p(x)$.

Remark 2. In this case E needs not necessarily to be a one-way function anymore because f needs not to be disclosed by Alice at all (PLUS and MIXED-MULT are sufficient). This further weakening of the requirements on the encryption scheme makes it easier to come up with such a scheme. On the other hand the protection of E against disclosure is rather weak: once an adversary gets to know $E(1)$ he may compute $E(x)$ for arbitrary x by applying MIXED-MULT to the pair $(E(1), x)$.

4.3 $\mathbb{Z}/n\mathbb{Z}$-Cryptosystems

We have seen that it is very useful for CEF to have encryption functions that are additively and mixed multiplicatively homomorphic. A simple but important observation is that for $\mathbb{Z}/n\mathbb{Z}$-cryptosystems the first property (additively homomorphic) implies the second one. This makes it possible to describe encryption schemes that can be used to realize computing with encrypted polynomials. In this section we discuss HES for the ring $\mathbb{Z}/n\mathbb{Z}$.

Lemma 1. *An additive homomorphic encryption function on $\mathbb{Z}/n\mathbb{Z}$ is also mixed multiplicative homomorphic.*

Proof. We have to construct an algorithm MIXED-MULT using PLUS only, such that MIXED-$Mult(E(x), y) = E(xy)$. Assume $y = \sum_{i=0}^{\log n} y_i 2^i$. First compute the list $E(x2^i), 1 \leq i \leq \log n$ by repeated addition using PLUS. To obtain $E(xy)$ add up those $E(2^i x)$ for which $y_i \neq 0$.

Corollary 1. *An additively homomorphic encryption scheme $E : \mathbb{Z}/n\mathbb{Z} \to \mathbb{Z}/m\mathbb{Z}$ allows CEF for polynomials.*

Proof. Combine proposition 3 and lemma 1.

4.4 Algebraic Schemes that are Additively Homomorphic

There already exist schemes on $\mathbb{Z}/n\mathbb{Z}$ that enable to compute $E(x + y)$ from $E(x)$ and $E(y)$ directly. An example is the Naccache-Stern public key encryption function [10]. However, this scheme can not be used for CEF. The Naccache-Stern approach is computationally infeasible because to guarantee the correctness of the results the polynomial many calls to PLUS that in general are needed to perform CEF require the system parameter p to be chosen exponentially large.

We propose a scheme that does not have these problems.

A Scheme Based on Exponentiation
The exponentiation map $E : \mathbb{Z}/(p-1)\mathbb{Z} \to \mathbb{Z}/p\mathbb{Z}, x \mapsto g^x$, for a prime p and g a generator of $(\mathbb{Z}/p\mathbb{Z})^\times$ is additively homomorphic: the function PLUS is the simple multiplication because $E(x + y) = E(x)E(y)$. To recover x from $y := E(x)$ one has to solve the discrete logarithm problem $y = g^x$ which is believed to be hard. Alice chooses a prime p such that the discrete log problem is easy to solve (e.g., if $p-1$ has only small prime factors she can use the Pohlig-Hellmann algorithm for computing discrete logarithms efficiently). She further chooses a generator g of $(\mathbb{Z}/p\mathbb{Z})^\times$ which she keeps secret. Alice can use corollary 1 to realize CEF.

Remark 3. The security of the scheme relies on the secrecy of g. An additively homomorphic encryption scheme based on discrete logarithms which does not have this shortcoming i.e., which can be published, is currently under development by Lipton and Sander [8] (see also [2]). Their scheme is furthermore probabilistic which significantly reduces the information leakage about the original polynomial.

4.5 Preliminary Conclusions

Non-interactive computing with encrypted functions is a challenge to cryptography. Although some theoretical results related to CEF were produced in the vicinity of computing with encrypted data, these findings seem to be impractical with respect to their computational feasibility as well as their interactiveness. Our approach of studying algebraic homomorphic encryption schemes (HES) yields a first and surprisingly simple scheme for CEF. Thus, by changing the conditions (looking at polynomials instead of Boolean circuits) we obtained a feasible and non-interactive solution. A more advanced scrutiny will have to show whether and under which conditions this scheme is secure. We should keep looking for other (and hopefully secure) additively homomorphic encryption schemes.

5   Offline Digital Signing in a Malicious Host

Can an agent carry and keep a secret? The answer is certainly yes as any secret data can be given to the agent as long as it remains encrypted. The important point is, however, that an agent would like to *use* the secret in public e.g., to compute the digital signature of an order form but without disclosing the secret needed to do so. In this section we introduce the concept of *undetachable digital signatures* and a possible realization of it that allows a mobile agent to effectively produce a digital signature inside a remote and possibly malicious host without the host being able to deduce the agent's secret or to reuse the signature routine for arbitrary documents.

5.1   Making Digital Signatures "Undetachable"

Let us assume for the moment that we have a way to conceal a function s that produces a digital signature e.g., using the CEF approach. The problem then is that even if the real signature routine could be kept secret, still the whole (encrypted but operational) routine might be abused to sign arbitrary documents which simply would make the signing process worthless. We therefore need a way to glue the signature routine to the function f that produces the output that is to be signed. How could a practically useful remotely signed document look like? The output producing routine f could for example add to each document a prefix saying that the following digitally signed order form is valid only for a single airline ticket issued for a specific date and costing less than a certain amount of dollars. Thus, our intention is to "cast" into the general purpose signing routine some task specific information which is enforced to be part of the signed document.

We give now the outline of an idea how one can sign the output of a function f securely, where f is given by a rational function. Let s be a rational function used by Alice to produce the digital signature $s(m)$ of an arbitrary message m. Furthermore we want the message m to be the result of a rational function f applied to some input data x. Finally we need a function v that Alice publishes in order to let others check the validity of the digital signature, i.e., z is regarded to be a valid signature of m if and only if $v(z) = m$. For letting her mobile agent create "undetachable" signatures, Alice computes the dense representation of $f_{signed} := s \circ f$. She sends f and f_{signed} to Bob who evaluates both $f(x)$ and $z = f_{signed}(x)$.

A valid output of this algorithm is the pair $(f(x), z := f_{signed}(x))$. Applying the verification function v to z every user can check that the message $f(x)$ indeed is a valid output of the function f. If Bob wants to pretend that a message n is a valid output of Alice's function f, he would have to construct $s(n)$. So the security of the method lies in Bob's inability to construct $s(n)$ for a given n. Unfortunately there are at least four attacks against this scheme:

- *Left decomposition attack:*
  Given the rational functions $h := s \circ f$ and f determine s.
- *Interpolation attack I:*
  The function v is public. So an adversary can produce a list of pairs $(z, v(z))$. Because s is a rational function it is feasible to reconstruct s by interpolation techniques. (Observe that s has to be a function of low degree, because else the size of $s \circ f$ in a dense representation will explode. So the interpolation attack is in fact a realistic threat for the secrecy of s.)
- *Interpolation attack II:*
  An adversary can produce pairs $(l, s(l))$ where he obtains l by using the output function f. Again, a rational function s could be reconstructed.
- *Inversion attack:*
  If Bob is able to find a preimage x of n under f, i.e., $f(x) = n$, he can produce a valid signature z for n by computing $z := f_{signed}(x)$.

The *Interpolation attack I* applies to every signature scheme based on low degree rational functions used for the signing routine. Shamir, who also introduced the signature schemes where the signature routine is given by rational functions, had an interesting idea how to overcome this difficulty that we are also going to use below. To secure our scheme against these attacks we first switch to a multivariate context using the following notation:

(i) Let $s = (s_1, \ldots, s_k) : R^k \to R^k$ be a bijective function whose components are given by rational functions (R is a ring or a field). s is a so called birational map. (To be more precise, s is defined as $s : U \to R^k$ where U is a Zariski–open subset of R^k).

(ii) Let $v = (v_1, \ldots, v_k) : R^k \to R^k$ be the inverse function of s, i.e., $s \circ v = v \circ s = id_{R^k}$.

(iii) Let $f : R^l \to R^t$ be the function whose output Alice wants to be signed.

(iv) We further assume that rational functions $G_2, \ldots G_k : R^t \to R$ are known to the public. (These functions can be used by many users like Alice to obtain signing routines for their mobile programs).

Now we are ready to describe how the modified scheme works:

Public key Alice's public key for the signature verification is given by the function $v_2, \ldots v_k$. (Observe that Alice does not publish v_1).

Construction of the signed program Alice chooses a random rational function $r : R^l \to R$. She constructs the map $f_{signed} : R^l \to R^k$ with components given by $f_{signed,i} := s_i(r, G_2 \circ f, \ldots, G_k \circ f), 1 \le i \le k$. Alice computes the dense representation of f_{signed}. She sends the tuple of functions (f, f_{signed}) to Bob.

Execution of the signed program Bob computes $y := f(x)$ and
$z := f_{signed}(x)$. (y, z) is then a signed output of the program.

Verification of the signature Compute $G_i(y), 2 \leq i \leq k$ and $v_i(z), 2 \leq i \leq k$.
z is a signature of y if and only if $v_i(z) = G_i(y)$ for $2 \leq i \leq k$.

Let us briefly describe how these modifications yield a scheme that is strengthened against the attacks mentioned above. The key point is that an adversary
does not know the functions r and v_1.

(i) Because an adversary does not know r the left decomposition attack to
obtain s_i from the i'^{th} component of f_{signed} has become even harder.

(ii) Because an adversary does not know v_1 he can not compute input/output
pairs for the interpolation of the s_i.

(iii) Because an adversary does not know r he can not compute input/output
pairs for the interpolation of the s_i as described in the second interpolation
attack.

(iv) Even if an adversary is able to invert f the scheme is not broken. Because
an adversary does not know r he does not know how to compute preimages
of $(r, G_2 \circ f, \ldots, G_k \circ f) : R^l \to R^k$. (Note that already to invert the rational function f an adversary has to solve a multivariate system of algebraic
equations. This problem is known to be very hard. So an adversary will not
be able to invert f except for some very simple choices of f.)

Ways to construct birational functions s that are easy to invert have been
described by Shamir in the second part of [13]. However, the schemes resulting from those constructions have been successfully attacked by Coppersmith,
Stern and Vaudenay [4]. So there is a need to find new constructions for secure birational functions to put our ideas to work. We expect that other ways
to construct secure birational maps can be found e.g., based on concepts from
Algebraic Geometry where birational maps are extensively studied.

A detailed analysis of the security of the proposed scheme remains to be
given.

6   Conclusions

Although we do not claim to have a general solution for the main problem of
mobile agent protection, we produced evidences that code can at least partially
be protected against a malicious host. We identified a special class of functions –
polynomials and rational functions – together with encryption schemes that
lead to a first non-trivial example of cryptographically hiding a function such
that it can nevertheless be executed with a non-interactive protocol. We also
described an approach to hide a signing function and to make digital signatures
"undetachable" which prevents that the signing procedure can be abused for
signing arbitrary documents. While a more thorough analysis of the security
properties of our schemes remains to be done, we hope that they represent a first
step towards fully software based mobile code protection. We expect interesting
and surprising results from a field that might be called "mobile cryptography".

References

1. M. Abadi and J. Feigenbaum. Secure circuit evaluation. *Journal of Cryptology*, 2(1):1–12, 1990.
2. J. Benaloh. Dense probabilistic encryption. In *Proceedings of the Workshop on Selected Areas of Cryptography*, pages 120–128, 1994.
3. D. Chess, B. Grosof, C. Harrison, D. Levine, and C. Parris. Itinerant agents for mobile computing. Technical Report RC 20010, IBM, March 1995.
4. Don Coppersmith, Jacques Stern, and Serge Vaudenay. Attacks on the birational permutation signature schemes. In Douglas R. Stinson, editor, *Proceedings of CRYPTO'93*, number 773 in LNCS, pages 435–443, 1993.
5. Dave Dyer. Java decompilers compared. http://www.javaworld.com/javaworld/jw-07-1997/jw-07-decompilers.html, June 1997.
6. J. Feigenbaum and M. Merritt. Open questions, talk abstracts, and summary of discussions. *DIMACS Series in Discrete Mathematics and Theoretical Computer Science*, 2:1–45, 1991.
7. Don Libes. *Obfuscated C and other mysteries*. Wiley, 1993.
8. Richard Lipton and Tomas Sander. An additively homomorphic encryption scheme or how to introduce a partial trapdoor in the discrete log, November 1997. Submitted for publication.
9. Catherine Meadows. Detecting attacks on mobile agents. In *Proceedings of the DARPA workshop on foundations for secure mobile code, Monterey CA, USA*, March 1997.
10. David Naccache and Jacques Stern. A new public-key cryptosystem. In *Advances in Cryptology - EUROCRYPT'97*, LNCS, pages 27–36, 1997.
11. Franco P. Preparata. Generation of near-optimal universal boolean functions. *Journal of Computer and System Sciences*, 4:93–102, 1970.
12. Ronald L. Rivest, Len Adleman, and Michael L. Dertouzos. On data banks and privacy homomorphisms. In R. A. DeMillo, D. P. Dobkin, A. K. Jones, and R. J. Lipton, editors, *Foundations of Secure Computation*, pages 169–179. Academic Press, 1978.
13. Adi Shamir. Efficient signature schemes based on birational permutations. In Douglas R. Stinson, editor, *Proceedings of CRYPTO'93*, number 773 in LNCS, pages 1–12, 1993.
14. K. B. Sriram. Hashjava - a java applet obfuscator. http://www.sbktech.org/hashjava.html, July 1997.
15. Giovanni Vigna. Protecting mobile agents through tracing. In *Proceedings of the Third ECOOP Workshop on Mobile Object Systems, Jyväskylä Finnland*, June 1997.
16. Joachim von zur Gathen and Gadiel Seroussi. Boolean circuits versus arithmetic circuits. *Information and Computation*, 91:142–154, 1991.
17. Ingo Wegener. *The Complexity of Boolean Functions*. Eiley-Teubner, 1987.
18. Bennet S. Yee. A sanctuary for mobile agents. In *Proceedings of the DARPA workshop on foundations for secure mobile code, Monterey CA, USA*, March 1997.
19. Richard E. Zippel. Rational function decomposition. In *Proceedings of the International Symposium on Symbolic and Algebraic Computation*, pages 1–6. ACM Press, July 1991.

Safe, Untrusted Agents Using Proof-Carrying Code *

George C. Necula and Peter Lee

Carnegie Mellon University, School of Computer Science
Pittsburgh, PA 15217, USA
necula,petel@cs.cmu.edu

Abstract. Proof-Carrying Code (PCC) enables a computer system to
determine, automatically and with certainty, that program code provided
by another system is safe to install and execute without requiring interpretation or run-time checking. PCC has applications in any computing
system in which the safe, efficient, and dynamic installation of code is
needed. The key idea is to attach to the code an easily-checkable proof
that its execution does not violate the safety policy of the receiving system. This paper describes the design and a typical implementation of
Proof-Carrying Code, where the language used for specifying the safety
properties is first-order predicate logic. Examples of safety properties described in this paper are memory safety and compliance with data access
policies, resource usage bounds, and data abstraction boundaries.

1 Introduction

Proof-Carrying Code (PCC) enables a computer system to determine, automatically and with certainty, that program code, also referred to as an *agent*, provided
by another system is safe to install and execute. The key idea behind PCC is
that the external system, which we shall henceforth refer to as the *code producer*,
provides an encoding of a proof that the code adheres to a safety policy defined
by the recipient of the code, which we shall call the *code consumer*. The proof is
encoded in a form that can be transmitted digitally to the consumer and then
quickly validated using a simple, automatic, and reliable proof-checking process.

PCC is useful in many applications. It enhances the ability of a collection
of software systems to interact flexibly and efficiently by providing the capability to share executable code safely. Typical examples of code consumers include

---

* This research was sponsored in part by the Advanced Research Projects Agency
CSTO under the title "The Fox Project: Advanced Languages for Systems Software,"
ARPA Order No. C533, issued by ESC/ENS under Contract No. F19628-95-C-0050.
The views and conclusions contained in this document are those of the authors and
should not be interpreted as representing the official policies, either expressed or
implied, of the Advanced Research Projects Agency or the U.S. Government.

operating system kernels and World-Wide Web browsers, which must allow untrusted applications and Internet hosts to install and execute code. Indeed, PCC is useful in any situation where the safety in the presence of newly installed code is paramount.

PCC has several key characteristics that, in combination, give it an advantage over previous approaches to safe execution of foreign code:

1. *PCC is general.* The code consumer defines the safety policy, and this policy is not limited to a particular notion of "safety." We have experimented both with simple safety properties, such as memory and type safety, and with properties that are normally difficult to verify, such as time limits on execution and resource usage bounds.

2. *PCC is low-risk and automatic.* The proof-checking process used by the code consumer to determine code safety is completely automatic, and can be implemented by a program that is relatively simple and easy to trust. Thus, the *safety-critical infrastructure* (also referred to as the *trusted computing base*) that the code consumer must rely upon is reduced to a minimum.

3. *PCC is efficient.* In practice, the proof-checking process runs quickly. Furthermore, in contrast to previous approaches, the code consumer does not modify the code in order to insert costly run-time safety checks, nor does the consumer perform any other checking or interpretation once the proof itself has been validated and the code installed.

4. *PCC does not require trust relationships.* The consumer does not need to trust the producer. In other words, the consumer does not have to know the identity of the producer, nor does it have to know anything about the process by which the code was produced. All of the information needed for determining the safety of the code is included in the code and its proof.

5. *PCC is flexible.* The proof-checker does not require that a particular programming language be used. PCC can be used for a wide range of languages, even machine languages.

This paper describes Proof-Carrying Code and how it can be used to enforce safety in the presence of untrusted agents. We begin with a general overview of the basic elements of PCC. Then, each of the major components of PCC is described in the subsequent sections. For a more concrete presentation of the implementation details of PCC, we introduce in Sect. 5 a stripped-down example of a safety policy and an associated agent that can be used for agent-based shopping. After we complete the discussion of PCC we review the agent example in the context a more complex safety policy (Sect. 8). We conclude with a comparison with related work and a presentation of the experimental result showing that agents using PCC can be much faster than agents whose safety is enforced through run-time checking.

2   Basic Elements of Proof-Carrying Code

Proof-Carrying Code has many applications, and each such application may entail some variations on the precise details of the approach. We will have more to say about some of these variations in the next section. In this section we describe at a high-level a canonical implementation of PCC which is general enough that any of the variations can be seen as optimizations or special cases.

In its most general form PCC involves, in addition to a *code consumer* and *code producer*, a *proof producer*. In practice, it often turns out that the code producer and proof producer are the same system, though in general they may be separate entities.

A central component of any PCC implementation is the *safety policy*, which is specified once and for all by the code consumer, in advance of any interaction with mobile code. In this paper, we use the term "safety policy" in two distinct ways. First, we use it to refer informally to the set of safety rules that the code consumer desires to enforce for any untrusted code. We also use the term "safety policy" to denote the concrete realization of these safety rules. In PCC, the concrete realization of the safety policy is used not only by the code consumer, but is also exported to the producers, thereby allowing the consumer and each producer to work cooperatively. Details about the implementation of the safety policy are given in Sect. 4.

Once the safety policy is defined, PCC involves a two-stage interaction process. In the first stage, the code consumer receives the untrusted code and extracts from it a *safety predicate* that can be proved only if the execution of the code does not violate the safety policy. This predicate is then sent to the proof producer who proves it and returns its proof back to the consumer. In the second stage, the code consumer checks the validity of the proof using a simple and fast proof checker. If the proof is found to be a valid proof of the safety predicate, then the untrusted code is installed and executed.

This two-stage verification process is a key design element contributing to the advantages listed in the previous section. In particular, this is the reason PCC can be used to certify code properties that would be very difficult, or even impossible, to infer from the code directly. Also, by staging the verification into a difficult phase (proof generation) and a simple phase (proof checking), we are able to minimize the complexity of the safety-critical infrastructure. That is, the implementation of the proof-checking process is simplified, thereby greatly reducing the risk that a bug in the system leads to the failure to detect unsafe programs. In fact, we have made it a design goal of PCC that any task whose result can be more easily checked than generated should be performed by an untrusted entity (the code or the proof producer), and then checked by the code consumer.

We now give a step-by-step description of a typical PCC session, glossing over many implementation details. These details are deferred to later parts of this paper. Fig. 1 shows a session based on the canonical PCC implementation, where the sequence of steps is determined by the arrows.

Step 1. A PCC session starts with the code producer preparing the untrusted code to be sent to the code consumer. As part of this preparation, the producer adds *annotations* to the code. This can be done manually, or else automatically by a tool such as a *certifying compiler* (which we shall discuss

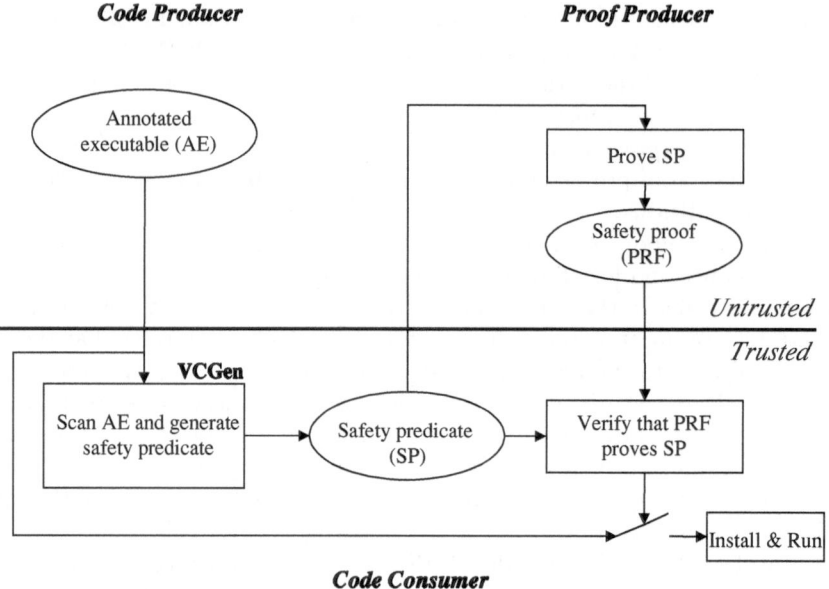

Fig. 1. Overview of Proof-Carrying Code.

later, and for which a full description is given in [15]). The annotations, whose exact nature is discussed in a later section, contain information that helps the code consumer understand the safety-relevant properties of the code. The code producer then sends the annotated code to the code consumer, requesting its execution.

Step 2. Upon receiving the annotated code, the code consumer performs a fast but detailed inspection of the annotated code. This is accomplished using a program, called *VCGen*, which is one component of the consumer-defined safety policy. VCGen performs two tasks. First, it checks simple safety properties of the code. For example, it verifies that all immediate jumps are within the code-segment boundaries. Second, VCGen watches for instructions whose execution might violate the safety policy. When such an instruction is encountered, VCGen emits a predicate that expresses the conditions under which the execution of the instruction is safe. Following the standard terminology from the field of automatic program verification, we refer to such predicates as *verification conditions* (and hence VCGen can be seen as a classical verification condition generator). The collection of the verification conditions, together with some control flow information, make up the *safety predicate*, a copy of which is sent to the proof producer.

Step 3. Upon receiving the safety predicate, the proof producer attempts to prove it, and in the event of success it sends an encoding of a formal proof back to the code consumer. Because the code consumer does not have to trust the proof producer, any system can act as a proof producer. In particular the code producer can also act as the proof producer.

Step 4. The next step in a PCC session is the proof validation step performed by the code consumer. This phase is performed using a program which we refer to as the *proof checker*. The proof checker verifies that each inference step in the proof is a valid instance of one of the axioms and inference rules specified as part of the safety policy. In addition, the proof checker verifies that the proof proves the same safety predicate generated in Step 2. This prevents an attacker from circumventing the PCC system by submitting, for example, a valid proof of a trivial predicate.

Step 5. Finally, after the executable code has passed both the VCGen checks and the proof check, it is trusted not to violate the safety policy. It can thus be safely installed for execution, without any further need for run-time checking.

3   Variants of Proof-Carrying Code

The process described above and depicted in Fig. 1 present a canonical view of Proof-Carrying Code. However, this approach to PCC is not the only one. By redistributing the tasks between the entities involved we can adapt PCC to special practical circumstances while maintaining the same safety guarantees. In this section we briefly discuss several such variations. Then, in the subsequent sections, we present details of the implementation of each component of PCC.

- In one variant of PCC the code producer runs VCGen itself and then submits the resulting predicate to the proof producer. Then the code and the proof are sent together to the code consumer, who in turn runs VCGen again and verifies that the incoming proof proves the resulting safety predicate. This arrangement is possible because there is nothing secret about VCGen and it can therefore be given to untrusted code producers to use. To retain the safety guarantees of original PCC, it is necessary that the code consumer repeats the VCGen step in order to produce a trustworthy safety predicate. Because this version saves a communication step in generating the safety predicate, it is preferred over the interactive version when the latency of the verification must be minimized.

- In another variant of PCC the code consumer does the proof generation. For this to be possible it must be the case that the safety predicate be relatively easy to prove automatically without extra knowledge about the program. This variant of PCC is useful in situations when the generated proof would be too large to send over the communication channel between the proof producer and the code consumer.

  Even though the code consumer does more work in this variant of PCC, the safety-critical infrastructure, consisting of VCGen and the proof checker, remains the same. One could be tempted to save the cost of generating, storing and verifying the proof altogether by trusting the theorem prover on the consumer side. But this savings is at the expense of greatly increasing the size and complexity of the safety-critical infrastructure, and our experience suggests that relying on the correctness of a complex theorem prover is a dangerous game.

– Yet another scheme for employing PCC is to use one of the variants above to establish the safety of the code on given code consumer system C, and then to forward this code for execution to any other system that trusts C. This trust can be established by any convenient means such as digital signatures. This scheme might be useful in enclaves where there are some trusted machines with the computational power to perform the VCGen and proof-checking phases, and other machines that do not have this power but still want to execute the untrusted code. For example, a firewall might certify external code using PCC and then forward the code to other machines inside the firewall.

No matter which of these or other variants are chosen, they all share the same characteristic of depending on a small and well-defined safety-critical infrastructure, given by a simple proof checker and VCGen.

4   The Safety Policy

Starting with this section, we consider in more detail the main building blocks of a PCC system. We start with the safety policy, and then continue in the next sections with descriptions of the VCGen, proof checker, and proof generator components.

As we mentioned earlier, the term "safety policy" is used in two distinct ways, first to refer informally to the set of safety requirements demanded of all incoming mobile programs, and second to refer to the concrete realization of the safety policy in a running PCC system. This concrete realization consists of four elements, as follows:

– An *agent language* in which the mobile agents must be written. PCC does not restrict the language that can be used, although all of the examples presented in this paper use DEC Alpha assembly language, in part to emphasize the fact that PCC can accommodate a wide range of languages. In practice, higher-level languages might be used to increase portability. Also, a given code consumer might accept agents written in multiple languages, in which case a safety policy is defined for each language.

– A *logic* that is able to describe the conditions under which an agent is considered safe. In principle, any program logic can be used. In the current instantiation of PCC, we use first-order predicate logic extended with predicate symbols as dictated by the safety properties to be proved. For example, in a safety policy for which read-access must be controlled, a predicate symbol saferd (*mem, addr*) might be added to the logic, to specify the conditions under which it is safe to read the cell in memory state *mem* at address *addr*. The logic is described as a set of syntactic predicate constructors along with a set of axioms and inference rules that define provability.

- A *specification* for each function implementing the interface between the code consumer and the agent. This includes the functions that the consumer provides to agents and the agent entry points. The specification for a function is given as a pair of a precondition and a postcondition, expressed as predicates in the selected logic.
  A function precondition describes the state of the variables and actual arguments at the moment when the function is invoked. The precondition must be established prior to invoking the function. This enables the callee to assume that it holds without verifying it first.
  A function postcondition describes relationships between variables, actual arguments and the result values. The postcondition predicate must be established prior to returning from a function. This enables the caller to assume that it holds upon return.
- Finally, the safety policy must also contain a method for inspecting the agent code and for discovering the potential safety violations that can occur during its execution. This is accomplished by the *verification condition generator* (VCGen), which performs syntactic checking and produces a *verification condition* (VC) predicate that is provable within the selected logic only when the agent code is considered safe to execute.

We now describe the design of the VCGen component.

5   Design Details of VCGen

The purpose of VCGen is twofold: to perform simple checks on the untrusted code, and to emit verification conditions for all checks that are mandated by the safety policy but difficult to perform at this time. In order to simplify the adaptation of VCGen to different safety policies, it is useful to restrict the checks performed by VCGen to those code properties that are likely to be encountered in many safety policies (e.g., that branch targets are within the code boundaries, or that the function invocations follow a stack discipline). All other checks should be emitted as general verification conditions, whose interpretation is left to the logic used in the proofs of the safety predicates.

For example, we have found it to be useful to assume that some form of memory safety is always going to be part of the safety policy. However, we do not want to hard-wire in VCGen a particular form of memory safety. Hence, we have designed VCGen to emit a generic verification condition $\mathtt{saferd}\,(mem, addr)$ for each attempted read access from address $addr$ in memory state mem. Then, it is left to the proof logic to determine the meaning of the $\mathtt{saferd}$ predicate. As an extreme example, a given logic might even say that $\mathtt{saferd}$ is never true, thus effectively disallowing memory reads.

Several techniques for implementing VCGen have been described in the literature [3, 8]. As shown in Fig. 2, our approach to implementing VCGen involves two main components. One is the language-dependent *parser*, whose purpose is to translate the instructions of the untrusted annotated code to a stream of instructions in a generic *intermediate language* (IL) that is understood by the

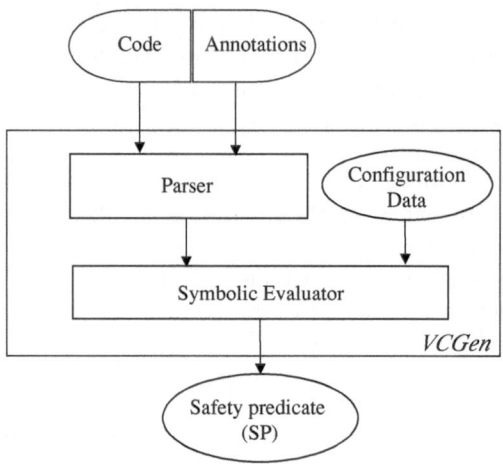

Fig. 2. The structure of VCGen

second component, the *symbolic evaluator*. VCGen can be customized to a particular safety policy by using a configuration file that is provided as part of the safety policy by the code consumer.

Example: An Agent-Based Travel Agency. For a more concrete presentation of the implementation details that follow, we introduce here a simple example of a safety policy and an associated agent that can be used for agent-based shopping.

Assume that a travel agency host records a database of pricing information for airline tickets between various destinations. A distinguishing feature of this particular travel agency is that mobile untrusted agents are allowed to scan the database and then communicate back to their parent host. To control the access to the information in the database, the travel agency implements a multi-level access protection scheme for the database. For this purpose, it assigns access levels to the agent and to each record in the database, and requires that an agent can only access those records whose access level is less or equal to its own access level. And to make things even more interesting the travel agency decides not to mediate at all the interaction between the agent and the database, but instead to use Proof-Carrying Code to select the agents that obey the safety policy from those whose behavior is uncertain.

For the purpose of this paper, we are using a simple agent that computes the best available price for a trip. The actual agent is expressed in DEC Alpha assembly language, but for clarity we only show here the C source code (Fig. 3). We make the simplifying assumption that the database is an array of pricing entries, each entry containing four 32-bit fields encoding the entry access level, the source and destination airport and the associated price, in that order. We focus here only on the operation of reading the price fields. This agent will be used in future sections to exemplify the operation of the building blocks of PCC. For the purpose of providing a simple example, we initially ignore the communication between the agent and its parent host. Then in Sect. 8, we will expand the safety policy to allow communication and to restrict the agent's use of CPU cycles and network bandwidth.

```
int main(ENTRY tab[], int len, ACCESS acc) {
  for(j=0;j<len;j++) {
    if(tab[j].access <= acc) {int p = tab[j].price; ... }
  }
}
```

Fig. 3. A fragment of an agent that computes the best available price for a trip.

5.1   The Code Annotations

Some of the code properties of interest are, in general, difficult to infer from the code directly. In such cases VCGen relies on the code annotations provided by the producer as an extra source of information about the code behavior. As we mentioned earlier, these annotations can be inserted manually or automatically generated by a tool such as a compiler [15]. No matter how this is accomplished, we must be careful to ensure that incorrect annotations will not cause unsafe program behavior to be hidden.

There are several kinds of annotations that we currently use, some of them mandatory and others used only for optimization purposes. The most important mandatory annotations are the *loop invariants*. Their main purpose is to associate with each loop a set of properties that are preserved by the execution of the loop body, and that are sufficient for proving the safety of the code. The presence of a loop invariant for each loop in the code makes it possible for VCGen to extract the safety predicate in just one pass through the code. The requirement that every loop has an associated invariant can be easily satisfied by associating an invariant with every backward-branch target.

For each loop invariant two verification conditions are emitted as part of the safety predicate: one verifies that the invariant holds on loop entry and the other verifies that it is preserved through one loop iteration. If both these are proved, then, by induction, the loop invariant can be assumed valid for the purpose of inspecting the loop body and the code following the loop.

There are other less important annotations that we do not describe here. However, they all share the property that they are untrusted and, following the model of the loop invariants and call-target annotations, they are checked using verification conditions.

5.2 The VCGen Configuration File

In order to reduce the need for dynamic checking of parameters, the code consumer usually declares a *precondition*, which is essentially a description of the calling convention the consumer will use when invoking the untrusted code. For example, if the untrusted code needs to access Ethernet network packets, the code consumer might declare that the first argument passed to the code is an array of length at least 64 bytes. With this assumption array accesses to most packet header fields can be proved safe without the need for run-time array-bounds checking. The safety policy can also declare *postconditions* for the untrusted code. These are constraints on the final execution state of the untrusted code.

Both the precondition and postcondition are parameters of VCGen and are part of the safety policy. The preconditions and the postconditions for all the functions declared by the untrusted code, as well as for the functions exported by the code consumer, are expressed as first-order logic predicates in a VCGen configuration file. The code consumer guarantees that the code precondition holds when the untrusted code is invoked. In turn, the untrusted code must ensure that the postcondition holds on return. For functions exported by the consumer the situation is reversed and the precondition is a predicate that the untrusted code must establish before calling the function while the postcondition is a predicate that the untrusted code may assume to hold upon return from the function.

Example: The Safety Policy for the Agent-Based Travel Agency. We return now to the example introduced before, with the purpose of defining the necessary precondition and postcondition. We define the predicate $\texttt{entry}(m, e, a)$ to denote that, in memory state m and for an agent whose access level is a, the address e points to an entry in the pricing database. This is described formally as follows:

$$\texttt{entry}(m, e, a) = \texttt{saferd}(m, e + 0) \wedge \texttt{saferd}(m, e + 4) \wedge \texttt{saferd}(m, e + 8) \wedge$$
$$(sel(m, e + 0) \leq a \supset \texttt{saferd}(m, e + 12))$$

Informally, the above definition says that the 32-bit words situated at offsets 0, 4 and 8 from the start of the entry are always readable, while the word situated at offset 12 (the price) is only readable if the value of the first word (the access level) is less than or equal to the agent's own access level.

For this application, the VCGen has been constructed to check that each agent contains a function $\texttt{main}(tab, len, acc)$ that expects as arguments the starting address of the table, the number of entries in the table and the access level that was assigned to this agent. No postcondition is assigned to the agent at this time, meaning that **H** imposes no requirements on the agent's result. This calling convention is expressed as a pair of a precondition and a postcondition, as shown below:

$$Pre_{\texttt{main}} = \forall i.0 \leq i \wedge i < len \supset \texttt{entry}(mem, tab + i \times 16, acc)$$
$$Post_{\texttt{main}} = \texttt{true}$$

This safety policy could be enforced at run time only if each access to the table is mediated by the host. In our example, the untrusted agent performs the access checks itself without invoking the host, thus greatly reducing the run-time penalty for enforcing safety.

5.3   The Code Parser

The purpose of the code parser is to provide a machine and language-independent interface to the symbolic evaluator. In fact, the parser is the only language-dependent component of a PCC system. While translating instructions from the incoming language to the intermediate language it abstracts over language and code details that are not relevant to the safety policy.

The intermediate language (IL) syntax is shown in Tab. 1. To simplify the parsing of machine code, we use a generic assembly language as the IL. The examples presented in this paper require one distinguished variable *mem* for denoting the state of the memory during symbolic evaluation. If the safety policy makes explicit use of other state components besides memory, then they should be modeled in a similar fashion. Beyond this requirement the sets of variables and labels are left abstract at this time because they depend on the particular source language being parsed.

Variables	*Vars*	x
Variable sets	$\mathcal{P}(\textit{Vars})$	s
Labels	*Label*	l, f
Expressions	*Expr*	$e ::= x \mid n \mid e_1 + e_2 \mid e_1 - e_2 \mid$
		$\mathtt{sel}\,(e_1, e_2) \mid \mathtt{upd}\,(e_1, e_2, e_3)$
Predicates	*Pred*	$P ::= \mathtt{true} \mid \mathtt{false} \mid P_1 \wedge P_2 \mid P_1 \supset P_2 \mid \forall x.P_x \mid$
		$e_1 = e_2 \mid e_1 \neq e_2 \mid e_1 \geq e_2 \mid e_1 < e_2 \mid$
		$\mathtt{saferd}\,(e_1, e_2) \mid \mathtt{safewr}\,(e_1, e_2, e_3)$
Instructions	*Instr*	$c ::= \mathtt{SET}\ x, e \mid \mathtt{ASSERT}\ P \mid \mathtt{CALL}\ l \mid \mathtt{RET} \mid$
		$\mathtt{BRANCH}\ P_1 \to l_1 \square\ P_2 \to l_2 \mid$
		$\mathtt{INV}\ P, s \mid \mathtt{MEMRD}\ e \mid \mathtt{MEMWR}\ e_1, e_2$

Table 1. The syntax of the intermediate language (IL).

For expository purposes, the intermediate language presented here is restricted to the few constructors that we shall use in our examples. In practice, expressions for most arithmetic and logical operation would also need to be included. Also, depending on the needs of the safety policy, an extension of first-order logic might be used, such as temporal, linear or higher-order logic. Two special expression constructors merit some discussion. The expression $\mathtt{sel}\,(e_1, e_2)$ denotes the contents of memory address e_2 in the memory state denoted by e_1.

The expression upd (e_1, e_2, e_3) denotes the new memory state obtained from the old state e_1 by updating the location e_2 with the value denoted by e_3.

At the level of predicates we introduce two special predicates for dealing with memory safety. The predicate saferd (e_1, e_2) is valid if in the memory state denoted by e_1 it is safe to read from the address denoted by e_2. The predicate safewr is used similarly for memory writes, with the extra argument denoting the value being written.

The invariant instruction INV P, s requires that predicate P be valid at the corresponding program point, and it also declares the maximal set of variables that might be modified on all loop paths that contain this instruction.[1] The instructions MEMRD and MEMWR are used by the parser to signal to the symbolic evaluator that a memory access instruction was decoded. They can be safely ignored if the safety policy is not concerned with memory safety because their state-changing semantics is redundantly expressed via the SET instruction (see Tab. 2 for examples). The CALL , RET , and BRANCH instructions denote procedure call, procedure return, and conditional branching, respectively. The ASSERT instruction tests the given predicate, allowing program execution to continue only if the predicate is found to be valid.

For example, Fig. 4 shows a possible IL representation of the agent of Fig. 3. The loop invariant for the main loop is $j \geq 0$ and the only changed variable in the loop is j.

```
           SET     j, 0
  Loop : INV     j ≥ 0, {j}
           BRANCH j < len → L₁ □ j ≥ len → Done
  L₁ :    BRANCH sel(mem, tab + 16 × j) ≤ acc → L₂ □ ... < acc → Next
  L₂ :    MEMRD   tab + 16 × j + 12
           SET     p, sel(mem, tab + 16 × j + 12)
           ...
  Next : SET     j, j + 1
           BRANCH true → Loop
```

Fig. 4. The intermediate language representation for the agent shown in Fig. 3.

---

[1] The set of modified variables is an optimization allowing the symbolic evaluator to construct smaller safety predicates. If it is missing then it is conservatively approximated by the set of all variables in scope.

$DEC\,Alpha$	IL	$Observations$
start of function	SET sp_0, sp SET ra_0, ra	At the start of function save the values of the stack pointer and return address.
addl r_1, r_2, r_d	SET $r_d, r_1 + r_2$	Most arithmetic and logical instructions are done similarly.
ANN_CALL (f) jsr $ra, (pv)$	ASSERT $sp = sp_0 - \mathit{fsz}$ ASSERT $pv = f$ CALL f SET $ra, pc + 4$	Require a CALL annotation. Emit checks for the stack pointer and the correctness of the annotation. The return address register is changed by the call.
jsr $zero, (ra)$	ASSERT $sp = sp_0$ ASSERT $ra = ra_0$ RET	On return, verify the stack pointer and the return address.
ANN_INV (P, s)	INV P, s	Invariant annotations are propagated unchanged.
ldl $r_d, n(sp)$	ASSERT $sp = sp_0 - \mathit{fsz}$ SET r_d, f_j	Check that $0 <= n < \mathit{fsz}$ and $n \bmod 4 = 0$. Let $j = n/4$. Emit check for the stack pointer.
ldl $r_d, n(r_b)$	MEMRD $r_b + n$ SET $r_d,$ sel $(mem, r_b + n)$	For other load instructions signal the read and its effect of the state.
stl $r_s, n(sp)$	ASSERT $sp = sp_0 - \mathit{fsz}$ SET f_j, r_s	Check that $0 <= n < \mathit{fsz}$ and $n \bmod 4 = 0$. Let $j = n/4$. Emit check for the stack pointer.
stl $r_s, n(r_b)$	MEMWR $r_b + n, r_s$ SET $mem,$ upd $(mem, r_b + n, r_s)$	For other store instructions signal the write and its effect on the memory state.
beq r_s, n	BRANCH $r_s = 0 \rightarrow$ $L(pc + n + 4)$ $\Box\ r_s \neq 0 \rightarrow L(pc + 4)$	L is a mapping from DEC Alpha machine code addresses to labels within the stream of IL instructions.

Table 2. Parser for DEC Alpha machine code. The current function being parsed is declared to use a frame of size fsz. At each line, pc is the machine code index of the DEC Alpha instructions.

Example: Parsing DEC Alpha Machine Code. As an example we describe a parser from a subset of DEC Alpha machine code to the intermediate language IL. The set of variables in this case are the 32 machine registers of the DEC Alpha plus the special memory variable mem. In order to simplify the resulting safety predicate we might want to let the parser interpret the spill area of the stack

frame as an extension of the register file.[2] For this purpose we extend the set of
IL variables with $f_0, \ldots, f_{F-1}$ where F is a limit we impose on the number of
spill slots. In order to keep the parser simple, we require the untrusted code to
declare its frame size fsz. In the same spirit of simplicity, only memory accesses
through the register sp will be interpreted as accesses to the stack. All other
accesses are treated as ordinary memory accesses.

For the purpose of checking procedure calls and returns we define two other
special variables, sp_0 and ra_0, that are used to keep the initial values of the
stack pointer and return address registers. The DEC Alpha has only indirect
procedure calls that are difficult to translate to the IL call syntax, which requires
an immediate label. This information gap is bridged by requiring, in the position
immediately preceding the call instruction, a call-target annotation ANN_CALL
that declares the actual call target.

Table 2 shows the definition of the parser for the DEC Alpha machine code as
a mapping from sequences of DEC Alpha machine instructions and annotations
to sequences of IL instructions. Each line in the table is assumed to occur at
label pc in the machine code. For convenience we assume that annotations are
in-lined in the machine code. In practice, the actual implementation stores the
annotations off-line in the data segment.

5.4   The Symbolic Evaluator

The symbolic evaluator executes the intermediate code produced by the parser.
As opposed to a concrete evaluator, it does not actually perform the basic operations of the IL, but instead it computes the result as a symbolic expression.
The symbolic evaluator can be implemented as a linear pass through the code
because all loops are required to have an invariant.

The output of the symbolic evaluator is the safety predicate, which consists
mainly of verification conditions. A verification condition is emitted, for example, whenever the symbolic evaluator encounters memory operations. Besides
verification conditions, the symbolic evaluator also emits predicates corresponding to taken branches and invariants reflecting the control structure of the code.
In many respects, the safety predicate is an expression of that part of the operational semantics of the untrusted code that is relevant to the safety policy.

In order to define the symbolic evaluator, we introduce some notation. The
mapping Π associates function labels to triplets, each triplet containing a precondition, a postcondition and a set of modified global variables. We write
$\Pi_f = (Pre, Post, s)$ when function f is declared with the precondition Pre,
postcondition $Post$ and the set of modified global variables s.

The state of the symbolic evaluator consists of the current label i in the IL
instruction stream and a partial mapping from variables to symbolic expressions
$\rho \in VarState = Vars \rightarrow Expr$. We write $\rho[x \leftarrow e]$ to denote the state obtained
from ρ by setting the variable x to e and we write $\rho(e)$ to denote the expression

---

[2] To avoid the danger of aliasing in the spill area the safety policy must ensure that
this area is not declared as "safe-to-access" by arbitrary memory operations.

resulting from the substitution of variables in e with their values in ρ. We extend this substitution notation to predicates.

For the evaluation of the invariant instructions, the symbolic evaluator keeps track of the invariants seen so far on the path from the start to the current instruction. For each such invariant, the symbolic evaluator also remembers the execution state at the time the invariant was encountered. This is accomplished with a mapping $\mathcal{L}$ from instruction labels to states $\mathcal{L} \in \textit{Loops} = \textit{Label} \rightarrow \textit{VarState}$, such that at any moment during symbolic execution $\textit{Dom}(\mathcal{L})$ is the set of invariants on the current path from the start. The symbolic evaluator is also parameterized by the current function being evaluated and the mapping Π, although we shall often omit these subscripts:

$$SE_{f,\Pi} \in (\textit{Label} \times \textit{VarState} \times \textit{Loops}) \rightarrow \textit{Pred}$$

To simplify the presentation of the evaluator we assume that prior to the evaluation we prepend to the IL representation of each function f the instruction INV $\textit{Pre}, s$, where $\textit{Pre}$ and s are the precondition and the set of modified registers of f.

$SE(i+1, \rho[x \leftarrow \rho(e)], \mathcal{L})$	if $IL_i = $ SET x, e
$\rho(P) \wedge SE(i+1, \rho, \mathcal{L})$	if $IL_i = $ ASSERT P
$(\rho(P_1) \supset SE(i_1, \rho, \mathcal{L})) \wedge (\rho(P_2) \supset SE(i_2, \rho, \mathcal{L}))$	if $IL_i = $ BRANCH $P_1 \rightarrow i_1 \square P_2 \rightarrow i_2$
	$\quad i_1 < i \supset IL_{i_1} = $ INV P_1
	$\quad i_2 < i \supset IL_{i_2} = $ INV P_2
$\textbf{saferd}\ (\rho(m), \rho(e)) \wedge SE(i+1, \rho, \mathcal{L})$	if $IL_i = $ MEMRD e
$\textbf{safewr}\ (\rho(m), \rho(e_1), \rho(e_2)) \wedge SE(i+1, \rho, \mathcal{L})$	if $IL_i = $ MEMWR e_1, e_2
$\rho(P) \wedge \forall y_1 \dots y_k.\rho'(P) \supset SE(i+1, \rho', \mathcal{L}[i \leftarrow \rho'])$	if $IL_i = $ INV $P, \{x_1, \dots, x_k\}$ and
	$\quad i \notin \textit{Dom}(\mathcal{L})$
	$\quad \{y_1, \dots, y_k\}$ are new variables
	$\quad \rho' = \rho[x_1 \leftarrow y_1, \dots, x_k \leftarrow y_k]$
$\rho(P) \wedge \textbf{checkEq}\ (\rho, \mathcal{L}_i, s)$	if $IL_i = $ INV P, s and $i \in \textit{Dom}(\mathcal{L})$
$\rho(\textit{Pre}) \wedge \forall y_1 \dots y_k.\rho'(\textit{Post}) \supset SE(i+1, \rho', \mathcal{L})$	if $IL_i = $ CALL l
	$\quad \Pi_l = (\textit{Pre}, \textit{Post}, \{x_1, \dots, x_k\})$
	$\quad \{y_1, \dots, y_k\}$ are new variables
	$\quad \rho' = \rho[x_1 \leftarrow y_1, \dots, x_k \leftarrow y_k]$
$\rho(\textit{Post}) \wedge \textbf{checkEq}\ (\rho, \mathcal{L}_f, s)$	if $IL_i = $ RET and $\Pi_f = (\textit{Pre}, \textit{Post}, s)$

Table 3. The definition of $SE_{f,\Pi}(i, \rho, \mathcal{L})$, a symbolic evaluator for generic memory safety.

Table 3 presents the symbolic evaluation function $SE_{f,\Pi}(i, \rho, \mathcal{L})$ by cases depending on the instruction being evaluated (IL_i). For each kind of instruction there is one case, except for the invariant instructions, which are treated differently the first time when they are encountered.

The evaluation of a SET instruction consists of updating the state and continuing with the next instruction. In the case of an assertion the symbolic evaluator emits the asserted predicate with variables substituted according to the current state. For a conditional branch the symbolic evaluator considers both branches recursively and then builds the safety predicate as a conjunction of implications. The left side of each implication is the guard predicate of the branch. This way control flow information is made available for the purpose of proving the verification conditions arising from the evaluation of the branches. For MEMRD and MEMWR instructions the evaluator emits appropriate verification conditions for the safety of the memory access.

The evaluation of a loop invariant instruction that is encountered for the first time (its label is not in $Dom(\mathcal{L})$) consists of asserting the invariant, then altering the values of the variables that might be changed by the loop and finally processing the loop body in the new state. The invariant predicate is also assumed to hold before considering the loop body and the new state is recorded in $\mathcal{L}$. When the same invariant instruction is encountered again, the evaluator asserts the invariant predicate and checks that variables not declared as modified have not been changed. The verification conditions corresponding to these equality checks are generated by the auxiliary function checkEq :

$$\text{checkEq } (\rho, \rho', s) = \bigwedge_{x \in (Dom(\rho) \cap Dom(\rho')) - s} \rho(x) = \rho'(x)$$

Not surprisingly, the function call and return instructions are processed in a manner similar to the loop invariants, with just a few minor differences. In processing the RET instruction the reference state for the equality check is recovered from $\mathcal{L}$. This is possible because the first instruction in each function (at label f) is the invariant instruction INV Pre, s.

As an optimization, the evaluator might itself verify some of the simple verification conditions. This has the effect of reducing the safety predicate size and implicitly the proof size. The cost of this optimization is increased code complexity in the symbolic evaluator, and so it must be employed only when the verification conditions are trivial to check. One such case are those variable-equality checks emitted by checkEq that are syntactic identities.

Finally, the safety predicate of a function is obtained by evaluating it symbolically starting in a state that maps the global variables[3] and function formal parameters to new variables $y_1, \ldots, y_k$. Then the resulting predicate is quantified over $y_1, \ldots, y_k$:

$$SP_f = \forall y_1 \ldots y_k.SE_{f,\Pi}(f, [g_1 \leftarrow y_1, \ldots, g_k \leftarrow y_k], \{\})$$

As an example we show in Fig. 5 the safety predicate obtained from the symbolic evaluation of the agent whose IL code is shown in Fig. 4. The first three lines of the safety predicate represent, in order: the final quantification, the precondition and the initial invariant. The rest of the predicate originates from the evaluation of the loop body.

---

[3] The special memory variable *mem* is also a global variable.

$\forall mem. \forall tab. \forall len. \forall acc.$
$\quad (\forall i.\ 0 \le i \wedge i < len \supset \text{entry}(mem, tab + 16 \times i, acc)) \supset$
$\quad\quad (0 \ge 0 \wedge$
$\quad\quad \forall j.\ (j \ge 0 \supset$
$\quad\quad\quad\quad (j < len \supset ((\text{sel}(mem, tab + 16 \times j) \le acc \supset$
$\quad\quad\quad\quad\quad\quad\quad\quad\quad\quad\quad\quad \text{saferd}(mem, tab + 16 \times j + 12)) \wedge$
$\quad\quad\quad\quad\quad\quad (\text{sel}(mem, tab + 16 \times j) > acc \supset j + 1 \ge 0)) \wedge$
$\quad\quad\quad (j >= len \supset \text{true}))$

Fig. 5. The safety predicate of the function **main** of Fig. 3.

6   Encoding and Checking Proofs

The next building block of PCC that we describe is the proof checker. Its purpose is to verify that the proof supplied by the untrusted proof producer uses only allowed axioms and inference rules and that it is a proof of the required safety predicate and not another one. In order to isolate the dependencies on the safety policy we have built a generic proof checker parameterized by a configuration file. The proof checker itself does not contain *any* details of the safety policy, not even of the logic being used. All such details are segregated to the configuration file.

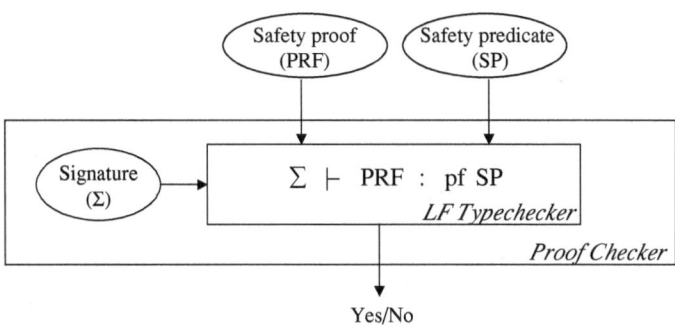

Fig. 6. The structure of the proof checker

To achieve the independence of the safety policy and logic we are currently encoding both the safety predicates and their proofs in the *Edinburgh Logical Framework* [11] (LF), which was specifically designed as a metalanguage for high-level specification of logics. In the rest of this section we only give a brief overview of LF and its use for PCC. The reader interested in a more comprehensive discussion of the subject, including numerous implementation details, should consult [14].

The Logical Framework is a simple typed language (dependent-typed λ-calculus) with four expression constructors (variables, constants, functions and function applications), and a similar set of type constructors:

$$\text{Types } \quad A ::= a \mid A\,M \mid \Pi x{:}A_1.A_2$$
$$\text{Objects } M ::= c \mid x \mid M_1 M_2 \mid \lambda x{:}A.M$$

To encode the syntax of a particular logic (the predicates) and its semantics (the axioms and inference rules), the safety policy declares a set of LF object constants together with their types. We refer to this set of constant declarations as the *LF signature* Σ that defines the logic. Fig. 7 shows a small fragment of the signature that defines the first-order predicate logic with integers. The first two lines declare the constant 0 to be an object (the representation of the numeral 0), and plus to be a binary object constructor. If M_1 and M_2 are the LF representations of respectively e_1 and e_2, then the LF object "plus M_1 M_2" is the LF representation of $e_1 + e_2$. The middle section of the figure shows some predicate constructors.

The particular feature that makes LF an excellent choice for proof checking is the richness of the type system, and in particular its ability to encode predicates as LF types. If P is a predicate then pf P is the type of proofs of P in our logic. In the bottom third of Fig. 7 we show the declaration of two proof constructors. true_i is a nullary proof constructor (a proof constant) that represents the axiom that the predicate true is always valid. The proof constructor mp is used to represent the "modus ponens" proof of a predicate. For example, if M_1 and M_2 are the LF representations of the proofs of $P_1 \supset P_2$ and P_1, respectively, then the LF object "mp P_1 P_2 M_1 M_2" is the LF representation of a proof of the predicate P_2.

```
0      : exp
plus   : exp → exp → exp
...
true   : pred
impl   : pred → pred → pred
=      : exp → exp → pred
...
true_i : pf true
mp     : Πp:pred.Πr:pred.pf (impl p r) → pf p → pf r
```

Fig. 7. A fragment of the LF signature describing the syntax and semantics of first-order logic.

The actual proof-checking operation is done by verifying that the proof object PRF has type pf SP, where SP is the safety predicate of interest. This LF typechecking operation, written as $\vdash_{\Sigma} PRF : \text{pf } SP$, verifies both the facts that the proof contains only proof constants declared in Σ, and that it proves the right predicate.

An important feature of LF type-checking is that it is very simple and can be completely described by fifteen inference rules and implemented in less than five pages of C code [14]. Furthermore, because the LF type checker is completely independent of the particular logic being used by the safety policy, we can reuse it for checking proofs in other logics. A standing proof of reusability is that in all of our past and present experiments with PCC we have used the same unmodified implementation of LF type-checking with safety policies ranging from memory safety and type safety to termination and resource usage bounds. Furthermore, because LF type-checking is simple and abstract, it is possible to prove formally its adequacy for proof checking [11, 14].

In our PCC implementation the LF signatures are expressed in proof-checker configuration files using a format that is virtually identical to the one used in Fig. 7. To further increase our confidence in the proof-checking infrastructure, the configuration file must itself pass the LF type-checker before being used for type-checking proofs.

7   Generating Proofs for PCC

The safety predicates are expressed using first-order logic, with all of the language and machine details either abstracted or modeled in the logic, so the proof generator must be a theorem prover for a fragment of first-order logic. For first-order logic, many theorem-proving systems have been implemented [2, 4, 5, 7, 9, 18]. To our knowledge, all of these are able to prove typical safety predicates, sometimes with the help of additional tactics that might be provided by a human or code consumer. However, for some safety properties, automatic decision procedures do not exist or are not effective. In such cases it is more practical to use a semi-interactive theorem prover guided by a person with a deep understanding of the reasons underlying the safety of the untrusted code.

To be usable as a PCC proof producer, a theorem prover must not only be able to prove safety predicates but must be also capable of generating detailed proofs of them. Furthermore these proofs must be expressed in the particular logic (i.e., using the axioms and inference rules specified as part of the safety policy) used by the code consumer. The major difficulty here is to make the theorem prover output the proof, because once we have all the proof details, it is generally easy to transform them in the format expected by the consumer.

In our implementations of PCC, we have used two different theorem provers so far. The first, and most primitive, theorem prover that we used was developed using the Elf [19] implementation of LF. The Elf system is able to read an LF signature describing a logic and then answer queries of the form: *Is there any LF object M having type* pf *P?* If P is the representation of the predicate that we want to prove and the answer to the query is yes, then M is a representation of the proof, and by construction it is a valid proof. So basically, the theorem prover consists of the Elf system together with the LF signature part of the safety policy.

The major problem with the Elf approach to theorem proving is that Elf uses a very simple search algorithm that is inappropriate for many logics. In some cases, mostly having to do with integer arithmetic, we had to add redundant inference rules to the safety policy so that Elf could find a proof.

Lately we have switched to our own implementation of a theorem prover based on the Nelson-Oppen architecture for cooperating decision procedures [16], also implemented in the Stanford Pascal Verifier [6] and the Extended Static Checking [7] systems. The distinguishing feature of our implementation is that it outputs an LF representation of the proof of successfully proved predicates.

The theorem prover uses several decision procedures, the most notable ones being Simplex, for deciding linear inequalities, and the congruence closure, for deciding equalities. In addition, it also incorporates a decision procedure for modular arithmetic and a simple matcher. The theorem prover is a complicated system implementing complex algorithms, so it is of great practical importance that we do not have to rely on its soundness. We just have to check every proof that it outputs. In fact, by doing so we were able to discover subtle bugs in the theorem prover. With this theorem prover we are currently able to prove completely automatically most safety predicates arising from our PCC experiments.

8   Controlling Resource Usage with PCC

Previous sections describe Proof-Carrying Code and an example of its use for certifying the memory safety and the conformance with a simple access protection scheme for a simple shopping agent. In this section we expand the safety policy to allow communication from the agent to its parent host and also to restrict the agent's use of CPU cycles and network bandwidth. Then we consider an agent that exploits this extended policy to gather and send to its parent all entries satisfying an arbitrary predicate.

8.1   Extending the Safety Policy with Resource Usage Bounds

In order to control the total execution time of an agent we extend VCGen to perform a simple timing analysis of the agent's code. To keep things simple we use instruction counts as estimates for execution time and we define a pseudo-variable in the IL, *icount*, that is incremented by one for every instruction that is being parsed.[4] Then we change the parser to prepend a "SET *icount, icount* + 1" instruction to the translation of every instruction from the agent's code. For example, the translation of an add instruction from the DEC Alpha machine language to the IL is now described as follows:

$$\texttt{addl}\ r_1, r_2, r_d \longrightarrow \textbf{SET}\ icount, icount + 1$$
$$\textbf{SET}\ r_d, r_1 + r_2$$

---

[4] A more precise estimate of the execution time could be obtained by increasing the increment amounts for instructions that are likely to take more time to complete.

The instruction-count variable can be referred to in preconditions and postconditions in order to specify timing constraints. For example, to limit the execution of the agent to maximum MAXRUN instructions we add the predicate $icount \leq icount^0 + \text{MAXRUN}$ to the agent's postcondition. (The superscript 0 on a variable refers to its value at function entry.) However, this is not quite enough because the symbolic evaluator of Sect. 5 enforces only partial correctness, and thus the postcondition is enforced only in the event the function terminates. Total correctness is important not only for termination but for a large class of program properties, usually referred to as *liveness* properties, that require the occurrence of certain events during the execution (as opposed to safety properties that prevent the occurrence of certain events).

Fortunately, with only a minor change to the symbolic evaluator we can also enforce total correctness. If the symbolic evaluator automatically adds the predicate $icount \leq icount^0 + \text{MAXRUN}$ to every loop invariant and function postcondition, then a valid safety predicate ensures the termination of every loop or function, and therefore the postconditions can be used to express total correctness properties.[5]

Next, we extend the safety policy to allow communication between an agent and its parent host. For this purpose the host **H** supplies the function sendBack, which the agent can invoke with a memory address and the number of words to be sent. The precondition of sendBack states that the entire memory range referred to by the actual arguments is agent readable. To address the resource usage issues arising during the communication, the safety policy limits both the memory and network bandwidth usage. This is achieved in a conservative manner by limiting the size of a single message and the timing between successive invocations. Concretely, the safety policy requires that the length argument passed to sendBack is less than MAXSEND and that at least $\text{MINWAIT} \times len$ instructions have to have passed since the previous communication before a message of length len can be sent. This conservatively limits the memory buffer usage to MAXSEND and the network bandwidth used to $\text{Freq}/(\text{MINWAIT} \times \text{CPI})$, where Freq is the processor's clock frequency and CPI is the average number of cycles-per-instruction for the agent execution.

The implementation of the sendBack function has to be customized for every individual agent, for example with the address of the parent host. A simple way to do this is for the code consumer to prepare a closure data structure containing the customization information, and to give a pointer to it to the main function of the untrusted code. Then the agent is required to use this closure every time it invokes sendBack. The safety issue that arises is how can we ensure that the untrusted agent does not invoke sendBack with a phony or tampered closure argument? The answer is inspired by abstract types. We define an abstract type closureSB with no constructors and we require that one argument to the sendBack function have this type. The untrusted code must then prove that the

---

[5] Programs that are intended not to terminate but which must have certain liveness properties can be structured as a function that is invoked repeatedly by the host. The liveness properties are then verified on this function.

type of the actual argument to the sendBack function has the abstract closure type, and the only way it can do that is by passing along the closure that was supplied by the host.

Finally, we extend the safety policy with a host-provided function sleep that the agent can use to delay its execution for the equivalent of a number of instructions passed as an argument.

Having described the safety policy informally, we proceed now with its formalization in first-order logic. We start with the simpler task of formalizing the abstract closure type for sendBack and continue with the formalization of the bandwidth limitation.

The logic counterpart of an abstract type with no constructors is an uninterpreted unary predicate symbol with no introduction axioms. Thus we introduce the predicate closureSB(x) to denote that the expression x is a valid closure for the sendBack function.

To formalize the bandwidth limitation we consider the more general problem of restricting the timing between various events during execution. For our particular example we use two event constructors: start, to denote the start of agent execution, and send, to denote a communication event. Then we define a pseudo-variable log that is used to keep a log of events and their occurrence times. This is a global variable and, just like the memory and instruction count pseudo-variables, it is implicitly passed to, and potentially modified by every function. Valid values of the log variable are expressions of the form new(l, e, c), denoting that a new event e occurred when the instruction count was c in the state of the log denoted by l.

In order to manipulate the event occurrence times we define the expression timeOf(l, e) to denote, in a log state l, the value of the instruction count at the last occurrence of event e. If the event e never occurred, the function is undefined. This meaning of timeOf is expressed using the following axioms:

$$\frac{}{\texttt{timeOf}(\texttt{new}(l,e,c),e) = c} \qquad \frac{e \neq e'}{\texttt{timeOf}(\texttt{new}(l,e,c),e') = \texttt{timeOf}(l,e')} \qquad \frac{}{\texttt{send} \neq \texttt{start}}$$

To conclude the safety policy description we show in Tab. 4 the preconditions and postconditions for the functions involved. Recall that only main is untrusted, and as such the precondition of main and the postconditions of sendBack and sleep are used as assumptions in the safety predicate; the postcondition of main and the preconditions of sendBack and sleep are actual verification conditions in the safety predicate, along with the verification conditions arising from loop invariants and memory operations.

Function	Precondition	Postcondition
main(cl,tb,ln,sl)	closureSB(cl) $\forall i.0 \le i \wedge i < ln \supset$ $\quad$ entry($mem, tb + 16 \times i, sl$) timeOf($log$, start) $= icount$ timeOf(log, send) $= icount$	$icount \le icount^0 +$ MAXRUN
sendBack(cl,dt,ln)	closureSB(cl) $\forall i.0 \le i \wedge i < ln \supset$ $\quad$ safeRd($mem, dt + 4 \times i$) $ln \le$ MAXSEND $icount -$ timeOf(log, send) $\ge$ $\quad\quad ln \times$ MINWAIT	$icount \le icount^0 +$ MAXSB $icount \ge icount^0 +$ MINSB $log =$ new(log^0, send, $icount$)
sleep(c)	$c \ge 0$	$icount = icount^0 + c$

Table 4. The extended travel agency safety policy. Each precondition and post-condition is shown as a list of conjuncts. The pseudo-variables *mem*, *log* and *icount* are considered implicit inputs and outputs of all functions.

8.2   Extending the Shopping Agent

We now swap the travel-agency administrator's hat with that of the code pro-ducer's and we design a shopping agent that uses an arbitrary predicate to select database records to be sent to the parent host. Then we discuss a few key points in proving the safety predicate for the new agent and finally, we describe our experimental results gathered from the actual implementation of the agents.

For the purpose of this paper we stick with the agent design that leads to a simpler proof of safety. Our agent, whose main function is shown in Fig. 8, keeps track explicitly of the instruction counts by using the variables timeout, which conservatively estimates the number of instructions that are still avail-able for execution, and timesend, which conservatively estimates the number of instructions that must pass before a new communication can be initiated. The constants MINSB, MAXSB, MINFIL and MAXFIL are the minimum and maximum number of instructions required for the execution of the functions sendBack and filter respectively. The decrement operations from line 6 account for the in-structions in lines 3–8, while those from line 11 account for the program lines 9–11. Note that the variable timeout is always decremented by the maximum possible execution time, while timesend is decremented by the minimum. The purpose of the constant 6 in the initialization of timeout is to account for the loop preamble and exit (lines 2 and 4). The loop terminates when all the en-tries have been scanned (line 5), or when not enough instructions are left to perform one more iteration through the loop (line 4). The constant MAXLOOP is a conservative estimate of the number of instructions executed in a loop iteration (MAXLOOP = MAXFIL + MAXSB + $4 \times$ MINWAIT) assuming a maximum length wait has to be performed in line 10.

```
1    void main(cl, tab, len, acc) {
2      timesend = 4 * MINWAIT; timeout = MAXRUN - 6; i = 0;
3      while(true) {
4        if(timeout < MAXLOOP) return;
5        if(i >= len) return;
6        i+=; timeout -= 8 + MAXFIL; timesend -= 8 + MINFIL;
7        if(tab[i-1].access > acc) continue;
8        if(!filter(&tab[i-1])) continue;
9        if(timesend >= 0) { sleep(timesend); timeout -= 2 + timesend;}
10       sendBack(cl, & tab[i-1], 16);
11       timeout -= (4 + MAXSB); timesend = 4 * MINWAIT;
12 }}
```

Fig. 8. The skeleton of a shopping agent that attempts to send back to its parent host all pricing table entries that match a certain predicate.

We conclude the presentation of the new agent with the loop invariant of the main loop:

$$Inv = i \geq 0 \wedge \texttt{timeout} \geq 0 \ \wedge$$
$$\texttt{MAXRUN} - 3 - \texttt{timeout} \geq icount - \texttt{timeOf}(log, \texttt{start}) \ \wedge$$
$$0 \leq 4 \times \texttt{MINWAIT} - \texttt{timesend} \ \wedge$$
$$4 \times \texttt{MINWAIT} - \texttt{timesend} \leq icount - \texttt{timeOf}(log, \texttt{send})$$

The first conjunct of the invariant is inherited from the simple agent presented before. The third conjunct specifies that $\texttt{MAXRUN} - 3 - \texttt{timeout}$ is a conservative estimate of the total number of instruction executed (three instructions are being subtracted to allow for the time-out return of line 4). The last two conjuncts of the invariant claim than $4 \times \texttt{MINWAIT} - \texttt{timesend}$ is always positive and a conservative estimate of the number of instructions executed since the last communication operation. The modified symbolic evaluator is adding to the above invariant the predicate $icount - icount^0 \leq \texttt{MAXRUN}$. This additional conjunct is weaker than our loop invariant and we ignore it from now on.

8.3   Proving the Safety of the Extended Agent

The safety predicate and the safety proof corresponding to this agent are too large to show here. Instead we only discuss a key point in the proof and then we report the data obtained from the actual implementation.

When the symbolic evaluator encounters the call to **sendBack** (line 10) it emits the verification condition obtained by substituting the symbolic values of variables in the precondition of **sendBack**. From this verification condition we focus on the conjunct that specifies the timing of **sendBack**. This conjunct is shown below the horizontal line in Fig. 9. Line-number subscripts on variables denote the value of the variable right before the execution of the corresponding line. The proof of this conjunct is by cases, depending whether the **sleep** function is called or not. For the case when `sleep` is called, the proof follows by adding the assumptions shown above the horizontal line in Fig. 9. The first assumption is the loop invariant, the second is from the postcondition of `filter` and the third is from the postcondition of `sleep`.

$$
\begin{array}{c}
icount_4 - \texttt{timeOf}(log_4, \texttt{send}) \geq 4 \times \texttt{MINWAIT} - \texttt{timesend}_4 \\
icount_9 \geq icount_4 + 7 + \texttt{MINFIL} \\
icount_{10} = icount_9 + (\texttt{timesend}_4 - 8 - \texttt{MINFIL}) + 3 \\
\hline
icount_{10} - \texttt{timeOf}(log_4, \texttt{send}) \geq 4 \times \texttt{MINWAIT}
\end{array}
$$

Fig. 9. A fragment of the proof that the precondition of `sendBack` holds at line 10, in the case when the test at line 9 succeeds. Above the line we have assumptions that when added yield the desired conclusion, shown below the line.

The other case of the proof of the precondition of `sendBack`, as well as all the other verification conditions arising from the symbolic evaluation of `main` are proved in a similar manner.

9   Experimental Results

We have implemented the extended safety policy presented in this section in our Proof-Carrying Code system. We constructed a configuration file for VCGen describing the functions involved in the experiment and their preconditions and postconditions. This file is literally a transcription of Tab. 4. We have also created an LF signature describing the first-order logic and the axioms that define the predicates `entry`, and `timeOf`. This is again a literal transcription in the LF syntax of the axioms presented in this paper.

We wrote the agents first in C and then we compiled them to DEC Alpha assembly language. The program for the extended agent then had to be manually edited to adjust for the discrepancy between the number of instructions counted at the C source level and the number of assembly language instructions. We also had to manually add the loop invariant annotations. The resulting programs were submitted to VCGen, which produced a safety predicate for each agent.

We finally proved the safety predicates using a theorem prover developed by us for other applications of PCC. The proof of the safety predicate for the simple agent was done completely automatically. For proving the timing verification conditions for the extended agent we had to customize the theorem prover by providing it with a list of axioms for `timeOf`.

There are two purposes for the experiments presented here. First, we want to show the costs that are specific to PCC, that is the safety predicate generation

time, the proof generation time, the proof size and the cost of proof checking.[6]
Second, we want to quantify the run-time penalty imposed on agent execution
by other techniques that are typically used to enforce the same level of safety.
Finally, we want to integrate the data obtained in these two experiments to
compute, for the simple agent, the minimum number of table entries such that
the cost of safety predicate generation and proof checking is amortized.

The first set of experiments was done to ascertain the costs of proof generation and proof checking. It is important to note that these costs are incurred
only once per agent, independently how many times the agent is executed by the
consumer. For this experiment we have measured the proof size and the times required for VCGen, for proof generation and for proof checking. To put the proof
size into context we also report the machine code size for the agents. As in other
experiments with PCC we obtain proofs that are between three and ten times
larger than the code, with the larger factors observed for more complex safety
policies. These experiments confirm the usual intuition that proof generation is
more expensive than proof checking.

Experiment	Code size (bytes)	Proof size (bytes)	VCGen (ms)	Proof Generation (ms)	Proof Checking (ms)
Simple agent	112	370	0.4	40	1.2
Extended agent	250	2012	1.5	800	12.3

Table 5. The cost of PCC for the two example agents presented in this paper.

The second set of experiments compared agents using PCC to agents implemented in Java [10] and agents isolated using either hardware-memory protection
or Software Fault Isolation (SFI) [20]. The comparison is not entirely fair because
Java and SFI cannot enforce the database access policy, and thus offer weaker
safety guarantees than PCC and hardware-memory protection. All of the measurements are done for the implementation of the simple agent on a 175 MHz
DEC Alpha running DEC OSF 1.3.

For the Java experiment we have embedded the code of Fig. 3 in a simple
Java applet containing timing code. The Java measurements were done using
the bytecode interpreter of Netscape 4.0. Clearly, a JIT compiler would provide
better performance at run time, at the cost of increasing installation time and
the size of the safety-critical infrastructure.

Software Fault Isolation is a technique by which the code consumer inspects
the untrusted agent code and inserts instructions for memory-bounds checking
before each memory operation. This code inspection process is similar to VCGen.
To simulate the effects of SFI, we have instructed the compiler to insert bounds-
checking operations for all memory accesses.

---

[6] We assume that the cost of inserting annotations in the code is negligible, as supported by our experiences with a certifying compiler that does this automatically. [15]

To simulate an agent that runs in a hardware-protected memory space, we have modified the agent to invoke a consumer-supplied function that checks the access level and then copies the entry to the agent's memory space. To simulate more accurately the cost of a function call across different protection domains we have inserted an idling loop lasting 50 instructions in the checking function.

Experiment	Running time (us)	Slowdown	Cross-over (# table entries)
Proof-Carrying Code	0.030	1.0x	-
Software Fault Isolation	0.036	1.2x	200,000
Indirect Access to Data	0.280	9.3x	8,400
Java Interpretation	1.230	41.0x	1,200
Java JIT	–	–	–

Table 6. A comparison of the per-table-entry running time of the simple agent of Fig. 3 when the safety policy is enforced using PCC, SFI, Java and consumer-intermediated access to data. The last column, computes the number of table entry to amortize the cost of VCGen and proof checking (1.6ms). See the text for caveats regarding these experiments.

Table 6 shows the running time divided by the number of table entries of the simple agent of Fig. 3 when the safety policy is enforced using PCC, SFI, Java and hardware-memory protection. These times are the average of 100 runs. These results are in-line with those measured in other similar experiments.

In addition to the running time of agents, PCC differs from the other techniques considered here in the one-time cost incurred for VCGen and proof checking. In some cases, especially for short-running agents or for agents that are only executed once, it is more efficient to use one of the other techniques. In the case of our example, this might happen for a small database. The last column in Tab. 6 shows the minimum size of a table for which that the checking time (1.6ms for the simple agent) added to the running time of the PCC agent is smaller than the running time of the agent using a competing technique. In the case of SFI we have considered that the cost of scanning the code and instrumenting it is the same as the cost of VCGen. However, note that only PCC and the Indirect Access method can enforce the desired safety policy.

10   Discussion and Future Work

The most important consideration in the design of the extended agent of Sect. 8.2 is the ultimate requirement that we must prove that it satisfies the safety policy. This imposes a delicate balance between code optimizations and the difficulty of the proof, because the safety predicate for an optimized agent is usually more difficult to prove than for an unoptimized version. The safety policy does not unduly restrict the optimizations that can be applied to an agent, and should we decide to spend more effort for proof generation we can develop more optimized agents.

We were forced to write the extended agent to maintain explicit instruction counts because the safety policy specifies very strict timing requirements. If the safety policy is relaxed to impose an instruction count limit that varies with the size of the database, the timing constraints have to be proved only for the loop body, making it unnecessary to maintain explicit instruction counts at run-time.

The most unpleasant aspect of writing the extended agent is for the programmer to keep track of assembly language instruction counts. We think that it is feasible to write an automatic tool to do this and to insert the appropriate decrement instructions and loop termination tests. For this to be possible we need to find a simpler way to specify timing constraints, maybe as code or typing annotations.

In the direction of automation of PCC, we have obtained promising results by using a prototype implementation of an optimizing compiler from a type-safe subset of the C language to DEC Alpha assembly language [15]. Not only is the performance of the resulting code comparable to that of cc and gcc with all optimizations enabled, but it produces all of the required annotations completely automatically as well as a proof of type safety and memory safety. Automation was possible in this case because the compiler need only preserve these properties from the source language. Similar technology might be used to certify more complex safety policies if we start with a restricted or a domain specific source language.

The most unpleasant aspect of the experimental results are the proof sizes, which can be an order of magnitude larger than the code, and in certain cases can grow exponentially with the size of the code. This worst case occurs when the program has long sequences of conditionals without intervening loop invariants. For many safety properties, however, and in fact for all of our experiments carried out to-date, the size of the proof is observed to grow only linearly with the size of the program.

At the moment, we have only scratched the surface of proof representation optimizations that can be applied to reduce the size of the proofs. For example, it is very common for the proofs to have repeated sub-proofs that should be hoisted out and proved only once as lemmas. Also, common subproofs can be identified among proofs from different experiments for the same safety policy. These common parts can be proved once and then assumed as theorems of a given safety policy. Finally, one can apply compression algorithms to the binary representation of proofs. In our superficial experiments with compression we observed a reduction by a factor of 2 in the proof size. We believe that by serious proof optimization, the size of the proofs for memory and type safety will approach the size of the code.

Another direction of future work is in identifying more examples of code properties that can be verified using PCC. The most challenging properties to verify seem to be the liveness properties and those involving dynamic safety requirements. In this direction we have obtained promising results in dealing with locks and memory allocation by extending the model of a log of events presented here. The greatest challenge in this area is the serious difficulty of proving the resulting safety predicates.

Proof-Carrying Code compares favorably with other techniques used to prevent untrusted code to step outside a safety policy. When compared with run-time techniques such as hardware or software memory protection [20] and interpretation [12, 17, 10] the advantage is the run-time performance and the simplicity of the safety-critical infrastructure. Another advantage over run-time checking is that PCC avoids the possibility that the untrusted code must be terminated abruptly because of a run-time error before it has a chance of cleaning-up the modified state. Furthermore, certain safety properties (e.g. compliance with data abstraction boundaries) cannot be checked at run-time without significant penalties.

When compared with approaches based on type-safety [1, 13] the advantage of PCC is the increased expressiveness of first-order logic over traditional type systems, which, for example, cannot express resource usage bounds or the arithmetic properties that enable the elimination of array-bounds checking.

Finally, using Proof-Carrying Code is qualitatively better than using digital signatures for the purpose of certifying the safety of agents, because it does not rely on the assumption that the owner of a particular encryption key writes only well-behaved code.

11   Conclusion

This paper presents the details of Proof-Carrying Code and its use in certifying the safety of untrusted code. The safety properties that are explored here are memory safety, compliance with simple data access policies and resource usage bounds, and data abstraction. PCC, however, can be used for any safety and liveness properties that can be expressed in first-order logic.

Proof-Carrying Code has the potential to free the host-system designer from relying on run-time checking as the sole means of ensuring safety. Traditionally, system designers have always viewed safety simply in terms of memory protection, achieved through the use of rather expensive run-time mechanisms such as hardware-enforced memory protection and extensive run-time checking of data. By being limited to memory protection and run-time checking, the designer must impose substantial restrictions on the structure and implementation of the entire system, for example by requiring the use of a very restricted agent-host interaction model (to intermediate the access to critical data and resources, for example).

Proof-Carrying Code, on the other hand, provides greater flexibility for designers of both the host system and then agents, and also allows safety policies to be used that are more abstract and fine-grained than memory protection. We believe that this has the potential to lead to great improvements in the robustness and end-to-end performance of systems.

Acknowledgments

The authors are grateful to Trevor Jim for his many helpful suggestions on an earlier draft of this paper. The authors also thank the reviewers for their comments and suggestions.

References

[1] Brian Bershad, Stefan Savage, Przemyslaw Pardyak, Emin Gun Sirer, David Becker, Marc Fiuczynski, Craig Chambers, and Susan Eggers. Extensibility, safety and performance in the SPIN operating system. In *Symposium on Operating System Principles*, pages 267–284, December 1995.

[2] Robert Boyer and J. Strother Moore. *A Computational Logic*. Academic Press, 1979.

[3] R.M. Burstall and P.J. Landin. Programs and their proofs: an algebraic approach. *Machine Intelligence*, (4), 1969.

[4] R. L. Constable, S. F. Allen, H. M. Bromley, W. R. Cleaveland, J. F. Cremer, R. W. Harper, D. J. Howe, T. B. Knoblock, N. P. Mendler, P. Panangaden, J. T. Sasaki, and S. F. Smith. *Implementing Mathematics with the Nuprl Proof Development System*. Prentice-Hall, 1986.

[5] Thiery Coquand and Gerard Huet. Constructions: A higher order proof system for mechanizing mathematics. In *Proc. European Conf. on Computer Algebra (EUROCAL'85), LNCS 203*, pages 151–184. Springer-Verlag, 1985.

[6] D.C. Luckham et al. Stanford Pascal verifier user manual. Technical Report STAN-CS-79-731, Dept. of Computer Science, Stanford Univ., March 1979.

[7] David Detlefs. An overview of the Extended Static Checking system. In *Proceedings of the First Formal Methods in Software Practice Workshop*, 1996.

[8] Edsger W. Dijkstra. Guarded commands, nondeterminancy and formal derivation of programs. *Communications of the ACM*, 18:453–457, 1975.

[9] Michael Gordon. HOL: A machine oriented formulation of higher-order logic. Technical Report 85, University of Cambridge, Computer Laboratory, July 1985.

[10] James Gosling, Bill Joy, and Guy L. Steele. *The Java Language Specification*. The Java Series. Addison-Wesley, Reading, MA, USA, 1996.

[11] Robert Harper, Furio Honsell, and Gordon Plotkin. A framework for defining logics. *Journal of the Association for Computing Machinery*, 40(1):143–184, January 1993.

[12] Steven McCanne and Van Jacobson. The BSD packet filter: A new architecture for user-level packet capture. In *The Winter 1993 USENIX Conference*, pages 259–269. USENIX Association, January 1993.

[13] Sun Microsystems. The Java Virtual Machine specification. Available as ftp://ftp.javasoft.com/docs/vmspec.ps.zip, 1995.

[14] George C. Necula and Peter Lee. Efficient representation and validation of logical proofs. Technical Report CMU-CS-97-172, Computer Science Department, Carnegie Mellon University, October 1997.

[15] George C. Necula and Peter Lee. The design and implementation of a certifying compiler. In *ACM SIGPLAN'98 Conference on Programming Language Design and Implementation*, June 1998.

[16] Greg Nelson and Derek Oppen. Simplification by cooperating decision procedures. *ACM Transactions on Programming Languages and Systems*, 1(2):245–257, October 1979.

[17] John R. Ousterhout. *Tcl and the Tk Toolkit*. Addison Wesley, 1994.

[18] S. Owre, J. M. Rushby, and N. Shankar. PVS: A prototype verification system. In Deepak Kapur, editor, *11th International Conference on Automated Deduction (CADE)*, volume 607 of *Lecture Notes in Artificial Intelligence*, pages 748–752, Saratoga, NY, June 1992. Springer-Verlag.

[19] Frank Pfenning. Elf: A meta-language for deductive systems (system description). In Alan Bundy, editor, *12th International Conference on Automated Deduction*, LNAI 814, pages 811–815, Nancy, France, June 26–July 1, 1994. Springer-Verlag.

[20] R. Wahbe, S. Lucco, T. E. Anderson, and S. L. Graham. Efficient software-based fault isolation. In *14th ACM Symposium on Operating Systems Principles*, pages 203–216. ACM, December 1993.

Time Limited Blackbox Security: Protecting Mobile Agents From Malicious Hosts[1]

Fritz Hohl

Institute of Parallel and Distributed High-Performance Systems (IPVR),
University of Stuttgart, Germany

`Fritz.Hohl@informatik.uni-stuttgart.de`

Abstract. In this paper, an approach to partially solve one of the most difficult aspects of security of mobile agents systems is presented, the problem of malicious hosts. This problem consists in the possibility of attacks against a mobile agent by the party that maintains an agent system node, a host. The idea to solve this problem is to create a blackbox out of an original agent. A blackbox is an agent that performs the same work as the original agent, but is of a different structure. This difference allows to assume a certain agent protection time interval, during which it is impossible for an attacker to discover relevant data or to manipulate the execution of the agent. After that time interval the agent and some associated data get invalid and the agent cannot migrate or interact anymore, which prevents the exploitation of attacks after the protection interval.

1   Introduction

Mobile agent systems are expected to become a possible base platform for an electronic services framework (see e.g. [5]), especially in the area of Electronic Commerce. In this application area, security is a crucial aspect since all parties involved require the confirmation that none of the other parties will break the rules without being punished. This requirement is not always fulfilled even in the traditional, non-electronic commerce. The anonymity of a worldwide communication network and the ease of automatic exploitation of security gaps in electronic applications make it necessary to meet this demand in the area of commercial transactions done by computers.

Mobile agents are entities that consist of code, data and control information (e.g. thread states). Mobile agent systems are platforms that allow mobile agents to migrate between different nodes of the agent system. From a more technical view, mobile agents can be compared to programs that migrate to nodes autonomously, while nodes offer the runtime environment of these programs including the program interpreters.

As in Mobile Code systems (e.g. the Java applet system), one aspect of security is the protection of the node, or *host*, against possible attacks of the mobile agent. Therefore, some of the security mechanisms developed in this field can also be applied to mobile agent systems. An example is sandbox security, i.e. the need of authorizing security-sensitive commands like the deletion of a file by a designated component. Other security mechanisms like authentication of single agents instances do not have a counterpart

---

[1]This work was funded by the German Research Community (DFG)

in mobile code systems and have to be designed using standard cryptographic techniques like encryption or digital signatures.

The reverse security issue, the protection of a mobile agent from possible attacks by a malicious host, is new as there are barely other areas where this aspect is important. Nevertheless, the protection of mobile agents from malicious hosts is — at least from the viewpoint of the owner of the agent — as important as the protection of the host from malicious agents. As we will see, apart from organisational solutions, no technical approaches to solve this problem without special secure hardware exist so far. The solubility of this problem which is called the *problem of malicious hosts* is even estimated to be very low [1].

This paper presents an approach to solve most of the aspects of the problem of malicious hosts. This approach will cost both execution time and communication bandwidth and will require some time-critical restrictions, but gives the agent the possibility to do some security sensitive work without the danger of an immediate exploitation of sensitive data by the host.

The rest of the paper is organized as follows: Section 2 presents the problem of malicious hosts, Section 3 describes existing approaches and lists their problems. Section 4 explains how blackbox protection can solve the problem of malicious hosts and Section 5 shortly describes a blackbox approach which is called Mobile Cryptography. Section 6 presents a special blackbox approach that uses time-limited blackboxes. Section 7 describes the changes that occur by the introduction of time limitedness. Section 8 explains how time limited blackbox protection can be reached, Section 9 presents further protection mechanisms. After examining potential attacks against this approach and listing the costs of the mechanism in Section 10 and 11, the paper concludes and presents future work.

2 The Problem of Malicious Hosts

The fact that the runtime environment (the host) may attack the program (the agent), plays hardly a role in existing computer systems. Normally, the party that maintains the hosts also employs the program. But in the area of open mobile agents systems, an agent is operated in most cases by another party, the agent owner. This environment leads to a problem, that is vital for the usage of mobile agents in open systems: the *problem of malicious hosts* A malicious host can be defined in a general way as a party that is able execute an agent that belongs to another party and that tries to attack that agent in some way. The question of what action is considered to be an attack depends on the question which assurances an agent owner needs in order to use a mobile agent. If we try to achieve a protection level that is comparable to the one of agents that run on non-malicious, or *trusted* hosts, we can identify the following attacks:

1. spying out code
2. spying out data
3. spying out control flow
4. manipulation of code
5. manipulation of data

6. manipulation of control flow
7. incorrect execution of code
8. masquerading of the host
9. denial of execution
10. spying out interaction with other agents
11. manipulation of interaction with other agents
12. returning wrong results of system calls issued by the agent

To illustrate these attacks we will use a small purchase agent as an example. The purchase agent contains a data and a code block. Entries in the data block may include:

```
Address home = "PDA, sweet PDA"
Money wallet = 20$
float maximumprice = 20.00$
good flowers = 10 red roses
Address shoplist[] = empty list
int shoplistindex = 0
float bestprice = 20.00$
Address bestshop = empty
```

The central procedure startAgent, that is called by the host every time the agent arrives, could look like this:

```
1  public void startAgent() {
2
3    if (shoplist == null) {
4      shoplist = getTrader().
5       getProvidersOf("BuyFlowers");
6      go(shoplist[1]);
7      break;
8    }
9    if (shoplist[shoplistindex].
10     askprice(flowers) < bestprice) {
11      bestprice = shoplist[shoplistindex].
12                   askprice(flowers);
13      bestshop = shoplist[shoplistindex];
14    }
15    if (shoplistindex >= (shoplist.length - 1)) {
16      // remote buy
17      buy(bestshop,flowers,wallet);
18      // go home and deliver wallet
19      go(home);
20      if (location.getAddress() = home) {
21        location.put(wallet);
22      }
23    }
24    go(shoplist[++shoplistindex]);
25 }}
```

Using this example, the attacks listed above can be illustrated.

1. Spying out code

The code of the agent has to be readable by the host. Although this requirement can be restricted to the next instruction at a single point of time, this does not solve the problem since some hosts see almost all of the code because they execute most of the commands. In our example the host visited last executes nearly all the code. If the agent code is characteristic not only for a single, but a whole class of agents, the whole code of the agent may be known even before execution time. If an agent is generated out of standard building blocks (which is a good idea regarding code migration costs and ease of agent construction), the detail specification is available for building blocks like libraries or classes. Furthermore, these blocks can be explored by blackbox tests. Knowing the code leads to knowledge about the execution strategy of the agent, knowledge about the exact physical structure of code and data in the memory of the host and sometimes (by using data statements like initial variable assignments) to knowledge about parts of the agent data.

2. Spying out data

The threat of a host reading the private data of an agent is very severe as it leaves no trace that could be detected. This is not necessarily true for the consequences of this knowledge, but they can occur a long time after the visit of the agent on the malicious host. This is a special problem for data classes such as secret keys or electronic cash, where the simple knowledge of the data results in loss of privacy or money. In our example, the money variable would be security sensitive when it is represented in a way that the binary number of the "coin" **is** the money and therefore can be used as real world cash. But there are also other classes of data, which can be used for an attack although they have not the nature of classes like e-cash. In our example, the knowledge of the maximum price or the best price so far can be used by a malicious host to offer flowers for a slightly lower amount than the competitors, although the regular price is much lower.

3. Spying out control flow

As soon as the host knows the entire code of the agent and its data, it can determine the next execution step at any time. Even if we could protect the used data somehow, it is rather difficult to protect the information about the actual control flow. This is a problem, because together with the knowledge of the code, a malicious host can deduce more information about the state of the agent. In our example, we can recognize whether an offer is better or worse than the best offer so far by simply watching the control flow, even if we could not read any data.

4. Manipulation of code

If the host is able to read the code and if it has access to the code memory, it can normally modify the program of an agent. It could exploit this either by altering the code permanently, thus implanting a virus, worm or trojan horse. It could also temporarily alter the behaviour of the agent on that particular host only. The advantage of the latter approach consists in the fact, that the host to which the agent migrates cannot detect a manipulation of the code since it is not modified. Applied to our example, a malicious host could modify the code of the agent with the effect that it prefers the offer of a certain flower provider, regardless of the price.

5. Manipulation of data

If the host knows the physical location of the data in the memory and the semantics of the single data elements, it can modify data as well. In our example, the host could cut down the shop list after setting the offer of the local flower provider as the best offer.

6. Manipulation of control flow

Even if the host does not have access to the data of the agent, it can conduct the behaviour of the agent by manipulating the control flow. In our example, the host could simply alter the flow at the second or third if statement, forcing the agent to choose the offer of the shop preferred by the host as the best.

7. Incorrect execution of code

Without changing the code or the flow of control, a host may also alter the way it executes the code of an agent, resulting in the same effects as above.

8. Masquerade

It is the liability of a host that sends an agent to a receiver host to ensure the identity of that receiver. Still, a third party may intercept or copy an agent transfer and start the agent by masking itself as the correct receiver host. A masquerade will probably be followed by other attacks like read attacks.

9. Denial of execution

As the agent is executed by the host, i.e. passive, the host can simply not execute the agent. This can be used as an attack e.g. in the case that a host knows about a time limited special offer of another host. The host simply can prevent the detection of this offer by the agent by delaying its execution until the offer expires.

10. Spying out interaction with other agents

The agent may buy the flowers remotely from a shop situated on another host. If the interaction between agent and the remote flower shop is not protected, the host of the agent is able to watch the buy interaction even in case the host cannot watch the execution of the agent. In our example, the host could read e.g. `wallet` and spend the stored money.

11. Manipulation of interaction with other agents

If the host can also manipulate the interaction of the agent it can act with the identity of the agent or mask itself as the partner of the agent. In our example the host can e.g. redirect the buying interaction to another shop, or it can interrupt the interaction e.g. to prevent spending the money by the agent.

12. Returning wrong results of system calls issued by the agent

In line 20 of the example code ("`if (location.getAddress() = home)`"), the agent requests the name of the current location. Here the host could mask itself as the agent's home location by returning the corresponding address. The agent then thinks that it is at home and delivers the wallet to the host.

After stating the problem we will now have a look on possible solutions. First we will examine some approaches that try to prevent single attacks. In the next section we will see an approach that try to restore the autonomy of the agent, the so called *blackbox approach.*

3 Existing Approaches

As mentioned above, a malicious host is defined as a party that is able execute an agent that belongs to another party and that tries to attack that agent in some way. This also means that malicious hosts are only a problem for agents that cannot trust a host in advance. In this case *trust* means, that the owner either knows or hopes that the operator will not attack. Therefore, some approaches (see e.g. [1]) exist that try to circumvent the problem of potentially malicious hosts by not allowing agents to move to nontrusted hosts. There are also approaches that use a trust approach to protect hosts from agents by not allowing to accept agents that have been on non-trusted hosts before. The problem of these approaches are that trust in this context is absolute (you do not hide anything from a trusted node), and that it is not always clear in advance whether a host is trusted or not. This can severely reduce the number of hosts an agent might migrate to. Even if an owner trusts a big company when it comes e.g. to accounting, it may not want them to see its secret communication key. If an agent has to obtain prices for a flight, it cannot trust the host of an air line or any other host that is maintained by a company related to an air line and so forth.

Another "trust" approach is the *organizational* solution: the agent system is not open in the sense that everybody can open a host, but only trustworthy parties can operate hosts. This is the approach General Magic [2] used for its agent system application, e.g. PersonaLink[2], that was operated by AT&T [5].

As trust is a relationship between agent and host which often cannot be determined in advance, a commonly used notion of trust, *reputation,* is used in another approach [8]. This also is problematic, as we have seen that trust depends on the task an agent has to fulfill. A reputation approach, where betrayed agents can complain about malicious hosts, that in turn, lose reputation, can also result in a new security problem. Agents could attack hosts using a "character assassination" attack, by simply complaining about being betrayed.

Another approach [13] enables an agent to *detect and prove modification attacks*in order to allow the owner to use legal or organizational ways to get its damage refunded. But this approach cannot prevent other attacks, and it assumes an organizational or legal framework for an agent system. In the first case, such an organizational framework may not exist in an open agent system without a central organization. In the second case it seems to be not realistic to assume such a legal framework on an international level, since also other laws required by new technologies, e.g. for data protection and privacy, are far from being homogeneous or even widespread.

Since the problem is the wrong behaviour of the executing environment, in contrary to

---

[2]PersonaLink was a service that allowed users to send electronic mails that carried agents. It was based on the Telescript mobile agent system.

a behaviour that meets the specification, another class of approaches (e.g. [7]) uses specialized, attack-proven *hardware* that can ensure its integrity. These approaches therefore require the usage of this hardware in every host, which is currently a too restricting assumption.

As the presented approaches either do not protect from all the attacks, or do not allow open mobile agent systems, a more adequate approach is needed.

4   Blackbox Security: The Idea

In this section we will discuss an approach that is able to protect an agent from most of the attacks mentioned in Section 1. The central idea of this approach is to generate an executable agent from a given agent specification which cannot be attacked by read or manipulation attacks. This agent is considered to be a "blackbox", if the following applies:

Def: Blackbox Property

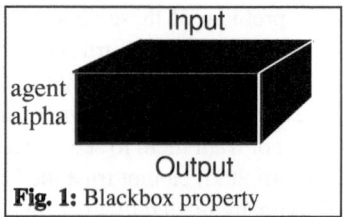

Fig. 1: Blackbox property

- an agent is a blackbox if:
  1. at any time
  2. code and data of the agent specification cannot be read
  3. code and data of the agent specification cannot be modified

If this definition can be applied to an agent, only input to and output from the blackbox can be observed.

The "conversion mechanism" that generates an agent with the blackbox property uses configuration parameters that allow to create different blackboxes out of the same specification (see Figure 2). These parameters allow to prevent dictionary attacks. Dictionary attacks guess the attributes of the blackbox by converting a number of agent specifications and compare the created blackboxes with the attacked one.

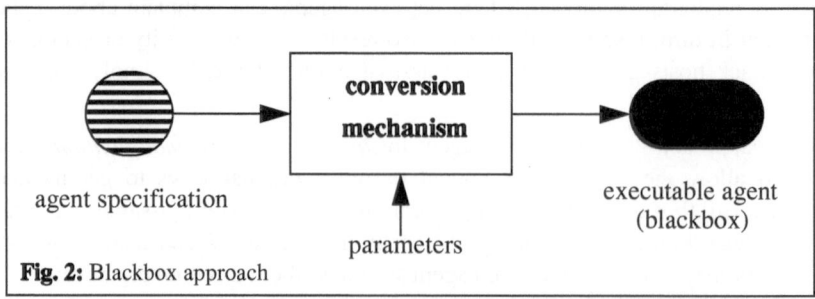

Fig. 2: Blackbox approach

If an agent fulfills the blackbox property defined above, it is autonomous in the sense that if a hosts executes that agent, the host cannot interfere with this execution in a directed way. If an agent reaches that level of autonomy, it can be protected from other attacks. Masking of the host or reading and manipulating the interaction of the agent with other parties can then be prevented by using conventional mechanisms from the area of stationary distributed systems.

The problem now is to ensure the blackbox property. Currently, there is no known algorithm to fully provide blackbox protection even if one other approach exists that seems to proceed in this direction. It is called Mobile Cryptography.

5 Mobile Cryptography

This approach does not call itself a blackbox approach, but it can be classified in this category. Sander and Tschudin describe in [10] and [11] a way to use *encrypted programs* as a means to protect agents from malicious hosts. Encrypted programs are programs that consist of operations that work on encrypted data. Agents are produced by converting a agent specification into some executable code plus initial, encrypted data. Since the attacker cannot break the encryption of the data, it cannot read or manipulate the original data. See [10] in this book for a detailed description of the Mobile Cryptography approach.

The advantages of this approach over the one that will be presented in the next section are:
*   the protection of the agent is easily provable
*   the costs of the protection are probably small
*   the protection is not time-limited

The current restrictions of the Mobile Cryptography approach are:
*   random programs cannot be used as the input specification; currently only polynomial and rational functions can be used for this purpose
*   the interaction model of the agent suffers the restriction that cleartext data can be sent only to trusted hosts

The extension of the approach to recursive functions and Turing machine program equivalent mechanisms are subject to future work. As soon as the latter can be used as an input to the conversion function, encrypted programs have also the blackbox property. However, even now most of the aspects described in this article, which do not rely on the specific conversion mechanism, apply also for encrypted programs.

The second restriction (cleartext data can be sent only to trusted hosts) is not mentioned explicitly. Still, receivers can only read encrypted output of the agent when they know the decryption function (which includes a potential key). If an attacker is able to decrypt the output of an protected agent, it is likely that it can also attack the agent itself.

6 Time Limited Blackbox Protection

As we have seen, the only known approach that tries to provide fully blackbox protection is currently not applicable to every existing agent. In order to remove this restriction[3], we redefine the blackbox property definition in a way which differs in the statement about how long the blackbox property is valid. Now we do not assume that the protection holds forever, but only for a limited, known minimal time interval

---

[3]Although it might seem that Mobile Cryptography is an earlier approach, the first public document about it [9] dates some months after the first publication [3] describing the time limited blackbox approach.

known in advance. Therefore the definition is now:

Def: Time Limited Blackbox Property
- an agent is a blackbox if:
    1. *for a certain known time interval*
    2. code and data of the agent specification cannot be read
    3. code and data of the agent specification cannot be modified
- *attacks after the protection interval are possible*
    4. *but these attacks do not have effects*

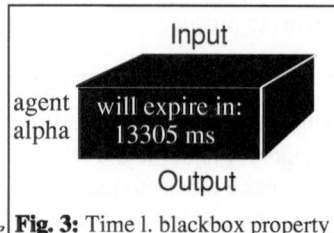

Fig. 3: Time l. blackbox property

To make the protection time interval explicit, an *expiration date* is attached to the blackbox.

Although this definition is weaker than the original blackbox property and results, as we will see, in more complex mechanisms, it has one big advantage: there is a way to achieve this. Before this way is sketched, we examine what changes if blackboxes are time-limited.

7   What Is Changing If the Blackbox Is Time Limited?

For achieving the requirement that attacks after the protection interval do not have effects, we have to examine the circumstances under which time limitedness affects processing. To do this, four different interaction scenarios are introduced. It will be argued that effects of an attack can only occur when information of the agent is communicated to third parties.

7.1   No communication with a third party

In this scenario neither the agent nor the host communicates with a third party. Although this is a merely academic setting, it demonstrates that the temporal aspect is of no importance in this context. Even if the host successfully attack the agent, nothing results from these attacks.

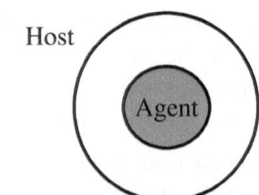

Fig. 4: No communication

7.2   Communication only with trusted servers

Here the agent communicates only with a *trusted third party.* A party can be considered as trusted if this party never attacks. These two partners can establish a secure communication channel to prevent attacks by the host. Time limitedness of the agent plays a role in this scenario since the communication partner has to know whether it can still trust the agent or not. If the host would have been able to attack the agent, the attacker could use the agent to mask itself as the agent. Since attacks can only take place after the protection interval, the trusted server has to know the expiration date associated with the agent before it starts communication. This can be done using an extended key certificate (see Figure 6). The resulting overhead is acceptable since secure communication requires already authentication of the partners.

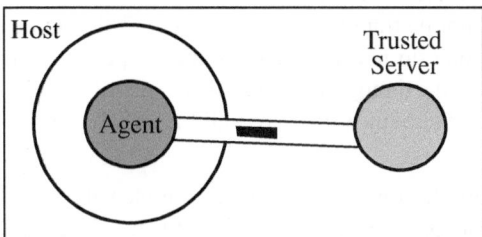

Fig. 5: Communication only with trusted server

| Version |
| Serial Number |
| Certification Alg. |
| Certification Par. |
| Name of CA |
| Validity of Certific. |
| Name of Agent |
| **Expiration Date** |
| Public Key of Agent |
| Signature of CA |

Fig. 6: Extended key certificate

7.3   Communication with untrusted servers

In this scenario the agent communicates with either an untrusted third party or with the host, which is by definition untrusted (see Fig. 7).

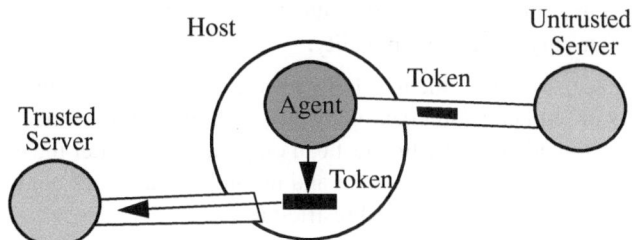

Fig. 7: Communication with untrusted servers

We have to distinguish two kinds of data that can be communicated: token and non-token data.

Token data are self-contained documents that depend on the identity of the issuer. Therefore they often bear digital signatures. Examples for tokens are electronic money coins, secret keys and capabilities. The problem with tokens is, that an attacker may use or trade them without having obtained them regularly. Therefore, also tokens have to bear expiration dates to prevent the usage of tokens that could have been obtained by attacking the agent. Every party that receives a token by another party

Fig. 8: Token structure

thus has to check whether the expiration date of the token has passed or not. To do that, this party has to be able to get the correct global time. This means that time limitedness always require synchronized clocks. Note that it is not necessary for the party that sends a token to know the current time. Only the party that issues a token and the party that receives a token have to have this information. The issuer needs it to add the protection interval to it. The receiver needs the current time since if a party accepts an outdated token, no other party will accept it in return. The drawback of the expiration date is, that a token cannot be protected after the expiration date. Thus, tokens which need a larger protection interval must not be transported by the agent. This can be the case for some existing token systems that do not include expiration aspects or which cannot be extended by this aspect. A good example for tokens that cannot be protected in agents are secret keys of an agent owner since they are valid normally for a long time.

Non-token data is everything else. Examples for this category are simple values that do not need to be protected and values that are security sensitive like the maximum price. The blackbox property guarantees that they cannot be read or modified before the expiration date has passed. They cannot be used against the agent or its owner since they not depend on the identity of the issuer. Since non-token data cannot be used to interact with third parties, it does not need to be protected against modification attacks after the protection interval. Although nothing has to be done to protect non-token data, there is a restriction for these elements: an agent must not transport non-token data, that can be used to attack the owner of the agent and whose protection interval has to be larger than the lifetime of the agent. An example for such data could be a variable describing the maximum price for a good that is valid for all purchasing agents of a user ever used. Fortunately, data elements with a larger protection need do not seem to occur very frequently in reality.

Note that this scenario does include both planned interaction of the agent with an untrusted party or unplanned interaction by an attack of the host. Since an "unplanned interaction", i.e. a read attack by the host can only take place after the expiration date, all allowed tokens are also outdated then and non-token data does not have to be protected any longer due to the mentioned restriction.

7.4   Migration of the agent

The last scenario comprises the remaining possibility to explicitly communicate agent information: the migration of the whole agent to a new host. The problem here is, that the agent may have been "overtaken" or tampered by the host after the expiration date. Although it is unlikely that the code of the agent was manipulated by the host since it is rather easy to protect constant code from manipulation attacks by using digital signature techniques, an attacker could have been altered values that are not protected by the signature, i.e. mainly variable data.

Therefore, the receiving host has to ensure that the arriving agent is still valid, i.e. that its expiration date has not passed already. As we have seen the agent will probably be protected by a signature, and all we have to do is to either include the expiration date into the constant part of the agent allowing the signature to also protect this date or to use the extended key certificates we introduced above. The receiver then can simply check the signature of the agent and the validity of the agent by checking the expiration date.

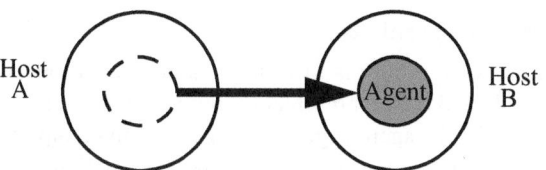

Fig. 9: Agent migration

As we have seen, it is possible to compensate most of the effects that occur when agents are subject of time-limitedness. The next question to answer is how such a protection can be reached.

8 How Can We Reach Time Limited Blackbox Protection?

The lack of approaches that protect agents from host attacks is based on the observation that a host is always able to read every bit of the memory and the content of every variable and to know the memory location of every line of code. Therefore, some authors conclude, it is impossible to prevent e.g. read attacks.

While this observation is always true for the "semantics in the small", i.e. the meaning of these elements for the next execution step, it is not necessarily true for the "semantics in the large", i.e. the meaning of these elements to the overall semantics of the application. An example for this difference is the code in Figure 10 where you can of course put the finger on every statement and every variable, but to explain the meaning of a statement or a variable in relation to the overall result, you have to think about it (the code fragment computes the difference of two two-bytes-numbers).

```
w[6] = b[3] - b[5];

w[7] = b[2] * 256;

w[8] = w[7] + w[6];

w[5] = w[8] - b[4] * 256;

b[0] = w[5] DIV 256;

b[1] = w[5] MOD 256;
```

Fig. 10: A code fragment

This effect results from the fact, that this overall semantics is not expressed by code, but by the "mental model" of the programmer or the reader of a program. To attack an agent, the human attacker has to have such a mental model of the code in order to find certain points in the code or values that are interesting for the attacker.

The central idea now is not to allow an attacker to build such a mental model of the agent in advance, i.e. before the agent arrives, and to make the process of building this model a time-consuming task. The first goal is reached by creating a new "form" of the agent dynamically, in an unpredictable, manner at the start of the protection interval. The second goal is reached by using conversion algorithms that produce a new form that is *hard* to analyse. In this context hard means that the analysis should take as much as time as possible. These conversion algorithms are therefore called *obfuscating* or *mess-up algorithms*. Note that the approach does not assume that it is impossible for the attacker to analyse the agent, the analysis simply takes time. The assumption is that a lower bound of this time can be determined and that this time interval is large enough for most agent applications on one host.

8.1   Agent mess-up algorithms

The task of a mess-up algorithm is to generate a new agent out of an original agent, which differs in code and data representation but yields the same results. This means, that the specification of the agent is given as an executable, unprotected agent. Agents consists of executable code and some data. To prevent dictionary attacks (see Section 2), it has to use a random parameter that allows the algorithm to create different new agents out of a single original one (see Figure 11).

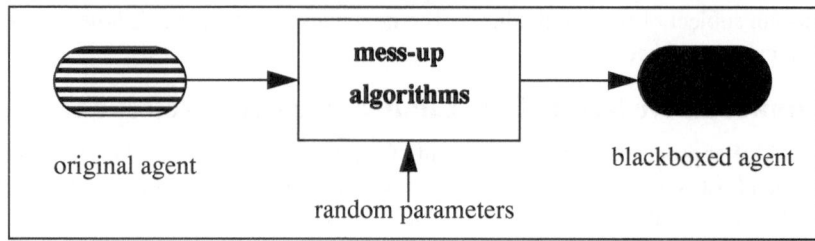

Fig. 11: Time-limited blackbox approach

To achieve the requirement that a blackbox protected agent that is hard to analyse, the designer of a mess-up algorithm has to take into account two key aspects: the attributes of an agent that can be modified and the abilities and characteristics of the attacker

8.2   Agent attributes that can be modified

Statements

A statement has a type and a location in a program (it also consists of data, but this aspect is viewed below). The *type of a statement* can be hidden until the statement is executed by dynamically creating it at runtime. This is possible by using e.g. self-modifiable code. The *location of a statement* can also be hidden, either implicitly by using dynamic code creation or explicitly by hiding a certain statement into other statements.

Data

Data, i.e. variables and constants, consist of a type, a value and a location. The *type of a data element* can be hidden until the data is needed. This is even normal for languages that use dynamic typing as e.g. Smalltalk. The *value of a data element* can be hidden. One way to achieve this is to replace element accesses by accesses on subelements and to translate operations on the data elements by operations on the subelements. This results in an execution where the value of an data element never occurs as a whole. Finally, the *location of a data element* can be hidden either statically, e.g. by splitting up the element and distributing the parts, or dynamically by e.g. allowing the element to move around in the data area.

8.3   Abilities and characteristics of the attacker

To model the properties of the attacker, we have to distinguish two cases.

In the first case, the attacker does not know the original version of the agent in advance. Therefore, a human has to analyse the blackbox to build up a mental model. Although it can use the aid of computerized tools to do this, humans tend to be far too slow compared to the execution speed of computer. This slowness cannot be reduced fundamentally since it is not possible to speed up humans. Therefore, the next case seems to be much more relevant.

In the second case, the attacker does know the exact specification of the agent in advance. This case is probably the common one if most agents in an agent system are instances of a set of standard agents. If it is possible to identify the type of an agent, i.e. the original agent, then the exact specification is accessible. If now an attacker knows the exact specification, it can automate the attack by generating a program that tries to compute only a few or even a single attribute of the agent, e.g. the current location of a certain variable in the blackboxed agent. In this case the attack can be accelerated by using faster computers or by employing several computers in parallel.

In both cases the generated code has to be constructed in a way that standard program analysing techniques such as program slicing, data flow analysis or program abstraction, cannot be used to analyse the agent before the expiration date has passed. Good mess-up algorithms do not allow the complete analysis to be done statically, but also require to run the agent at least partially.

Let us now have a look at three example algorithms.

8.4   Examples for mess-up algorithms

The most important aspects are the structure and attributes of the used mess-up algorithms, as they decide about the protection strength of the security mechanism. Therefore, three mess-up algorithms will be sketched here.

Variable Recomposition

This algorithm takes the set of program variables, cuts each variable content into segments and creates new variables that contain a recomposition of the original segments. The original variable accesses in the program code are then adapted correspondingly. In Figure 12a, you can see the original variable access, Figure 12b defines a scheme for recomposing two new variables v23 and v19 from the contents of three original variables.

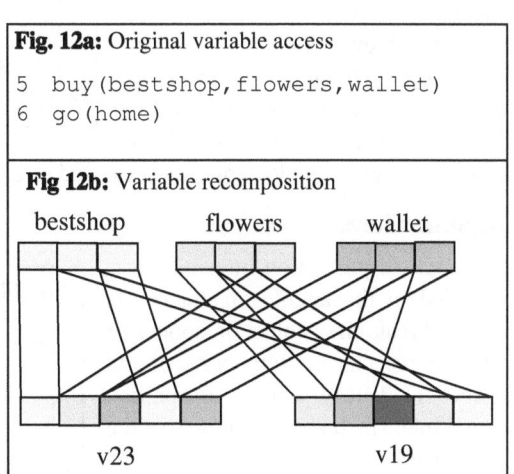

Fig. 12a: Original variable access

```
5  buy(bestshop,flowers,wallet)
6  go(home)
```

Fig 12b: Variable recomposition

bestshop   flowers   wallet

v23   v19

The access code for the new variables as displayed in Figure 12d can therefore be created automatically, given the recomposition scheme, by using conversion functions (see Figure 12c) that create the original values from the new variables. As a result, now there is no direct relationship between variables and processing model elements like the maximum price from our example. The variable names are now meaningless and the data representation is rather complicated.

Fig 12c: Conversion functions

```
public Address c7(Bitstring b)
public Good c4(Bitstring b)
public Money c3(Bitstring b)
public Address c34(Bitstring b)
```

Fig 12d: New variable access

```
5   buy(c7(v23[0]+v19[4]+v23[3])
        ,c4(v19[0]+v19[3]+v23[1]),
        c3(v23[2]+v19[1]+v23[4]))

6   go(c34(v21[4]+v19[2]+v21[2]))
```

Conversion of Control Flow Elements into Value-Dependent Jumps

The next presented mechanism is a *conversion of compile-time control flow elements into run-time data dependent jumps.* Control flow elements like `if` and `while` statements allow the programmer to imagine the potential control flow even at compile time as these statements make control flow explicit. If we convert these elements into a form that depends on the content of variables, the control flow cannot be determined as easily as before. This dependence can be achieved by the usage of jumps that are bound to variable contents, e.g. switch-statements. The effect can even be strengthened by using complex variable expressions instead of using simple variables.

Fig 13a: Original code

```
if (a(b) < c) {
    b = s(d(e) + f);
}
```

Fig 13b: Converted code

```
z= 0
DO
    if (z=0) then t1 = a(b); z=1; continue;
    if (z=1) then t2 = t1 < c; z=2; continue;
    if (t2) then t3 = d(e); z=3; continue;
    if (z=3) then t4 = t3 + f; z=4; continue;
    if (z=4) then b = t4; z=5; continue;
    if (z=5) then break;
LOOP
```

Deposited Keys

If the whole protection information is included in the agent, an attacker is able to break that protection sooner or later. If we can encrypt parts of the agent or identify other information, that is both small and important for the execution of the agent, we can "externalize" this information on another, trusted server. The idea is to let the agent request these information parts, or keys, from the trusted server by indicating the state of the agent. An example for

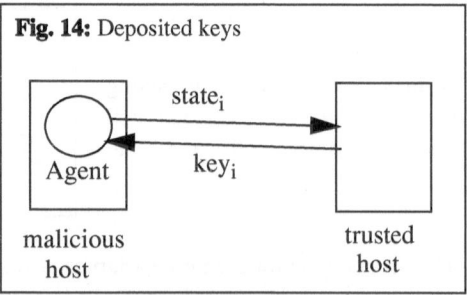

Fig. 14: Deposited keys

Agent

state$_i$

key$_i$

malicious host

trusted host

one type of keys can be found in Figure 13b where the numbers printed in bold denote data that "interconnects" the statements. If these numbers are not present in the code, the attacker is not able to analyse the agent and, therefore, to attack the agent before runtime. The trusted host will deliver them to the agent when the right state is indicated.

There are, of course, more and better algorithms, but the above examples demonstrate some of the principles they have to follow:

- the algorithm needs to be parametrizable with a very large parameter space in order to avoid dictionary attacks
- it must not be possible to break the protection without running the code
- it may be useful to take out parts of agent and to put these parts on trusted nodes

Each single of these algorithms may be not that strong if they would be used alone. It can be expected that a *combination* of these algorithms is much stronger than the sum of the single strengths. Therefore, our approach uses a "chain" of mess-up algorithms. To illustrate the effects of the mess-up algorithms, we want now to sketch possible algorithms that try to break the protection generated by the example algorithms.

8.5   Counter attacks

Having the three example mess-up algorithms in mind, we want now have a look at possible *counter attacks*. Counter attacks are algorithms that try to break the protection, i.e. mess-up algorithms.

Variable Recomposition

There are at least two possible approaches: we can try to guess the variable layout by analysing the access to a byte statistically over the operations known to access certain original variables. The other approach tries to read the original variables simply by reading the parameters of the calls of the known procedures. This means in our example, that the attacker sees the values of `bestshop`, `flowers` and `wallet` as soon as `buy` is called as these are the contents of the parameters of this procedure.

Both attacks assume knowledge about the original procedures. Fortunately, this attack is not that important as either the known procedure is a system call of the host or a call of an "internal" procedure. In the first case, the parameters do not have to be protected as they are by definition not secret (they are delivered to the host). In the second case we can dissolve the internal procedures into code of the main procedure, so that they are not visible any more.

Conversion of Control Flow Elements into Value-dependent Jumps

The presented version of this algorithm is rather easy to break as it can be analysed without having to run the code. All we have to do is to create the original statement out of the if-statements. The computational complexity of this is roughly proportional to the number of if-statements, which corresponds at most to the number of single language expression nodes of the syntax tree. We can prevent such an approach by replacing the constant numbers in the if-conditions by more complex expressions and by adding another algorithm that adds more dynamics to the computation of the conditions, e.g. the Deposited Keys mechanism.

Deposited Keys

We can attack this algorithm by creating every possible state of the agent and by requesting all the keys that are associated to these states. We then have all the runtime informations of the agent and can try to analyse it. The question is, how the attacker gains all the states of an agent. If the states can be associated to the execution of the agent (e.g. by computing a key that has to be delivered with the request), the host has to execute the agent. We then can control the attack by the trusted host since it can notice the execution of the agent.

8.6   Problems with mess-up algorithms

The first main problem is that the protection intervals have to be of a "useful" length. Useful in this context means the question of how long a protection interval has to be in order to allow the agent to do something useful. The answer depends of course on the task the agent has to fulfill on a host, but with an interval that allows two "long-range" migrations, some execution time and enough time for the protection overhead, most applications should be in range. If the protection interval is longer, the agent can migrate to more hosts or compute a longer time on every host. If the protection interval is much smaller, the possible application areas of the protected agent is severely restricted.

The second and even bigger problem is the question of how to determine these protection intervals from the used mess-up mechanism. Here, the usage of cryptography to protect data has a valuable advantage: it is possible to express the protection strength of the crypto algorithm in terms of the needed computational power. This is possible because there are known algorithms that are able to break the encryption. Sometimes (as with RSA), these algorithms are not necessarily the best possible mechanisms, but the best known, even after some decades of research. More often, the complexity class of the problem that breaks the encryption is known to be too hard to be computed, even in case of technological progress if the key is long enough.

Compared to cryptography, blackbox protection has two advantages:
*   there is no receiver that has to apply the reverse encryption process
*   the identity (and - in limits - the specification) and the order of the used algorithms does not have to be known in advance

We could now try to apply the same mechanism of determining the protection strength of crypto algorithms to mess-up algorithms. Unfortunately, this approach seems to be very difficult. The reason for that is the current lack of a formal model of the agent mess-up and the associated counter algorithms. While in traditional cryptography the problem of breaking an encryption can be tracked down to a well-defined mathematical problem, the possible attacks against a blackbox protected agent are numerous, and different in nature. Future research has to develop a model that expresses e.g. the hiding of the location of a variable on several places and that computes the complexity to find that location. Fortunately we do not have to formalize the process of building up a mental model of a program by a human as we have excluded this possibility due to the lack of attack performance of humans in Section 8.3.

However, the current lack of a formal model is not an immanent problem of the approach. It is an open problem that has to be solved in order to both estimate the strength of the protection and to compute the current protection interval for a specific agent. This computation will then take into account the average computational need for solving the problem of breaking the blackbox protection and estimate how much computational power an attacker will stake. Since the computation will be done before an agent migrates the first time, the estimation can be adjusted according to the existing technology.

8.7   How can a blackbox protected agent be created?

To create a protected agent, token type data has to be converted into tokens that bear an expiration date and that are signed digitally. In the next step all security sensitive library calls (like calls of an encryption function) have to be replaced by the corresponding library code. Afterwards the code mess-up algorithms are applied to the code and the data of the agent. Finally, the agent has to be signed digitally after receiving the agent expiration date. Now the agent is ready to migrate.

8.8   Recharging of protected agents

If the "maximum distance" of the agent is determined by its expiration date, is it possible to "recharge" the agent in order to allow it to migrate further? Due to the nature of the code mess-up algorithms, any host could convert the agent to a new form without having to know its internal structure or the contents of the original data. Therefore, we could assign this task to any host that does not cooperate with any malicious host the agent has visited or will visit. Unfortunately, the expiration dates of the agent and of the transported tokens are a problem as they cannot be modified that easily. The first problem is that the agent has to be assigned with a new expiration date and signed digitally by a party that the agent (or its owner) trusts. This also incurs, that the agent gets a new identity, as it differs at least in the expiration date. The second problem is, that the tokens have to be replaced by new ones. If you think of electronic money coins, you have to change them into new coins with a new expiration date, while tokens that have no real value like keys, can be easily created. All of this can only be done by a trusted host. If the agent has checked the identity of the trusted host, it delivers the tokens that have to be replaced and gets the new ones in return. An alternative to recharging an agent is to extract the state of a nearly expired agent and to "inject" it into a new agent "hull", thus creating a new agent that contains the state of the old one. The advantage of this alternative is that it prevents the delay that would be needed to mess-up the old agent after its arrival.

Now we have seen how to achieve time limited blackbox protection. But what can we do to prevent other attacks by the host?

9   Which Other Attacks by Malicious Hosts Can Be Prevented Using Blackbox Protection?

Even if an agent is protected by time-limited blackbox security, there are still some possible attacks:
- a malicious host can try to mask itself as another, perhaps trusted host

- a malicious can try to read and manipulate the interaction of a hosted agent with a third party and
- a malicious can return wrong results when the agent is calling system library procedures

While there is no known protection from the latter attack apart from verifying the answer by another third party (but then using library code seems to be rather redundant), the first two attacks can be prevented.

This is possible since a blackbox protected agent is autonomous again, i.e. that if a hosts executes that agent, the host cannot interfere in this execution. This allows us to use the same mechanisms to prevent the mentioned attacks as in distributed systems where the parties reside on different, and therefore autonomous, nodes.

We can prevent masking of hosts by using existing authentication methods using symmetric or asymmetric encryption schemes. We can even strip down these protocols a little bit since no third party can read the local communication between the agent and the host.

We can also prevent attacks against the interaction of an agent with another party by using secure channels between the interaction partners. These channels are obtained by exchanging session keys between the partners and by encrypting the traffic between them. Since in this scenario, the malicious host can be modeled as an attacker on a connection between two autonomous nodes, the protocols do not have to be modified.

10 New Attacks: Sabotage and Blackbox Testing

If there is an agent protection scheme like the one described in this paper, one can imagine attacks that rely on the characteristics of this scheme. One attack is *sabotage*, or the action of destroying parts of the agent without being detected. As an agent contains data that might change during execution, the attacker can simply modify single bits of the data area without knowing about the effects to the agent. Fortunately, this attack is very similar to the problem of data that is sent over an insecure network. Therefore, similar error detection or even correction mechanisms like CRC, computed by the agent itself, can be used as long as the attacker cannot detect the detail structure of the mechanism. It is easy to circumvent a CRC algorithm if the exact mechanism is known and if it the borders of the protected data elements can be seen.

Another attack is the *blackbox test*. Its aim is to determine characteristics of the inside of the "black box" by executing the box with different input parameters and by watching the effects. The recorded reactions can be formal results like output values or characteristic "activity patterns". In our example, the attacker could execute the agent until it tries to buy the flowers, starting over and over with the initial agent. The only value that is changed over the tests is the price for the flowers. When the agent finally wants to buy, the attacker knows the price that is both the lowest so far and that is below the maximum price. Even if the agent would not buy the flowers immediately (it might want to ask at least three different providers), the attacker can watch whether the data of the agent changes. If this is the case, it is very likely, that this agent has memorized a better price. If it comes to countermeasures, two goals have to be reached: first, the parallel execution of the same agent has to be suppressed, e.g. by using a trusted third party that is informed by the agent about its execution. Second, the very fast execution of an agent has to be prevented, e.g. by using a similar interaction with a trusted host. Finally, activity patterns can be covered up by inserting and executing dummy code.

11 What Blackbox Security Costs

Protecting agents using blackbox security is not for free. Since the costs mainly depend on the class of an agent, it has to be decided per class whether this kind of protection is appropriate or whether the agent should operate immobile from a trusted host via remote communication. For calculating the costs, we can distinguish four classes of costs that result from blackbox security:

costs at creation time
These are the costs for converting the original agent into the new form. These costs are not important for the execution time of the agent, only for the "delay" of starting the execution. If we get an agent with low execution time overhead, we can accept higher creation time costs.

costs at transmission time
This is the size overhead of the agent, since the transmission time is determined by the size. The main problem here is the fact, that agents have to transport all library code that is security sensitive instead of using the corresponding system library at the target host. An example are the J/Crypto libraries from Baltimore Technologies that implement cryptographic functions like DES, RSA, SHA-1 and MD-5 and which consist of 200 KB of Java bytecode.

costs at execution time
The execution time overhead results on the one hand from the computations that are introduced by the mess-up algorithms and on the other hand from the execution time of the transported libraries if this time is longer than the execution time of a system library call. There are also costs if communication with remote trusted nodes is needed (e.g. in the case of Deposited Keys).

"costs" by not using efficiency enhancing mechanisms
Due to the blackbox mechanism, it is possible, that mechanisms enhancing efficiency cannot be used by protected agents. One example is the fact, that blackbox agents are not modular and hence cannot use code caching mechanisms as the code is different for every agent even if providing exactly the same functionality.

12 Conclusions and Future Work

Blackbox security is a new approach to solve the problem of malicious hosts, a problem in the area of mobile agent security, that has been rated as not solvable by software means. The presented approach does not prevent every possible attack. It is still possible for the host to deny the execution and to return wrong system call results to the agent. It is further still possible to read and to manipulate data and code, but as the attacker cannot determine the role of these elements for the application, the attack results are random. The approach is able to guarantee a certain protection time interval. Therefore, the agent and its transported data get invalid after this "expiration date". For the purpose of comparing the expiration dates with the current time, synchronized clocks are necessary. As the strength of blackbox security depends on algorithms that "mess-up" code and data of the agent, these algorithms have to be constructed in a way that can guarantee the protection time interval, which also have to be of a useful length. As we have seen, this kind of security is not for free, but costs both in terms of execution and transmission speed. We expect therefore, that blackbox security will be applied only to agents that transport money-like values or security sensitive data such as secret keys.

We will implement a framework for blackbox security for our own Java-based agent system, Mole [6]. At the moment, no overall implementation of the approach exists as it is a complex framework that needs a lot of modifications in an agent system. Currently, we are finishing the implementation of a first combination of code mess-up algorithms [4], and we are starting to develop a formal model of the mess-up effects to be able to compute their protection strength. To prevent blackbox testing attacks, we are currently working on an extension of the blackbox mechanism, which will also allow agents to authenticate their hosts.

Acknowledgments

The author thanks Prof. Dr. Kurt Rothermel and Dr. Markus Schwehm for their help and for fruitful discussions.

References

[1]   Farmer, William; Guttmann, Joshua; Swarup, Vipin: Security for Mobile Agents: Authentication and State Appraisal, in: Proceedings of the European Symposium on Research in Computer Security (ESORICS), pp. 118-130, Springer LNCS 1146, 1996

[2]   General Magic: The Telescript Reference Manual. 1996. http://www.genmagic.com/Telescript/Documentation/TRM/

[3]   Hohl, Fritz: An approach to solve the problem of malicious hosts. Universität Stuttgart, Fakultät Informatik, Fakultätsbericht Nr. 1997/03, 1997. http://www.informatik.uni-stuttgart.de/cgi-bin/ncstrl_rep_view.pl?/inf/ftp/pub/library/ncstrl.ustuttgart_fi/TR-1997-03/TR-1997-03.bib

[4]   Röhrle, Klaus: Konzeption, Implementierung und Analyse von Verwürfelungsmechanismen für Quellcode, Diploma Thesis Nr. 1541, Faculty of Informatics, University of Stuttgart, Germany, 1997

[5]   Mobilis: Exploring Telescript - mobilis Reader Interview: General Magic's Jim White. Mobilis March 1996. http://www.volksware.com/mobilis/march.96/interv1.htm

[6]   Mole project page. http://www.informatik.uni-stuttgart.de/ipvr/vs/projekte/mole.html

[7]   Palmer, E: An Introduction to Citadel - a secure crypto coprocessor for workstations, in: Proceedings of the IFIP SEC'94 Conference, 1994

[8]   Rasmusson, Lars; Jansson, Sverker: Simulated Social Control for Secure Internet Commerce, in: New Security Paradigms '96, ACM Press, 1996

[9]   Sander, Tomas: Security! or "How to Avoid to Breath Life in Frankensteins Monster". Slides of a talk at the ICSI Inhouse Workshop on Auto Mobile Code, "Technology and Applications of Auto Mobile Code (AMC)", September 1997. http://www.icsi.berkeley.edu/~tschudin/amc/workshop97/security.html

[10]   Sander,Tomas; Tschudin,Christian: Protecting Mobile Agents Against Malicious Hosts, in: Vigna, Giovanni (Ed.): Mobile Agents and Security, Springer-Verlag, 1998. http://www.icsi.berkeley.edu/~sander/publications/MA-protect.ps

[11]   Sander,Tomas; Tschudin,Christian: Towards Mobile Cryptography. Technical Report 97-049, International Computer Science Institute, Berkeley. 1997. http://www.icsi.berkeley.edu/~sander/publications/tr-97-049.ps

[12]   Sander,Tomas; Tschudin,Christian: On Sofware Protection via Function Hiding. Submitted to the 2nd International Workshop on Information Hiding, Dec 1998. http://www.icsi.berkeley.edu/~sander/publications/hiding.ps

[13]   Vigna, Giovanni: Protecting Mobile Agents through Tracing, in: Proceedings of the Third ECOOP Workshop on Operating System support for Mobile Object Systems, 1997. To appear.

Authentication for Mobile Agents*

Shimshon Berkovits**, Joshua D. Guttman, and Vipin Swarup

The MITRE Corporation
202 Burlington Road
Bedford, MA 01730-1420
shim,guttman,swarup@mitre.org

Abstract. In mobile agent systems, program code together with some process state can autonomously migrate to new hosts. Despite its many practical benefits, mobile agent technology results in significant new security threats from malicious agents and hosts. In this paper, we propose a security architecture to achieve three goals: certification that a server has the authority to execute an agent on behalf of its sender; flexible selection of privileges, so that an agent arriving at a server may be given the privileges necessary to carry out the task for which it has come to the server; and state appraisal, to ensure that an agent has not become malicious as a consequence of alterations to its state. The architecture models the trust relations between the principals of mobile agent systems and includes authentication and authorization mechanisms.

1 Introduction

Currently, distributed systems employ models in which processes are statically attached to hosts and communicate by asynchronous messages or synchronous remote procedure calls. Mobile agent technology extends this model by including mobile processes, i.e., processes which can autonomously migrate to new hosts. Numerous benefits are expected; they include dynamic customization both at servers and at clients, as well as robust remote interaction over unreliable networks and intermittent connections [7,15,25].

Despite its many practical benefits, mobile agent technology results in significant new security threats from malicious agents and hosts. In fact, several previous uses of mobile agents have been malicious, e.g., the Internet worm. Security issues are recognized as critical to the acceptability of distributed systems based on mobile agents. An important added complication is that, as an agent traverses multiple machines that are trusted to different degrees, its state can change in ways that adversely impact its functionality.

---

* This work was supported by the MITRE-Sponsored Research Program.
** Shimshon Berkovits is also affiliated with the Department of Mathematical Sciences, University of Massachusetts–Lowell.

G. Vigna (Ed.): Mobile Agents and Security
LNCS 1419, pp. 114–136, 1998. © Springer–Verlag Berlin Heidelberg 1998

Threats, vulnerabilities, and countermeasures for the currently predominating static distributed systems have been studied extensively; sophisticated distributed system security architectures have been designed and implemented [13,21]. These architectures use the access control model, which provides a basis for secrecy and integrity security policies. In this model, objects are resources such as files, devices, processes, and the like; principals are entities that make requests to perform operations on objects. A reference monitor is a guard that decides whether or not to grant each request based on the principal making the request, the operation requested, and the access rules for the object.

The process of deducing which principal made a request is called *authentication*. In a distributed system, authentication is complicated by the fact that a request may originate on a distant host and may traverse multiple machines and network channels that are secured in different ways and are not equally trusted [13]. Because of the complexity of distributed authentication, a formal theory is desirable: The formal theory shows how authentication decisions may be made safely and uniformly using a small number of basic principles.

The process of deciding whether or not to grant a request—once its principal has been authenticated—is called *authorization*. The authentication mechanism underlies the authorization mechanism in the sense that authorization can only perform its function based on the information provided by authentication, while conversely authentication requires no information from the authorization mechanism.

In this paper, we examine a few different ways of using mobile agents, with the aim of identifying many of the threats and security issues which a meaningful mobile agent security infrastructure must handle. We identify three security goals for mobile agent systems and propose an abstract architecture to achieve those goals. This architecture is based on four distinct trust relationships between the principals of mobile agent systems. We present and prove conditions necessary to establish each trust relation and then create an architecture that establishes the conditions. We use existing theory—the distributed authentication theory of Lampson et al. [13]—to clarify the architecture and to show that it meets its objectives. Finally, we describe a set of practical mechanisms that implement the abstract architecture.

This paper draws heavily from two papers that we have published [6,5]. For related work on mobile agent security, see [3,4,16,22,23,24,11].

2   Mobile Agents

A mobile agent is a program that can migrate from one networked computer to another while executing. This contrasts with the client/server model where non-executable messages traverse the network, but the executable code remains permanently on the computer it was installed on. Mobile agents have numerous potential benefits. For instance, if one needs to perform a specialized search of a large free-text database, it may be more efficient to move the program to the database server rather than move large amounts of data to the client program.

In recent years, several programming languages for mobile agents have been designed. These languages make different design choices as to which components of a program's state can migrate from machine to machine. For instance, Java [15] permits objects to migrate. In Obliq [1], first-class function values (closures) can migrate; closures consist of program code together with an environment that binds variables to values or memory locations. In Kali Scheme [2], again, closures can migrate; however, since continuations [10,8] are first-class values, Kali Scheme permits threads to migrate autonomously to new hosts. In Telescript [25], functions are not first-class values; however, Telescript provides special operations that permit processes to migrate autonomously.

The languages also differ in their approach to transporting objects other than agents. When a closure or process migrates, it can either carry along all the objects (mutable data) that it references or leave the objects behind and carry along network references to the objects. Java lets the programmer control object marshalling. Object migration uses copy semantics which results in multiple copies of the same object; data consistency needs to be programmed explicitly if it is desired. In Obliq, objects remain on the node on which they were created and mobile closures contain network references to these objects; if object migration is desired, it needs to be programmed explicitly by cloning objects remotely and then deleting the originals. In Kali Scheme, objects are copied upon migration as in Java. In Telescript, objects can either migrate or stay behind when an agent that owns them migrates. However, if other agents hold references to an object that migrates, those references become invalid.

In this paper, we adopt a fairly general model of mobile agents. Agent servers are abstract processors, e.g., individual networked computers, interpreters that run on computers, etc. Agent servers communicate among themselves using host-to-host communication services. An agent consists of code together with execution state. The state includes a program counter, registers, local environment, control stack, and store.

Agents execute on agent servers within the context of global environments (called places) provided by the servers. The places provide agents with (restricted) access to services such as communication services or access to computational or data resources of the underlying server. Agents communicate among themselves by message passing. In addition, agents can invoke a special asynchronous "remote apply" operation that applies a closure to arguments on a specified remote server. Remote procedure calls can be implemented with this primitive operation and message passing. Agent migration and cloning can also be implemented with this primitive operation, using first-class continuation values.

3   Example: Travel Agents

In this section, we will study an example that is typical of many—though not of all—of the ways that mobile agents can be used effectively. We will try to draw out the most important security issues that they raise, as a concrete illustration of the problems of secure mobile agents.

Consider a mobile agent that visits the Web sites of several airlines searching for a flight plan that meets a customer's requirements. We focus on four servers: a customer server, a travel agency server, and two servers owned by competing airlines, for instance United Airlines and American Airlines, which we assume for the sake of this example do not share a common reservation system. The mobile agent is programmed by a travel agency. A customer dispatches the agent to the United Airlines server where the agent queries the flight database. With the results stored in its environment, the agent then migrates to the American Airline server where again it queries the flight database. The agent compares flight and fare information, decides on a flight plan, migrates to the appropriate airline server, and reserves the desired flights. Finally, the agent returns to the customer with the results.

The customer can expect that the individual airlines will provide true information on flight schedules and fares in an attempt to win her business, just as we assume nowadays that the reservation information the airlines provide over the telephone is accurate, although it is not always complete.

However, the airline servers are in a competitive relation with each other. The airline servers illustrates a crucial principle: *For many of the most natural and important applications of mobile agents, we cannot expect the participants to trust one another.*

There are a number of attacks they may attempt. For instance, the second airline server may be able to corrupt the flight schedule information of the first airline, as stored in the environment of the agent. It could surreptitiously raise its competitor's fares, or it could advance the agent's program counter into the preferred branch of conditional code. Current cryptographic techniques can protect against some but not all such attacks. Thus, the mobile agent cannot decide its flight plan on an airline server since the server has the ability to manipulate the decision. Instead, the agent would have to migrate to a neutral server such as the customer's server or a travel agency server, make its flight plan decision on that server, and then migrate to the selected airline to complete the transaction. This attack illustrates a principle: *An agent's critical decisions should be made on neutral (trusted) servers.*

A second kind of attack is also possible: the first airline may hoodwink the second airline, for instance when the second airline has a cheaper fare available. The first airline's server surreptitiously increases the number of reservations to be requested, say from 2 to 100. The agent will then proceed to reserve 100 seats at the second airline's cheap fare. Later, legitimate customers will have to book their tickets on the first airline, as the second believes that its flight is full. This attack suggests two additional principles: *A migrating agent can become malicious by virtue of its state getting corrupted;* and *unchanging components of the state should be sealed cryptographically.*

4   Security Goals

Security is a fundamental concern for a mobile agent system. Harrison et al. [7] identified security as a "severe concern" and regarded it as the primary obstacle to adopting mobile agent systems.

The operation of a mobile agent system will normally be subject to various agreements, whether declared or tacit. These agreements may be violated, accidentally or intentionally, by the parties they are intended to serve. A mobile agent system can also be threatened by parties outside of the agreements: they may create rogue agents; they may hijack existing agents; or they may commandeer servers.

There are a variety of desirable security goals for a mobile agent system. Most of these concern the interaction between agents and servers. The user on behalf of whom an agent operates wants it to be protected—to the extent possible—from malicious or inept servers and from the intermediate hosts which are involved in its transmission. Conversely, a server, and the site at which it operates, needs to be protected from malicious or harmful behavior by an agent.

Not all attractive goals can be achieved, however, except in special circumstances. In the case of mobile agents, one of the primary motivations is that they allow a broad range of users access to a broad range of services offered by different—frequently competing—organizations. Thus, in many of the most natural applications, many of the parties do not trust each other. In our opinion, some previous work (for instance [23]) is vitiated by this fact: It assumes a degree of trust among the participants which will not exist in many applications of primary interest.

Nevertheless, the special cases may be of interest to some organizations. A large organization like the United States Department of Defense might set up a mobile agent system for inter-service use; administrative and technical constraints might ensure that the different parties can trust each other in ways that commercial organizations do not. In this paper, however, we will focus on the more generic case, in which there will be mistrust and attempts to cheat.

We assume that different parties will have different degrees of trust for each other, and in fact some parties may be in a competitive or even hostile relation to one another. As a consequence, we may infer that one party cannot be certain that another party is running an untampered server. An agent that reaches that party may not be allowed to run correctly, or it may be discarded. The server may forge messages purporting to be from the agent. Moreover, the server may inspect the state of the agent to ferret out its secrets. For this reason, we assume that agents do not carry keys.

Existing approaches for distributed security [12] allow us to achieve several basic goals. These include authenticating an agent's endorser and its sender, checking the integrity of its code, and offering it privacy during transmission, at least between servers willing to engage in symmetric encryption.

However, at least three crucial security goals remain:

(1) *Certification that a server has the authority to execute an agent on behalf of its sender.* If executing an agent involves contacting other servers, then a server may have to authenticate that it is a legitimate representative of the agent. The sender of an agent may want to control which servers will be allowed to authenticate themselves in this role.

(2) *Flexible selection of privileges, so that an agent arriving at a server may be given the privileges necessary to carry out the task for which it has come to the server.* There are some applications in which a sender wants his agent to run with restricted authority most of the time, but with greater authority in certain situations. For instance, in the travel agent example of Section 3, a data-collection agent collecting flight information on an airline server needs only ordinary privilege. However, when it returns to its home server or a travel agency server, the agent must request privilege so that it can select a flight plan and purchase a ticket. Thus, there must be a mechanism to allow an agent to request different levels of privilege depending on its state (including its program counter).

(3) *State appraisal, to ensure that an agent has not become malicious as a consequence of alterations to its state.* Because a migrating agent can become malicious if its state is corrupted, as in the case of the travel agent of Section 3, a server may want to execute a procedure to test whether an agent is in a harmful state. However, the test must be application-specific, which suggests that reputable manufacturers of mobile agents may want to provide each one with an appropriate state appraisal function to be used each time a server starts an agent. The code to check the agent's state may be shipped under the same cryptographic signature that protects the rest of the agent's code, so that a malicious intermediary cannot surreptitiously modify the state appraisal function.

In the remainder of this paper, we will focus our attention on achieving these three goals.

5   Security for Mobile Agents: Theory

In this section, we will describe a security architecture for mobile agent systems that is designed to achieve the security goals listed in Section 4. The architecture consists of two levels. The first is the *authentication* level. The mechanisms at this level combine to meet the first of the above security goals. The other two goals are achieved via a pair of *state appraisal functions* together with the mechanisms of the *authorization* layer of the architecture which determine with what authorizations the agent is to run.

5.1   Authentication

Authentication is the process of deducing which principal has made a specific request. In a distributed system, authentication is complicated by the fact that a request may originate on a distant host and may traverse multiple machines and network channels that are secured in different ways and are not equally trusted. For this reason, Lampson and his colleagues [13] developed a logic of authentication that can be used to derive one or more principals who are responsible for a request.

Elements of a Theory of Authentication   The theory—which is too rich to summarize here—involves three primary ingredients. The first is the notion of *principal*. Atomic principals include persons, machines, and keys; groups of principals may also be introduced as principals; and in addition principals may be constructed from simpler principals by operators. The resulting compound principals have distinctive trust relationships with their component principals. Second, principals make *statements*, which include assertions, requests, and performatives.[1] Third, principals may stand in the *"speaks for"* relation; one principal P_1 speaks for a second principal P_2 if, when P_1 **says** s, it follows that P_2 **says** s. This does not mean that P_1 is prevented from uttering phrases not already uttered by P_2; on the contrary, it means that if P_1 makes a statement, P_2 will be committed to it also. For instance, granting a power of attorney creates this sort of relation (usually for a clearly delimited class of statements) in current legal practice. When P_1 speaks for P_2, we write $P_1 \Rightarrow P_2$. One of the axioms of the theory allows one principal to pass the authority to speak for him to a second principal, simply by saying that it is so:

$$(P_2 \text{ says } P_1 \Rightarrow P_2) \supset P_1 \Rightarrow P_2$$

This is called the *handoff* axiom; it says that a principal can hand his authority off to a second principal. It requires a high degree of trust.

Three operators will be needed for building compound principals, namely the **as**, **for**, and quoting operators. If P_1 and P_2 are principals, then P_1 **as** P_2 is a compound principal whose authority is more limited than that of P_1. P_2 is in effect a *role* that P_1 adopts. In our case, the programs (or rather, their names or digests) will be regarded as roles. Quoting, written $P \,|\, Q$ is defined straightforwardly: $(P\,|\,Q)$ **says** s abbreviates P **says** Q **says** s.

The **for** operator expresses *delegation*. P_1 **for** P_2 expresses that P_1 is acting on behalf of P_2. In this case P_2 must delegate some authority to P_1; however, P_1

---

[1] A statement is a *performative* if the speaker performs an action by means of uttering it, at least in the right circumstances. The words "I do" in the marriage ceremony are a familiar example of a performative. Similarly, "I hereby authorize my attorneys, Dewey, Cheatham and Howe, jointly or severally, to execute bills of sale on my behalf." Semantically it is important that requests and performatives should have truth values, although it is not particularly important how those truth values are assigned.

may also draw on his own authority. For instance, to take a traditional example, if a database management system makes a request on behalf of some user, the request may be granted based on two ingredients, namely the user's identity supplemented by the knowledge that the database system is enforcing some constraints on the request. Because P_1 is combining his authority with P_2's, to authenticate a statement as coming from P_1 **for** P_2, we need evidence that P_1 has consented to this arrangement, as well as P_2.

Mobile agents require no additions to the theory presented in [13]; the theory as it exists is an adequate tool for characterizing the different sorts of trust relationships that mobile agents may require.

Atomic Principals for Mobile Agents Five categories of basic principals are specifically relevant to reasoning about mobile agents:

- The *authors* (whether people or organizations) that write programs to execute as agents. Authors are denoted by C, C', etc.
- The *programs* they create, which, together with supplemental information, are signed by the author. Programs and digests of programs are denoted by D, D', etc.
- The *senders* (whether people or other entities) that send agents to act on their behalf. A sender may need a trusted device to sign and transmit agents. Senders are denoted by S, S', etc.
- The *agents* themselves, consisting of a program together with data added by the sender on whose behalf it executes, signed by the sender. Agents and digests of agents are denoted by A, A', etc.
- The *places* where agents are executed. Each place consists of an execution environment on some server. Places may transfer agents to other places, and may eventually return results to the sender. Places are denoted by I, I', etc.

Each author, sender, and place is assumed to have its own public/private key pair. Programs and agents are not allowed to have keys since they are handled by places that may be untrustworthy.

In addition to these atomic principals, the theory also requires:

- Public keys; and
- Compound principals built from keys and the five kinds of atomic principals given above, using the operators of the theory of authentication.

Three functions associate other principals with any agent A:

- The agent's program denoted as program(A).
- The agent's author (i.e., the author of the agent's program) denoted as author(A).
- The agent's sender denoted as sender(A).

Naturally, an implementation also requires certification authorities; the (standard) role they play is described in Section 7.

The Natural History of an Agent There are three crucial types of events in the life history of an agent. They are the creation of the underlying program; the creation of the agent; and migration of the agent from one execution site to another. These events introduce compound principals built from the atomic principals given above.

Program Creation. The author of a program prepares source code and a state appraisal function (denoted by max) for the program. The function max will calculate, as a function of the agent's current state, the maximum set of permissions to be accorded an agent running the program. Should max detect that the agent state has been corrupted, it will set the maximum set of permissions at a reduced level, possibly allowing no permissions at all.

In addition, a *sender permission list (SPL)* may be included for determining which users are permitted to send the resulting agent. In the event that the entire SPL is not known at the time the program is created, another mechanism such as a *sender permission certificate (SPC)* can be used.

After compiling the source code for the program and its state appraisal function, the author C then combines these compiled pieces of code with the SPL and her name, constructs a message digest D for the result, and signs that with her private key. D is regarded as a *name* of the program of which it is a digest. C's signature on D certifies that C is the one who created the program named by D. With this certification, any entity can later verify that the C did indeed create the program and that the program's code, state appraisal function, and SPL have not changed, either accidentally or maliciously. Should C wish to add a sender to the permission list, she creates and signs an SPC certificate containing the program name D and the sender's name S.

By signing D, the author is effectively making a statement about agents A whose programs are D and about senders S who appear on the SPL of D: The author C is declaring that the sender S of a signed agent $(A \textbf{ for } S)$ speaks for the agent. Formally, this is the statement

$$C\,|\,A\,|\,S \textbf{ says } [S\,|\,(A \textbf{ for } S) \Rightarrow (A \textbf{ for } S)]$$

for all C, A, and S such that $C = \mathsf{author}(A)$, $S = \mathsf{sender}(A)$, and S is on the SPL of $\mathsf{program}(A)$. The author's signature on an SPC makes a similar statement about the sender named in the certificate.

We assume as an axiomatic principle that the author of an agent speaks for the agent. Formally, this is the statement

$$C\,|\,A \Rightarrow A$$

for all C and A such that $C = \mathsf{author}(A)$.

Agent Creation. To prepare a program for sending, the sender attaches a second state appraisal function (denoted by req), called the *request* function. req will calculate the set of permissions the sender wants an agent running the program to have, as a function of the agent's current state. For some states Σ, $\mathsf{req}(\Sigma)$ may be a proper subset of $\mathsf{max}(\Sigma)$; for instance, the sender may not be certain how D will behave, and she may want to ensure she is not liable for some actions. The sender may also include a *place permission list (PPL)* for determining which places are allowed to run the resulting agent on the sender's behalf, either via agent delegation or agent handoff (see below under Agent Migration). One can also consider *place permission certificates (PPCs)* whereby the sender can essentially add such acceptable places to the PPL even after the agent has been launched.

The sender S computes a message digest A for the following items: the program, its digest D, the function req, the PPL, S's name, and a counter S increments for each agent she sends. A is regarded as a *name* of the agent of which it is a digest. She then signs the message digest A with her private key. S's signature on A certifies that S created the agent named by A to act on her behalf. The signed agent is identified with principal A **for** S.

By signing A, the sender S is effectively saying that it speaks for the signed agent (A **for** S). Formally, this is the statement

$$S \textbf{ says } [S\,|\,(A \textbf{ for } S) \Rightarrow (A \textbf{ for } S)]$$

for all A and S such that $S = \mathsf{sender}(A)$.

By signing the PPL within A, the sender S is saying that places I that appear on the PPL with an Agent Handoff tag can execute A as the principal (A **for** S), while places I that appear on the PPL with an Agent Delegation tag can execute A as the principal (I **for** A **for** S). Formally, these are the statements:

$$S\,|\,(A \textbf{ for } S) \textbf{ says } [I\,|\,(A \textbf{ for } S) \Rightarrow (A \textbf{ for } S)] \qquad \text{(Agent Handoff)}$$
$$S\,|\,(A \textbf{ for } S) \textbf{ says } [I\,|\,(I \textbf{ for } A \textbf{ for } S) \Rightarrow (I \textbf{ for } A \textbf{ for } S)] \text{ (Agent Delegation)}$$

for all A, S, and I such that $S = \mathsf{sender}(A)$ and I is on the PPL of A. The sender's signature on a PPC makes a similar statement about the place named in the certificate.

The act of creating the agent establishes the trust relationship embodied in the following theorem.

Theorem 1 *Let A be an agent such that $C = \mathsf{author}(A)$, $S = \mathsf{sender}(A)$, and S is on the SPL of $\mathsf{program}(A)$ or S holds an SPC for $\mathsf{program}(A)$. Then:*

$$S\,|\,(A \textbf{ for } S) \Rightarrow (A \textbf{ for } S)$$

Proof. The following assumptions hold:

(a) $C\,|\,A \Rightarrow A$ (axiom).
(b) $C\,|\,A\,|\,S \textbf{ says } [S\,|\,(A \textbf{ for } S) \Rightarrow (A \textbf{ for } S)]$ (derived from C's signature on $\mathsf{program}(A)$ and the SPL or SPC of $\mathsf{program}(A)$).
(c) $S \textbf{ says } [S\,|\,(A \textbf{ for } S) \Rightarrow (A \textbf{ for } S)]$ (derived from S's signature on A).

Applying (a) to (b) yields $A\,|\,S \textbf{ says } [S\,|\,(A \textbf{ for } S) \Rightarrow (A \textbf{ for } S)]$ (d). The delegation axiom $X \;\wedge\; (Y\,|\,X) \Rightarrow (Y \textbf{ for } X)$ applied to (c) and (d) yields $(A \textbf{ for } S) \textbf{ says } [S\,|\,(A \textbf{ for } S) \Rightarrow (A \textbf{ for } S)]$ (e). The result of the theorem then follows from (e) using the handoff axiom.

Before the sender dispatches A, she also attaches a list of parameters, which are in effect the initial state Σ_0 for the agent. The state is not included under any cryptographic seal, because it must change as the agent carries out its computation. However, S's request function req may impose invariants on the state.

Agent Migration. When an agent is ready to migrate from one place to the next, the current place must construct a request containing the agent A, its current state Σ, the current place I_1, the principal P_1 on behalf of whom I_1 is executing the agent, and a description of the principal P_2 on behalf of whom the next place I_2 should execute the agent starting in state Σ.

The statement $I_2 \mid P_2 \Rightarrow P_2$ asserts the expected trust relationship between I_2 and P_2, namely, that, whenever I_2 says P_2 makes a statement s, P_2 is committed to s. The authentication machinery can be construed as providing a proof of this statement. Depending on whether I_2 is trusted by I_1 or by the agent A, four different values of P_2 are possible, expressing four different trust relationships.

(1) *Place Handoff.* I_1 can hand the agent off to I_2. I_2 will then execute the agent on behalf of P_1. In this case, P_2 is P_1, and the migration request by I_1 is assumed to say $I_1 \mid P_1$ **says** $I_2 \mid P_2 \Rightarrow P_2$.

(2) *Place Delegation.* I_1 can delegate the agent to I_2. I_2 will combine its authority with that of P_1 while executing the agent.[2] In this case, P_2 is $(I_2$ **for** $P_1)$, and the migration request by I_1 is assumed to say $I_1 \mid P_1$ **says** $I_2 \mid P_2 \Rightarrow P_2$. The response by I_2 to accept the delegation is assumed to say $I_2 \mid P_1$ **says** $I_2 \mid P_2 \Rightarrow P_2$.

(3) *Agent Handoff.* The agent can directly hand itself off to I_2. I_2 will execute A on behalf of the agent. In this case, P_2 is $(A$ **for** $S)$, and A's PPL or a PPC must imply $S \mid (A$ **for** $S)$ **says** $(I_2 \mid P_2 \Rightarrow P_2)$. The migration request by I_1 does not assert anything and can be unsigned.

(4) *Agent Delegation.* The agent can delegate itself to I_2. I_2 will combine its authority with that of the agent while executing A. In this case, P_2 is $(I_2$ **for** A **for** $S)$, and A's PPL or a PPC must imply $S \mid (A$ **for** $S)$ **says** $(I_2 \mid P_2 \Rightarrow P_2)$. The response by I_2 to accept the delegation is assumed to say $I_2 \mid (A$ **for** $S)$ **says** $(I_2 \mid P_2 \Rightarrow P_2)$. The migration request by I_1 does not assert anything and can be unsigned.

In the first case, I_2 does not appear in the resulting compound principal. This requires I_1 to trust I_2 not to do anything I_1 would not be willing to do. In the third and fourth cases, because the agent itself is explicitly expressing trust in I_2, the resulting compound principal does not involve I_1. The agent trusts I_2 to appraise the state before execution. Assuming that the result of the appraisal is accepted, I_1 has discharged its responsibility. Place handoff and place delegation will usually be initiated directly by the server of the place, while agent handoff and agent delegation will usually be initiated by agent's code.

---

[2] After such delegation, where the agent travels after I_2 and what privileges it will be given thereafter may depend on input from I_2 or trust in I_2.

Agent launch may be regarded as place handoff where the sender's home place plays the role of I_2 and the sender herself acts as I_1.

Each time an agent migrates to a new place, the authentication machinery must verify that the statement $I_2 \mid P_2 \Rightarrow P_2$ is true. How this is done depends on which of the four cases of migration is involved. In each case, however, the verification is performed simply by checking to see if a small number of statements are true. The following four theorems show what these statements are in each of the four respective cases.

Let A be an agent such that $S = \mathsf{sender}(A)$, and assume that A migrates from place I_1 as principal P_1 to place I_2 as principal P_2.

Theorem 2 (Place Handoff) *Let* $P_2 = P_1$. *Then* $I_2 \mid P_2 \Rightarrow P_2$ *follows from the following assumptions:*

(a) $I_1 \mid P_1 \Rightarrow P_1$ *(derived from A's certificates).*
(b) $I_1 \mid P_1$ **says** $I_2 \mid P_2 \Rightarrow P_2$ *(derived from I_1's request).*

Proof. Applying (a) to (b) yields P_1 **says** $I_2 \mid P_2 \Rightarrow P_2$ (c). The result of the theorem follows from (c) using $P_1 = P_2$ and the handoff axiom.

Theorem 3 (Place Delegation) *Let* $P_2 = I_2$ **for** P_1. *Then* $I_2 \mid P_2 \Rightarrow P_2$ *follows from the following assumptions:*

(a) $I_1 \mid P_1 \Rightarrow P_1$ *(derived from A's certificates).*
(b) $I_1 \mid P_1$ **says** $I_2 \mid P_2 \Rightarrow P_2$ *(derived from I_1's request).*
(c) $I_2 \mid P_1$ **says** $I_2 \mid P_2 \Rightarrow P_2$ *(derived from I_2's response).*

Proof. Applying (a) to (b) yields P_1 **says** $I_2 \mid P_2 \Rightarrow P_2$ (d). The delegation axiom $X \wedge (Y \mid X) \Rightarrow Y$ **for** X applied to (d) and (c) yields P_2 **says** $I_2 \mid P_2 \Rightarrow P_2$ (e). The result of the theorem then follows from (e) using the handoff axiom.

Theorem 4 (Agent Handoff) *Let* $P_2 = A$ **for** S. *Then* $I_2 \mid P_2 \Rightarrow P_2$ *follows from the following assumption:*

(a) $S \mid (A \text{ for } S) \Rightarrow (A \text{ for } S)$ *(derived by Theorem 1).*
(b) $S \mid (A \text{ for } S)$ **says** $[I_2 \mid P_2 \Rightarrow P_2]$ *(derived from A's PPL or accompanying PPC).*

Proof. The result of the theorem follows from (a) and (b) using $P_2 = (A \text{ for } S)$ and the handoff axiom.

Theorem 5 (Agent Delegation) *Let* $P_2 = I_2$ **for** A **for** S. *Then* $I_2 \mid P_2 \Rightarrow P_2$ *follows from the following assumptions:*

(a) $S \mid (A \text{ for } S) \Rightarrow (A \text{ for } S)$ *(derived by Theorem 1).*
(b) $S \mid (A \text{ for } S)$ **says** $[I_2 \mid P_2 \Rightarrow P_2]$ *(derived from A's PPL or accompanying PPC).*
(c) $I_2 \mid (A \text{ for } S)$ **says** $[I_2 \mid P_2 \Rightarrow P_2]$ *(derived from I_2's response).*

Proof. Applying (a) to (b) yields $(A$ **for** $S)$ **says** $[I_2 \mid P_2 \Rightarrow P_2]$ (d). The delegation axiom $X \; \wedge \; (Y \mid X) \Rightarrow Y$ **for** X applied to (c) and (d) yield P_2 **says** $[I_2 \mid P_2 \Rightarrow P_2]$. The result of the theorem then follows using the handoff axiom.

We can now describe what happens when a place I_2 receives a request to execute an agent A with a state Σ on behalf of a principle P_2. First, I_2 will check the author's signature on the program of A and the sender's signature on A itself. This would be done using standard, well-understood, public key certification mechanisms [13]. Second, I_2 will authenticate P_2 by verifying that $I_2 \mid P_2 \Rightarrow P_2$ is true. This would be done by checking to see that the assumptions (given by the theorems above) which imply $I_2 \mid P_2 \Rightarrow P_2$ follow from A's PPL and PPCs, the certificates carried by A, and the certificates held by certification authorities. We have now met the first of the security goals proposed in Section 4, namely certification that a place has the authority to execute an agent, ultimately on behalf of its sender.

Admissible Agent Principals. Let an *admissible agent principal* be defined inductively by:

(1) A **for** S is an admissible agent principal if A is an agent and S is a sender.
(2) I **for** P is an admissible agent principal if I is a place and P is an admissible agent principal.

If we assume that an agent can be created and can migrate only in the ways described above, then an agent can only be executed on behalf of an admissible agent principal.

5.2   Authorization

The result of the *authentication* layer is a principal P_2 on behalf of whom I_2 has been asked to execute the agent. The purpose of the *authorization* layer is to determine what level of privilege to provide to the agent for its work. The authorization layer has two ingredients. First, the agent's state appraisal functions `max` and `req` are executed; their result is to determine what privileges ("permits") the agent would like to *request* given its current state. Second, the server has access control lists associated with these permits; the access control lists determine which of the requested permits it is willing to *grant*.

We will assume that the request is for a set α of permits; thus, a request is a statement of the form *please grant α*. In our approach, agents are programmed to make this request when they arrive at a site of execution; the permits are then treated as capabilities during execution: no further checking is required. We distinguish one special permit `run`. By convention, a server will run an agent only if it grants the permit `run` as a member of α.

The request is made by means of the two state appraisal functions. The author-supplied function `max` is applied to Σ returning a maximum safe set of permits. The sender-supplied appraisal function **req** specifies a desired set of permits; this may be a proper subset of the maximum judged safe by the author. However, it should not contain any other, unsafe permits. Thus, we consider P_2 to be making the conditional statement:

$$if \, \mathbf{req}(\Sigma) \subseteq \mathbf{max}(\Sigma) \, then \; please \; grant \; \mathbf{req}(\Sigma) \; else \; please \; grant \; \emptyset$$

I_2 evaluates $\mathbf{req}(\Sigma)$ and $\mathbf{max}(\Sigma)$. If either **req** or **max** detects dangerous tampering to Σ, then that function will request $\emptyset$. Likewise, if **req** makes an excessive request, then the conditional ensures that the result will be $\emptyset$. Since $\mathbf{run} \not\subseteq \emptyset$, the agent will then not be run by I_2. Otherwise, P_2 has requested some set α_0 of permits.

In the logic of authentication presented in [13], authorization—the *granting* of permits—is carried out using access control lists. Logically, an access control list is a set of formulas of the form $(Q \, \mathbf{says} \, s) \supset s$, where the statements s are requests for access to resources and Q is some (possibly compound) principal. If a principal $P \, \mathbf{says} \, s_0$, then I_2 tries to match P and s_0 against the access control list. For any entry $(Q \, \mathbf{says} \, s) \supset s$, if $P \Rightarrow Q$ and $s_0 \supset s$, then I_2 may infer s, thus effectively granting the request. This matching may be made efficient if P, Q, and s take certain restricted syntactic forms.

Since we are concerned with requests for sets of permits, if $\alpha \subseteq \alpha_0$ then *please grant* $\alpha_0 \supset$ *please grant* α. Hence, a particular access control list entry may allow only a subset of the permits requested. The permits granted will be the union of those allowed by each individual access control list entry

$$(Q \, \mathbf{says} \; please \; grant \; \alpha) \supset please \; grant \; \alpha$$

that matches in the sense that $P_2 \Rightarrow Q$ and $\alpha \subseteq \alpha_0$.

6   Example Revisited: Secure Travel Agents

We now return to our travel agents example (Section 3) and describe how the various trust relationships of that example can be expressed in our security architecture, and how state appraisal functions may be used to achieve their security goals.

6.1   Trust Relationships

In the example, a travel agency purchases a travel reservation program containing a state appraisal function from a software house. The state appraisal function determines when and how the agent will have *write privileges* to enter actual reservations in the databases of an airline, a hotel, or a car rental firm. Otherwise, it requests only *read privileges* to obtain pricing and availability information from those databases.

When a customer submits a tentative itinerary for a business trip or a vacation (via an HTML form, for example), the travel agency prepares to launch the travel reservation agent. It adds a permit request function. The agency has special relationships with certain airlines, hotels, car rental companies, and other travel agencies. The agency provides a PPL or PPCs to hand off or delegate authority to servers. For instance, the travel agency may be willing to hand off authority to its own server and to a neutral, trusted travel agency server, but it may wish only to delegate authority to Airline 1 and Airline 2 (since they have vested interests). Alternatively, the agency may get special commissions from Airline 2 and may be eager to accept anything that airline suggests. As a result, it may be willing to hand off to Airline 2. The travel agency launches the agent at its server, with an initial state containing the customer's desired travel plans.

As its first task, the agent migrates to the Airline 1 server I_1. The migration request is for place delegation to Airline 1, giving I_1 the authority to speak on the agent's behalf. Airline 1 accepts this delegation and runs the agent as I_1 **for** A **for** S. This ensures that Airline 1 takes responsibility while speaking for the agent, for instance, while deciding that it is to the customer's advantage to visit a hotel that Airline 1 owns before moving to Airline 2. This is an example of the *agent delegating its authority* to Airline 1 (Theorem 5).

Airline 1 owns a hotel chain and has strong trust in its hotels such as Hotel 1. It sends the agent to the Hotel 1 server I_2 and gives Hotel 1 whatever authority it has over the agent. Hotel 1 runs the agent as I_1 **for** A **for** S, which is the principal that I_1 hands it. This kind of trust relationship is an example of Airline 1's *server handing off its authority* to Hotel 1 (Theorem 2). As a consequence of this trust, I_2 may grant the agent access to a database of preferred room rates.

Next, the agent migrates to Airline 1's preferred car rental agency Car Rental 1, whose server is I_3. Since Airline 1 does not own Car Rental 1, it delegates its authority to Car Rental 1. Car Rental 1 runs the agent as I_3 **for** I_1 **for** A **for** S. This causes Car Rental 1 to take responsibility while speaking on Airline 1's behalf. It also gives the agent combined authority from I_1 and I_3; for instance, the agent can obtain access to rental rates negotiated for travelers on Airline 1. Airline 1's *server has delegated its authority* to Car Rental 1 (Theorem 3).

The agent now migrates to the Airline 2 server I_4. The agent's PPL includes Airline 2 or the agent holds a PPC that directly delegates to Airline 2 the authority to speak on the agent's behalf. Airline 2 accepts this delegation and runs the agent as I_4 **for** A **for** S, again agent delegation (Theorem 5). Airline 1's server I_1 has now discharged its responsibility; it is no longer an ingredient in the compound principal. Except that the agent is carrying the results of its inquiries at Airline 1, Hotel 1 and Car Rental 1, it is as if the travel agency had just delegated the agent to Airline 2.

Once the agent has collected all the information it needs, it migrates to the customer's trusted travel agency (Travel Agency 1) server I_5 to compare information and decide on an itinerary. The agent's PPL or a PPC permits directly handing Travel Agency 1 the authority to speak on its behalf. Travel Agency 1 can thus run the agent as A **for** S. This permits Travel Agency 1 to make critical decisions for the agent, for instance, to make reservations or purchase a ticket. This kind of trust relationship is an example of the *agent handing off its authority* to Travel Agency 1 (Theorem 4).

6.2   Authorization

We next illustrate how state appraisal functions may be used to achieve their security goals. In particular, we will stress the goals 2 and 3 of Section 4, namely flexible selection of permits and the use of state appraisal functions to detect malicious alterations.

In our first example, we will illustrate how the flexible selection of privilege may benefit the servers, in this case the airlines. Before any airline will grant write privileges for entering an actual reservation and payment information, it wants assurance that the agent has visited an acceptably neutral server to decide which reservation it should make. Since the author of the program knows best how these facts are stored in the agent's state, he knows how to perform this test. It may thus be incorporated into the state appraisal function `max`. Since the author is a disinterested, knowledgeable party, the server can safely grant the requested write privilege whenever it is within $\max(\Sigma)$. The airline is reasonably sure that it is not being tricked into making bogus reservations, thus tying up seats that actually could be and should be sold.

The flexible selection of privilege may also benefit the sender. For instance, when the agent returns to the travel agency's trusted server, it may attempt to book a ticket provided sufficient information has already been retrieved. Suppose it is the travel agency's policy not to make a booking unless at least four airlines have been consulted. Thus, the agency writes—or selects—a permit request function `req` that does not allow the write privilege unless four alternate bookings are available from which to choose the best. `max` may not allow write privileges to make a booking unless the agent has visited a neutral server to make a decision on which booking to make. It is `req`, however, which further limits the booking privilege if there were not four alternate itineraries from which the choice was made. An exception-handling mechanism will send the agent out for more information if it tries to make a booking without this permit.

State appraisal may also be used to disarm a maliciously altered agent. Let us alter our example slightly so that the agent maintains—in its state—a linked list of records, each of which represents a desired flight. The code that generates this list ensures that it is finite (free of cycles); the code that manipulates the list preserves the invariant. Thus, there is never a need for the program to check that this list is finite. However, when an agent is received, it is prudent for the state appraisal function to check that the list has not been altered in transit. For if it were, then when the agent began to make its reservations, it would exhaust the available seats, causing legitimate travelers to choose a different carrier.

7   Security for Mobile Agents: Practice

We next describe keys, certificates, and protocols that can be used to implement the abstract security architecture of Section 5.

7.1   Principals and Keys

In Section 5.1, we introduced atomic principals (which include persons, machines, and agents), keys, and compound principals constructed from other principals by operators. Of these, keys are the only principals that can make statements directly; they are the *simple* principals in the sense of Rivest and Lampson [20] that can certify statements made by other principals.

All other principals make statements indirectly. Their statements are validated via proof derivations in the theory of authentication (see Section 5.1). For example, a creator C of an agent A and its sender S, with their respective keys, can create the statements necessary to authorize another principal to speak for the compound principal A **for** S.

When an atomic principal signs a statement, the public key certificate of that principal serves to prove the identity of the principal making the statement. Similar proofs are needed when a compound principal makes a statement. The recipient of the statement must be able to determine who made the statement and whether that principal can be trusted with the statement. That is, the recipient must determine whether to act on the statement or not.

The proof authenticating the identity of an agent's principal may be complex, and its structure corresponds to the structure of the principal itself. The proof requires establishing the sequence of steps executed in building up the agent's compound principal. It examines how the agent's principal was modified at each step in the agent's migration from its launch to its current circumstance.

We assume the existence of a public key infrastructure with certification authorities (CAs) which issue certificates that bind two principals in a speaks-for relationship. Thus, a certification authority CA with key pair $K_{CA}, K_{CA^{-1}}$ might issue a certificate of the form *Cert(P, Q, CA, validity period)* where P and Q are principals. An identity certificate is a special case of this where P is a public key and Q is (the identity of) the owner of the key. These certificates can be stored in appropriate directory servers. We take this certificate to mean that K_{CA} **says** $P \Rightarrow Q$. If a principal trusts K_{CA}, then it can conclude that $P \Rightarrow Q$. Otherwise, a certification chain of CA certificates must be built. Each certificate in the chain attests to the identity of the owner of the public key in the preceding certificate. The chain extends trust in the local CA's signature to trust in the signature of the distant CA which signed the principal certificate being verified. Trust metrics for certificate chains have been studied in [19].

It is apparent from the previous section that certain other certifications are required to prove the authority of a server to speak for a principal. Basic (non-key) certificates include the creator's signature on the agent code, her signature on the SPL of acceptable senders, and sender SPC certificates. Similarly, the sender's certificates include her signature on the creator's signature of the code, and on Agent Handoff and Agent Delegation PPLs or PPC certificates. Finally, a place's certificates include Place Handoff and Place Delegation certificates. All these certificates are signed by the CA-certified, long-term key of the creator, sender, or place. Verifying signatures in a chain of authentication certificates, of course, requires validity checks for the long-term public key certificates used.

This presupposes an efficient validity/revocation infrastructure. The final word on building such an infrastructure is not yet in, but see [9,14,17,18].

The remainder of this section describes in some detail how sequences of these certificates are developed.

7.2   Authentication

We examine the mechanisms necessary to support handoff and delegation certificates when the only key pairs belong to atomic principals. We first describe in detail the certificates required for Place Handoff, Place Delegation, and Agent Launch. Then we look at what is needed for Agent Handoff and Agent Delegation.

We assume that I_j holds a certificate or a sequence of certificates that prove that $(I_j \mid P_k) \Rightarrow P_k$, where P_k is some principal. This is assumption (a) of both Theorem 2 and Theorem 3. All signatures on any certificates involved in this proof have been created by atomic principals using those principals' private keys. We represent the certificate or sequence of certificates that prove that $(I_j \mid P_k) \Rightarrow P_k$ as $Cert((I_j \mid P_k) \Rightarrow P_k)$. We use the symbol $\parallel$ to denote concatenation of data strings.

Form of a Migration Request All migration requests have the same form. It is *Migrate (requesting server's ID, agent ID, principal ID, target server's ID, flag, validity period)*. A request $Migrate(I_1, A, P, I_2, f, t)$ denotes that server I_1, which has the authority to run agent A as principal P, requests server I_2 to run agent A as a new principal which is determined by the flag f. The flag f consists of two bits and is used to indicate the type of migration being requested. We shall use HO for Place Handoff, Del for Place Delegation, AH for Agent Handoff, and AD for Agent Delegation. The validity period t indicates the intended lifespan of this handoff or delegation. At the end of the validity period, the target server no longer speaks for the agent's principal. Other servers should ignore any statements the target server has made quoting the principal, if those statements were made after the expiration of the validity period.

Place Handoff (HO) Suppose that a server I_1 possesses an agent A and a set of certificates $Cert((I_1 \mid P_1) \Rightarrow P_1)$ for A. I_1 can handoff the agent A to a server I_2 by sending I_2 those certificates together with a signed migration request $Migrate(I_1, A, P_1, I_2, HO, t)$. By this request, $(I_1 \mid P_1)$ **says** $[(I_2 \mid P_1) \Rightarrow P_1]$. Then, by Theorem 2,

$$Cert((I_2 \mid P_1) \Rightarrow P_1) = Migrate(I_1, A, P_1, I_2, HO, t)$$
$$\parallel Cert((I_1 \mid P_1) \Rightarrow P_1)$$

I_2, and any server that handles the agent after I_2, must check the signatures on the migration request by obtaining I_1's public key from a CA-signed certificate. As one possible implementation, the CA-signed certificate for I_1 can be included as part of the migration request and can be incorporated into $Cert((I_2 \,|\, P_1) \Rightarrow P_1)$. Otherwise, I_2 will have to obtain that key certificate from the CA or from some directory server.

Note that any server that checks the sequence of certificates can first examine the most recently added certificate and then work backwards in history. That way, if it encounters a server that it trusts to have checked all the preceding certificates, it can immediately cease its own verifications.

Place Delegation (Del) Suppose again that a server I_1 possesses an agent A and a set of certificates $Cert((I_1 \,|\, P_1) \Rightarrow P_1)$ for A. I_1 can delegate its authority over the agent A to a server I_2 by sending I_2 those certificates together with a signed migration request $Migrate(I_1, A, P_1, I_2, Del, t_1)$. By this request, $(I_1 \,|\, P_1)$ **says** $[(I_2 \,|\, (I_2 \text{ for } P_1)) \Rightarrow (I_2 \text{ for } P_1)]$.

If I_2 is willing to accept this delegation, it returns a signed response to I_1. The response, $Response(I_2, A, P_1, I_1, t_2)$, is signed by I_2's private key. The validity period t_2 in the response need not be the same as the period t_1 in the request. It is the period during which I_2 is willing to accept the delegation and must be a subset of t_1. I_1 checks I_2's signature on the response before sending the agent to I_2. This signature indicates that $(I_2 \,|\, P_1)$ **says** $[(I_2 \,|\, (I_2 \text{ for } P_1)) \Rightarrow (I_2 \text{ for } P_1)]$.

Then, by Theorem 3,

$$Cert((I_2 \,|\, (I_2 \text{ for } P_1)) \Rightarrow (I_2 \text{ for } P_1)) = Response(I_2, A, P_1, I_1, t_2)$$
$$\|\ Migrate(I_1, A, P_1, I_2, Del, t_1)$$
$$\|\ Cert((I_1 \,|\, P_1) \Rightarrow P_1)$$

along with CA-signed certificates in the case that the implementation requires their being sent from place to place.

I_2 verifies the signatures in $Cert((I_1 \,|\, P_1) \Rightarrow P_1)$ and the migration request just as in Place Handoff, above. Any other server that receives the agent after I_2 must also verify I_2's signature on the response as well as any other requests and responses of servers between I_2 and itself. Once again, if it encounters a server that it trusts, it may be able to stop checking certificates at that point.

Agent Launch In the above, we have discussed the certificates necessary for an agent's migration from one place to another using Place Handoff or Place Delegation. We now examine the certifications needed to launch an agent and note that they include precisely the same certifications required to support Place Handoff and Place Delegation.

Code Creation and Signature A creator of an agent's program prepares the source code for that agent and a state appraisal function called `max`. The function `max` is used to calculate the maximum permissions that are safe to afford an agent running the program. The creator then signs the combination of program and `max`. This insures the integrity of the code and of `max` and proves that the creator speaks for the program.

The creator may create a list of users, the sender permission list (SPL), who are permitted to send the resulting agent. That SPL can be included with the program and `max` as part of the object being signed. Subjects on the SPL may be individual users or groups of users.

Sender Permission Certificates As the creator may not know, a priori, all the users or groups of users who will want to employ the program, a mechanism for sender permission certificates (SPCs) is also needed. An SPC has the same syntax as an element of an SPL. However, it is signed as a separate entity with data to show to which program it refers and who the signer is. The signer is again the program creator.

The creator can, for example, sign and deliver an SPC to any buyer of his program who executes a licensing agreement. The SPC can even include a validity period to correspond to the lifetime of the license being issued. For a group license, the creator can specify in the SPC what determines group membership or who decides such membership.

Sender's Customization The sender may augment the signed code and sender SPL she has received from the creator. She may add a state appraisal function called `req`. The function `req` is used to calculate the minimum permissions that are required to run the agent program. The sender may include a list of places that are permitted to run the agent A with principal (A **for** S). She may also include a list of places I that are permitted to run the agent with principal (I **for** A **for** S). The two lists comprise the place permission list (PPL). To insure the integrity of the code and of `req` and to prove that the sender, quoting A **for** S, speaks for A **for** S, she signs the combination of the creator's signature on the program and `max`, the function `req`, and any PPL. Conceivably the sender can make separate place permission certificates (PPCs), one for each place that can accept Agent Handoff and one for each place that can accept Agent Delegation. This latter alternative, however, is quite unlikely. The sender should know at the time of launch which places are acceptable for Agent Handoff or Agent Delegation. If new places become available after the agent's launch, it is unlikely that the sender will be available to sign an appropriate PPC.

The creator's signature and the sender's signature, provided that the sender is on the creator list of authorized senders, together imply that $(S\,|\,(A$ **for** $S)) \Rightarrow$ (A **for** S) (see Theorem 1 for details of the proof of this statement). S is the initial place where the agent, with principal $P = A$ **for** S, exists. These signatures together form $Cert(S\,|\,P \Rightarrow P)$. The agent can now be sent to its first place by either Place Handoff or Place Delegation with S signing the appropriate migration request. For Place Delegation, the initial server creates and signs a response; whether or not that response is returned to the sender and verified is not important for this discussion.

Agent Handoff and Agent Delegation For both Agent Handoff and Agent Delegation, I_1 first checks that I_2 is on the PPL or is mentioned in a PPC. If it is, I_1 creates a request $Migrate(I_1, A, P_1, I_2, f, t_1)$ where the flag f is either AH or AD depending on the type of migration. Although this request takes the same standard form as the others, the agent principal P_1 at I_1 actually has no bearing on the migration.

If desired, I_1 may sign the request, and I_2 may verify the sequence of certificates $Cert((I_1 \mid P_1) \Rightarrow P_1)$ that allow I_1 to speak for P_1 and to make the migration request. I_2 may also recheck that it is on the proper sender-signed PPL or PPC. Ultimately, I_2 must decide if it wishes to run the agent with principal (A **for** S) if Agent Handoff is requested or with principal (I_2 **for** A **for** S) if Agent Delegation is the request.

How the agent reached I_2 is really of no consequence. In fact, the new certificate for Agent Handoff is

$$Cert(I_2 \mid (A \textbf{ for } S) \Rightarrow (A \textbf{ for } S)) = \text{the sender-signed PPL or PPC}$$

and for Agent Delegation is

$$Cert(I_2 \mid (I_2 \textbf{ for } A \textbf{ for } S) \Rightarrow (I_2 \textbf{ for } A \textbf{ for } S)) =$$
$$Response(I_2, A, (A \textbf{ for } S), S, t_2)$$
$$\| \text{ the sender-signed PPL or PPC}$$

The response is signed by I_2, of course, and can be sent to I_1 or to S for verification.

8 Conclusion

Many of the most important applications of mobile agents will occur in fairly uncontrolled, heterogeneous environments. As a consequence, we cannot expect that the participants will trust each other. Moreover, servers may disclose the secrets of visiting agents, and may attempt to manipulate their state.

Existing techniques, intended for distributed systems in general, certainly allow substantial protection within the broad outlines of these constraints. However, substantial investment in mobile agent systems may await further work on new security techniques specifically oriented toward mobile agents. These new techniques focus on three areas. The first is programming language and system support to improve the safety of mobile code. The second is support for tracking the state carried by mobile agents. The third is trusted execution environments within which agents can make critical decisions safely. With advances in these areas, we believe that mobile agents will be an important ingredient in producing secure, flexible distributed systems.

In this paper, we have described a framework for authenticating and authorizing mobile agents, building on existing theory. Our approach models a variety of trust relations, and allows a mobile agent system to be used effectively even when some of the parties stand in a competitive relation to others. We have introduced the idea of packaging state appraisal functions with an agent. The state-appraisal functions provide a flexible way for an agent to request permits, when it arrives at a new server, depending on its current state, and depending on the task that it needs to do there. The same mechanism allows the agent and server to protect themselves against some attacks in which the state of the agent is modified at an untrustworthy server or in transit. We believe that this is a primary security challenge for mobile agents, beyond those implicit in other kinds of distributed systems.

References

1. L. Cardelli. A language with distributed scope. In *Proceedings of the 22nd ACM Symposium on Principles of Programming Languages*, pages 286–298, 1995. http://www.research.digital.com/SRC/Obliq/Obliq.html.

2. H. Cejtin, S. Jagannathan, and R. Kelsey. Higher-order distributed objects. *ACM Transactions on Programming Languages and Systems*, 17(5):704–739, September 1995. http://www.neci.nj.nec.com:80/PLS/Kali.html.

3. D. Chess, B. Grosof, C. Harrison, D. Levine, C. Parris, and G. Tsudik. Itinerant agents for mobile computing. IEEE *Personal Communications Magazine*, 2(5):34–49, October 1995. http://www.research.ibm.com/massive.

4. D. Chess et al. Things that go bump in the net. Web page at http://www.research.ibm.com/massive, IBM Corporation, 1995.

5. W. M. Farmer, J. D. Guttman, and V. Swarup. Security for mobile agents: Authentication and state appraisal. In *Proceedings of the European Symposium on Research in Computer Security (ESORICS), LNCS 1146*, pages 118–130, September 1996.

6. W. M. Farmer, J. D. Guttman, and V. Swarup. Security for mobile agents: Issues and requirements. In *National Information Systems Security Conference*. National Institute of Standards and Technology, October 1996.

7. C. G. Harrison, D. M. Chess, and A. Kershenbaum. Mobile agents: Are they a good idea? Technical report, IBM Research Report, IBM Research Division, T.J. Watson Research Center, Yorktown Heights, NY, March 1995. http://www.research.ibm.com/massive.

8. C. Haynes and D. Friedman. Embedding continuations in procedural objects. *ACM Transactions on Programming Languages and Systems*, 9:582–598, 1987.

9. R. Housley, W. Ford, W. Polk, and D. Solo. Internet public key infrastructure X.509 certificate and CRL profile. Internet Draft <draft-ietf-pkix-ipki-part1-06.txt>, Work in Progress, October 1997.

10. IEEE Std 1178-1990. *IEEE Standard for the Scheme Programming Language*. Institute of Electrical and Electronic Engineers, Inc., New York, NY, 1991.

11. G. Karjoth, D. B. Lange, and M. Oshima. A security model for Aglets. In *IEEE Internet Computing*, pages 68–77, July/August 1997.

12. C. Kaufman, R. Perlman, and M. Speciner. *Network Security: Private Communication in a Public World*. Prentice Hall, 1995.

13. B. Lampson, M. Abadi, M. Burrows, and E. Wobber. Authentication in distributed systems: Theory and practice. *ACM Transactions on Computer Systems*, 10:265–310, November 1992.

14. S. Micali. Efficient certificate revocation. Technical Memo MIT/LCS/TM-542b, MIT, September 1997. See also US Patent 5666416.

15. Sun Microsystems. Java: Programming for the Internet. Web page available at http://java.sun.com/.

16. Sun Microsystems. HotJava: The security story. Web page available at `http://java.sun.com/doc/overviews.html`, 1995.
17. M. Myers. Internet public key infrastructure online certificate status protocol–OCSP. Internet Draft <draft-ietf-pkix-opp-ocsp-01.txt>, Work in Progress, November 1997.
18. M. Naor and K. Nissim. Certificate revocation and certificate update. In *7th USENIX Security Symposium*, San Antonio, CA, January 1998.
19. M. K. Reiter and S. G. Stubblebine. Toward acceptable metrics of authentication. In *IEEE Symposium on Security and Privacy*, pages 3–18, 1997.
20. R. L. Rivest and B. Lampson. SDSI – A simple distributed security infrastructure. `http://theory.lcs.mit.edu/~rivest/publications.html`.
21. J. G. Steiner, C. Neuman, and J. I. Schiller. Kerberos: An authentication service for open network systems. In *Proceedings of the Usenix Winter Conference*, pages 191–202, 1988.
22. J. Tardo and L. Valente. Mobile agent security and Telescript. In *IEEE CompCon*, 1996. `http://www.cs.umbc.edu/agents/security.html`.
23. C. Thirunavukkarasu, T. Finin, and J. Mayfield. Secret agents — a security architecture for KQML. In *CIKM Workshop on Intelligent Information Agents*, Baltimore, December 1995.
24. G. Vigna. Protecting mobile agents through tracing. In *Proceedings of the Third Workshop on Mobile Object Systems*, Finland, June 1997.
25. J. E. White. Telescript technology: Mobile agents. In *General Magic White Paper*, 1996. Will appear as a chapter of the book Software Agents, Jeffrey Bradshaw (ed.), AAAI Press/The MIT Press, Menlo Park, CA.

Cryptographic Traces for Mobile Agents

Giovanni Vigna

Dip. Elettronica e Informazione, Politecnico di Milano
P.za L. Da Vinci 23, 20133 Milano, Italy
vigna@elet.polimi.it

Abstract. Mobile code systems are technologies that allow applications to move their code, and possibly the corresponding state, among the nodes of a wide-area network. Code mobility is a flexible and powerful mechanism that can be exploited to build distributed applications in an Internet scale. At the same time, the ability to move code to and from remote hosts introduces serious security issues. These issues include authentication of the parties involved and protection of the hosts from malicious code. However, the most difficult task is to protect mobile code against attacks coming from hosts. This paper presents a mechanism based on execution tracing and cryptography that allows one to detect attacks against code, state, and execution flow of mobile software components.

1 Introduction

Mobile code technologies are languages and systems that exploit some form of code mobility in an Internet-scale setting. In this framework, the network is populated by several loosely coupled *computational environments*, or *sites*, that provide support for the execution of *executing units*, or *agents*. Agents represent sequential flows of computation which are characterized by a *code segment*, providing the static description of the behavior of a computation, and an *execution state*, containing control information related to the state of the computation, such as the call stack and the instruction pointer.

Mobile code technologies can be divided in two sets [6]. *Weakly mobile* technologies allow an application to send code to a remote site in order to have it executed there, or to dynamically link code retrieved from a remote site in order to execute it locally. The transferred code may be accompanied by some initialization data but no migration of execution state is involved. Examples of weakly mobile technologies are Java [19] and the Aglets system [16]. *Strongly mobile* technologies allow an executing unit that is running at a particular site to move to a different computational environment. In this case, the executing unit is stopped and its code and execution state are marshaled into a message that is sent to the remote site. The destination site restarts the unit from the statement that follows the invocation of the migration primitive. Examples of

G. Vigna (Ed.): Mobile Agents and Security
LNCS 1419, pp. 137–153, 1998. © Springer–Verlag Berlin Heidelberg 1998

strongly mobile languages are Telescript [30] and Agent-Tcl [12]. A survey of several mobile code languages and systems can be found in [10].

While the mobile code approach to designing and implementing distributed applications provides a greater degree of flexibility and customizability with respect to the traditional client-server approach [4], it raises some serious security issues. Agents travel across the network on behalf of users, visiting sites that may be managed by different authorities (e.g., a university or a company) with different and possibly conflicting objectives [20]. Therefore, mobile code systems must provide mechanisms to protect hosts and execution environments from misbehaviors or attacks coming from roaming agents as well as mechanisms to protect agents from malicious sites. In addition, agents should be protected against eavesdropping or tampering during migration from site to site.

Protection of agents while traveling over an untrusted network can be achieved using well-known cryptographic protocols (e.g., the Secure Socket Layer [9]). Mechanisms and policies to protect a site from code coming from an untrusted source have been the focus of recent research [28, 21, 32, 17]. Using suitable access control and sandboxing mechanisms, it is possible to protect execution environments effectively against a wide range of attacks.

By far, the hardest security problem is represented by the protection of agents from attacks coming from the computational environments that are responsible for their execution. In fact, execution environments must access agents' code and execution state to be able to execute them. As a consequence, it is very difficult to prevent disclosure, tampering, or incorrect execution of agents.

We propose a mechanism that allows for detecting possible misbehavior of a site with respect to a roaming agent by using cryptographic traces. Traces are logs of the operations performed by an agent during its lifetime. The proposed mechanism allows an agent owner to check, after agent termination, if the execution history of the agent conforms to a correct execution.

The paper is organized as follows. Section 2 presents some related work on mobile code and security. Section 3 introduces some concepts and assumptions underlying cryptographic tracing. In sections 4 and 5 we describe the mechanism and its applications. Section 6 discusses the applicability of the proposed approach and some of its limits. In Section 7 we describe a mobile code language that implements the tracing mechanism. The language is then used in a simple electronic commerce application. Section 8 draws some conclusions and illustrates future work.

2   Related Work

Protecting programs against attacks coming from the interpreter responsible for their execution is a challenging problem[1]. Some efforts have been devoted to determining which goals are achievable and which are not [5, 8]. For example, it

---

[1] Presently, most mobile code systems consider the site as a trusted entity and therefore they do not provide any mechanism to protect agent execution.

is not possible to guarantee that an environment will execute an agent correctly and to its completion, or to achieve total protection of agent data from disclosure.

Presently, solutions to the problem of protecting mobile agents against attacks coming from their execution environment are aimed at *prevention* or *detection*.

Prevention mechanisms try to make it impossible (or very difficult) to access or modify agents' code and state in a meaningful way. One possible approach is to adopt *tamper-proof devices* [31]. These devices are processors that execute agents in a physically sealed environment. The system internals are not accessible even by its owner without disrupting the system itself. While these systems can provide a high level of protection, they require dedicated (expensive) hardware. Therefore, they are not easily deployed on a large scale. A software-based approach is followed by *code scrambling* [14, 25] mechanisms. In this case, the mobile code is "rearranged" before it is moved to a remote site. The technique used to modify the code makes it difficult to re-engineer the code but preserves its original behavior. A simpler solution performs *partial encryption* of the agent's components. Using this mechanism, an agent protects data that must be used at a particular site by encrypting them with the site's public-key. This way, data are accessible only when the agent reaches the intended execution environment. Obviously, this approach requires that (at least part of) the route that will be followed by the agent is known in advance. A new and promising approach exploits *cryptographed functions* [23]. In this case, the mobile code performs an algorithm that, given some external inputs, computes a cryptographed value. The site has no clue about which is the function actually computed and therefore cannot meaningfully tamper with algorithm execution and computation results. Presently, this mechanism has been applied to the evaluation of polynomial and rational functions.

Detection mechanisms aim at detecting illegal modification of code, state, and execution flow of a mobile agent. While static code can be easily protected by using digital signatures, state and execution flow are dynamic components and therefore other mechanisms must be devised. For example, the *state appraisal* mechanism [7] associates a mobile agent with a state appraisal function. When a roaming agent reaches a new execution environment, the appraisal function is evaluated passing as a parameter the agent's current state. The appraisal function checks if some invariants on the agent's state hold (e.g., relationships among variables). This way, some malicious attempts to tamper with the agent's state can be detected.

We introduce a mechanism that aims at detecting *any* possible illegal modification of agent code, state, and execution flow. The mechanism is based on post-mortem analysis of data —called *traces*— that are collected during agent execution. Traces are used as a basis for program execution verification, i.e., for checking the agent program against a supposed history of its execution. This way, in case of tampering, the agent's owner can prove that the claimed operations could have never been performed by the agent.

3   Tracing Execution

The proposed mechanism assumes that all the involved principals, namely users and site owners, own a public and a secret key that can be used for encryption and digital signatures [22]. The public key of a principal A is denoted by A_p, while A_s is used for the corresponding secret key. Principals are users of a *public key infrastructure* [15] that guarantees the association of a principal identity with the corresponding public key by means of certificates. We assume that, at any moment, any principal can retrieve the certificate of any other principal and verify the integrity and the validity of the associated public key.

The process of encrypting[2] a message m with a key K is expressed by $K(m)$. In addition, we will use one-way hash functions in order to produce cryptographically secure compact representations of messages. The hash value obtained by application of the one-way hash function H to the message m is denoted by $H(m)$. The process of signing[3] a message with a secret key is denoted by $X_s(m)$, where X is the signing principal. Several examples of cryptosystems and one-way hash functions can be found in [24].

A moving agent is composed of a code segment p and the associated execution state S^i, which has been determined, at some specified point i, by code execution. The state includes global data structures, the call stack, and the program counter. We assume that the code is *static* with respect to the lifetime of the agent, that is, the agent cannot change its own code segment as the result of its execution. This constraint will be removed in Section 6. The code segment is composed of a sequence of *statements*, that can be *white* or *black*. A white statement is an operation that modifies the agent's execution state on the basis of the value of the agent's internal variables only. For example, the statement $x := y + z$, where x, y, and z are variables contained in the agent's execution state, is a white statement. A black statement modifies the state of the program using information received from the external execution environment. For example, the statement $read(x)$, that assigns to the variable x a value read from the terminal, is a black statement. This is not a new concept. For example, the Perl [18] language implements a security mechanism, called *tainting*, that allows the programmer to keep track of the variables whose value has been determined on the basis of information retrieved from the external environment (e.g., terminal input or environment variables).

A trace T^p of the execution of program p is composed of a sequence of pairs $\langle n, s \rangle$, where n represents a unique identifier of a statement, and s is a *signature*. When associated with a black statement, the signature contains the new values assumed by internal variables as a consequence of the statement

---

[2] Public-key cryptography is slow when compared to symmetric cryptography. In the sequel, when we will need bulk encryption using public keys we will assume that the message has been encrypted with a randomly generated secret key and that the key has been protected with the original public key. For example, if the application of a symmetric encryption process parameterized by a key K to a message m is represented by $K(m)$, then $A_p(m)$ is equivalent to $A_p(K), K(m)$.

[3] If not explicitly noted, $X_s(m)$ is considered equivalent to $m, X_s(H(m))$.

execution. For example, if the $read(x)$ instruction gets the value 3 from the terminal, the associated signature will be $x := 3$. The signature is empty for white statements.

We make some assumptions about the execution infrastructure. First of all, we assume that all the interpreter implementations are certified correct and respectful of the semantics of the language. For example, the interpreter owner must provide some kind of third-party certification of correct implementation of the language to be able to charge agents for the services used. This way, a site owner cannot claim that, in his/her interpreter implementation, the execution of a *while* statements means "buy two hundred shares of Microzooft in the stock market". Second, we assume that all the principals participating in the infrastructure respond to some trusted party that will be involved in case of (claimed) misbehaviors.

The following two sections address problems of increasing complexity, firstly considering *remote code execution*, and then *mobile agents*. In describing the protocols we employ the following notation:

$$X \xrightarrow{m_i} Y : F_1, F_2, \dots, F_n.$$

The expression above means that principal X sends message m_i to principal Y. The contents of the message are a sequence of fields $F_1, F_2, \dots, F_n$.

4   Remote Code Execution

Remote code execution, also known as *remote evaluation*, is a mechanism that allows an application to have code sent to a remote host and executed there. Remote execution is a well-known mechanism that dates back to the 70s, when it was used for remote job submissions [1], and has always been available to UNIX users by means of the `rsh` facility. Remote code execution represents the basis for several mobile code systems like Obliq [3] and M0 [29]. A formal definition of the remote evaluation mechanism is presented in [26].

Suppose now that principal A wants to execute program p on site B. Therefore, A sends B the following signed message:

$$A \xrightarrow{m_1} B : A_s(A, B, i_A, t_A, K_A(p), TTP).$$

The first two fields of the message specify that the message is coming from A and it is directed to B. When B receives m_1, it uses A's public key to verify the message signature. This way, B is assured that the message was actually sent by A and that the message was intended for itself. The third field (i_A) is a unique identifier used to mark all the messages that are involved in this execution request and to protect from replay attacks. The following field (t_A) is a timestamp to guarantee freshness[4]. The next field is the code to be executed,

---

[4] The timestamp may be associated to a time interval to limit execution time or the validity of the request.

encrypted using a random secret key K_A, chosen by A. The last field is the identifier of a trusted third party (TTP) that will be involved if A or B claim that the other principal is not playing fair.

B can reject or accept the request on the basis of the available information (the identity of the sender, the unique identifier, the timestamp, and the trusted third party chosen by A). In either case B replies with a signed message containing the outcomes of its decision, say M. If B rejects the request and refuses to execute the code, M contains the error message that motivates the rejection. If B accepts the request, M contains an acceptance statement that represents B's commitment to the execution of p and implicitly requests the decryption key K_A:

$$B \xrightarrow{m_2} A : B_s(B, A, i_A, H(m_1), M).$$

A receives m_2 and validates the message. Thus, A is assured that the message was sent by B, that it was intended for itself, and that the message refers to the execution request identified by i_A. If M is a rejection message the protocol ends. If the request has been accepted then A sends a signed message containing the key K_A protected using B's public key:

$$A \xrightarrow{m_3} B : A_s(A, B, i_A, B_p(K_A)).$$

When B receives the message, it checks message validity and then extracts the key K_A by using its own secret key. Then, B decrypts $K_A(p)$, retrieves the code to be executed, and sends A an acknowledgment message:

$$B \xrightarrow{m_4} A : B_s(B, A, i_A, H(m_3)).$$

Then, B executes code p and, during execution, it produces the associated trace T_B^p. The trace contains the identifiers of the executed statements and the signatures associated with black statements.

When the program terminates, B sends A a signed message containing the program's final state S_B encrypted using a random key K_B, chosen by B, a checksum of the execution trace T_B^p (whose extended form is stored —for a limited amount of time— by B), and a timestamp t_B:

$$B \xrightarrow{m_5} A : B_s(B, A, i_A, K_B(S_B), H(T_B^p), t_B).$$

When A receives the message, it replies with a signed acknowledgment message implicitly requesting the key to access the computation results:

$$A \xrightarrow{m_6} B : A_s(A, B, i_A, H(m_5)).$$

This message is A's commitment to pay for the services used by the mobile code if the execution was correct. B replies to m_6 with a signed message containing the key K_B, protected with A's public key:

$$B \xrightarrow{m_7} A : B_s(B, A, i_A, A_p(K_B)).$$

A verifies the signature on the message and then extracts K_B by using its own secret key. Then, A decrypts $K_B(S_B)$ and accesses the results of the computation.

After having accessed the results, if, for some reason, A suspects that B cheated while executing p, it can ask B to produce the trace. B cannot refuse because of its signed message m_5. After B delivers the complete trace T_B^p, A checks whether the trace is the one actually referenced in message m_5 by computing $H(T_B^p)$ and comparing it with the value contained in B's message. Finally, A validates the execution of p with respect to the trace T_B^p. That is, the code is re-executed step by step, and at each step the identifier of the current statement is compared with the one contained in the trace at the corresponding step. Every time a statement that involves some input from the outside environment must be executed, the input value is extracted from the corresponding signature. Note that the complexity of the validation process is linear with the size of the execution trace.

If, at some point, a discrepancy between the simulated execution and the trace is found or if the final state of the simulator does not match the value S_B provided by B then B cheated by modifying the code, by modifying some program variables, or by tampering with the code execution flow. If no difference between the simulated execution and the trace is found but B charged A for actions that the code did not perform during the simulation, then B cheated by overcharging A for services or resources that have not been used.

In both cases, A can prove B's misbehavior to the trusted third party. In fact, using message m_2, A can prove that B received code p and committed to its execution. Then, using message m_5, A can prove that B claimed to have executed p following trace T_B^p to obtain the final state S_B. In fact, B signed $H(T_B^p)$ and $K_B(S_B)$ and cannot provide a different trace or change the computation results. The proposed mechanism also provides a means to protect a well-behaving site against a cheating user. In fact, B can prove to the trusted third party that A requested the execution of code p by providing m_1 and that A accepted to pay for the resources consumed by showing message m_6.

The protocol described so far assumes that the participants are playing fair by following the protocol as expected. If A and/or B does not play fair, the trusted party must be involved to force the misbehaving participant to a correct behavior. In the following we analyze what these misbehaviors can be and how they are solved.

After A sends B message m_1, B should send message m_2. At this step there are two possible misbehaviors: (i) A could *claim* to have sent m_1 without actually having sent it; (ii) B omits producing message m_2 claiming that it has never received message m_1. In both cases, A —the party that is interested in having the code executed— contacts the trusted party TTP providing message m_1 and requesting its delivery to B. Note that TTP has no means of determining who is not playing fair and therefore cannot apply any sanction. Its role is simply to guarantee (and certify) that message m_1 was delivered to B.

After this step B must send a response message. Again, there are two possible misbehaviors: (i) B could *claim* to have sent m_2 without actually having sent it; (ii) A could omit sending message m_3 claiming that m_2 was never sent by B. In both cases, B —the party that is interested in charging A for the execution of p— contacts the trusted party and asks it to deliver message m_2 to A. Now A is committed to send message m_3. If A fails to send message m_3, B can contact the trusted party and ask it to force A to behave correctly. If A sent message m_3 but B claims it has never received it and for this reason it did not produce message m_4, A can ask the trusted party to deliver message m_3 and force B to provide a receipt.

After B executed the code, it should send message m_5 with the encrypted results. B can play unfair by pretending to have sent the message, while A can misbehave by pretending not to have received it. In both cases, B is in charge of contacting the trusted party and force the delivery, because B needs message m_6 to be able to charge A. If B omits sending message m_7 claiming it has never received m_6, A —the party that is interested in obtaining the results— can contact the trusted party, produce m_5 and m_6 as evidence, and force B to deliver message m_7.

The protocol described so far addresses the problem of detecting tampering in case of remote execution of code. Code execution involves two principals: the owner of the code and the remote site responsible for code execution. In the next section we will extend the protocol to take into account a computation that involves several sites and the transfer of intermediate execution states.

5   Mobile Agent

In the following we consider a scenario in which a mobile agent starts from an initial home site and then jumps from site to site to perform a particular task. Eventually the agent will terminate and the results will be delivered to its owner at its home site.

Let us suppose that the agent starts at site A (its "home" site) and, at some point, it requests to migrate to site B. As a consequence, the code p of the agent and its current execution state S_A are transferred to site B. That is, A sends B the following signed message:

$$A \xrightarrow{m_1} B : A_s(A, B, K_A(p, S_A), A_s(A, i_A, t_A, H(p), TTP)).$$

The first two fields state that the message is sent from A to B. The following field contains the agent code (p) and its initial state (S_A) encrypted with a random key K_A chosen by A. The fourth field is the *agent token* that contains some static data about the agent that will be used during further hops in the agent trip. The agent token (*agent$_A$* for short) contains A's identity, the agent's identifier i_A, a timestamp t_A indicating the time of agent dispatching, the hash value of the agent's code $H(p)$, and the identity of the trusted party (TTP) that will be involved in possible dispute resolution, similarly to the procedure described in the previous section. The token is signed by A.

When B receives m_1, it uses A's public key to check the signature on both the message and the agent token. As in the case of remote code execution, at this point B can refuse or accept agent execution on the basis of the information contained in the message. In both cases, B sends A the following signed message:

$$B \xrightarrow{m_2} A : B_s(B, A, i_A, H(m_1), M).$$

A validates the message and examines M. If M represents a rejection then the protocol ends. Otherwise, M is B's commitment to execute the agent and is an implicit request for the key K_A. In this case, A sends the key to B, protected with B's public key:

$$A \xrightarrow{m_3} B : A_s(A, B, i_A, B_p(K_A)).$$

B checks the message validity, extracts the key using its own secret key, and decrypts the agent's code and state. Then, B sends A a signed acknowledgment message:

$$B \xrightarrow{m_4} A : B_s(B, A, i_A, H(m_3)),$$

and begins agent execution.

B executes the agent until the agent requests to migrate to another site, say C. As a consequence, B stops the execution of the agent and sends C two consecutive signed messages:

$$B \xrightarrow{m_5} C : B_s(B, C, agent_A, H(T_B^p), H(S_B), t_B),$$

$$B \xrightarrow{m_5'} C : B_s(K_B(p, S_B), H(m_5)).$$

The first message contains the names of both the sender and the receiver, the agent token, a hash value of the trace T_B^p produced by agent execution on B, a hash value of the current state S_B, and a timestamp t_B. The next message contains the agent's code and the current state S_B, encrypted with a random key K_B chosen by B, followed by a hash of the previous message[5]. After having received both messages, C checks the corresponding signatures. In addition, C computes $H(m_5)$ and compares the result with the hash value contained in m_5'. Then C checks the signature on $agent_A$ using A's public key and verifies that the agent was sent originally by A at time t_A. C accepts or rejects the migration request with a signed message that replies to m_5 and m_5':

$$C \xrightarrow{m_6} B : C_s(C, B, i_A, H(m_5, m_5'), M).$$

If M represents a rejection, then B restarts the agent by returning an error message as the result of the statement that requested the migration. If M is an

---

[5] The two messages m_5 and m_5' are kept distinct because the verification procedure uses the data contained in m_5 only. This way it is possible to avoid retransmission of the whole code and state of the agent during trace validation.

acceptance message, then C commits to execute the agent and implicitly requests the decryption key K_B. Therefore, B replies with a signed message containing the requested key protected using C's public key:

$$B \xrightarrow{m_7} C : B_s(B, C, i_A, C_p(K_B)).$$

C receives the message and uses K_B to access the agent's state and code. Then it checks that the code has not been modified by B computing $H(p)$ and comparing the resulting value with the hash contained in the agent token. In addition, C checks if the hash of S_B matches the value contained in m_5. If both the code and the state of the agent have been sent correctly, C sends a signed acknowledgment that terminates the transfer:

$$C \xrightarrow{m_8} B : C_s(C, B, i_A, H(m_7)).$$

This protocol is repeated for every subsequent hop until the agent terminates. Upon termination, the final site, say Z, retrieves from the agent token the name of the "home site" of the agent (i.e., A) and contacts the home site to deliver the final state of the agent. Therefore Z sends A the following signed message:

$$Z \xrightarrow{m_n} A : Z_s(Z, A, agent_A, H(T_Z^p), K_Z(S_Z), t_Z).$$

A checks the message validity and requests K_Z with a signed acknowledgment message:

$$A \xrightarrow{m_{n+1}} Z : A_s(A, Z, i_A, H(m_n)).$$

Z provides the key K_Z —protected using A's public key— in a signed message that terminates the protocol:

$$Z \xrightarrow{m_{n+2}} A : Z_s(Z, A, i_A, A_p(K_Z), H(m_{n+1}))$$

After having examined the results of the computation or after having received the charges for the resources used by the agent during its execution, if A thinks that one or more of the sites involved cheated, it starts the verification procedure. Thus, A asks B (the first site in the agent route) to provide its trace T_B^p. B cannot deny receipt of the agent and having committed to its execution because of message m_2 and must provide the trace. A starts the simulation following the provided trace. The simulation eventually reaches the instruction that requests the migration to site C. The agent's simulated state, at that point, is S'_B. Then, A asks C to provide its trace and a copy of message m_5 (that is signed by B). C cannot deny acceptance of the migration request, because B has messages m_7 that states the commitment of C to agent execution. A extracts from message m_5 the hash values of S_B and T_B^p. Therefore, A can compare $H(S_B)$ to $H(S'_B)$. In addition A can verify the integrity of the trace previously provided by B. If both checks succeed, B did not cheat. As a consequence, A restarts the simulation of the agent's execution following the trace provided by C.

This process continues until it reaches agent termination. At the end of the simulation if state S'_Z and S_Z coincide and the trace provided by Z produces the same hash value $H(T^p_Z)$ contained in message m_n, then the agent has been executed correctly. Alternatively, if some discrepancy is found during the verification of the trace provided by site X, then X cheated.

6   Discussion

Cryptographic tracing is a mechanism for detection of illegal tampering with agent execution. By relying on this mechanism, the agent owner can verify with a high degree of certainty that his/her agent was executed conforming to its specification, that is, its code. Therefore, the agent's owner is protected against service overcharging. In addition, if the agent behaves incorrectly because its code and/or state has been modified in a malicious way against its original specification, the principal responsible for its execution can relinquish responsibility and determine who "brainwashed" the agent. Obviously, if there are ways to induce the agent to attack other sites by providing carefully crafted inputs, the agent's owner may be held responsible for the damage caused by the agent. In this respect, the developer of the agent's code must use the same caution required when developing privileged programs that could receive parameters by untrusted principals (e.g., SUID programs in the UNIX operating system [11] or CGI scripts that process inputs received from browsers [27]). Greater care must be used if the language being traced allows for dynamic evaluation of code, that is, if there exists some kind of *evaluate* statement that takes as a parameter a string and interprets it as code. This is a feature of most scripting language (e.g., Perl or Tcl) and represents both a danger and a blessing. In fact, while dynamic evaluation may allow a malicious site to drive an agent to execute arbitrary pieces of code, it makes it possible to remove the static constraint on code. If code can be managed as data, the code fragments determined by interacting with the computational environment during execution will be recorded in the execution trace and the corresponding statements will be traceable and verifiable as well.

Being able to detect mobile agent tampering is an asset. Yet there are some issues that limit the applicability of the tracing mechanism. Some limitations stem from the scope of the mechanism. First of all, cryptographic tracing is a mechanism that allows detection of tampering *after* agent execution. Therefore if timely detection of tampering is needed a different mechanism must be devised. In addition, the mechanism does not provide any means to determine *a priori* if tampering occurred. The decision to perform trace validation must rely on the evaluation of the outcomes of agent execution and on the charges received for agent operations[6]. The proposed protocol could be extended to include in the messages carrying the agent a list of signed hash values of the traces produced during execution at previously visited sites; this way, a site could refuse to execute the agent if it has visited certain sites, or perform trace validation

---

[6] This is somewhat similar to reconciling credit card statements.

of the agent's execution from its start to the current state before resuming the agent. Another issue is that the proposed mechanism does not offer any protection against disclosure. Differently from mechanisms based on code scrambling, partial encryption, or cryptographed functions, the code and the state of an agent are accessible by the site responsible for agent execution. Therefore if the mobile agent's code and state must be kept secret, then the tracing mechanism must be extended with the aforementioned mechanisms.

Some limits come from the assumptions made in Section 3. In particular, the mechanism requires that all the sites participate in some kind of infrastructure that allows for key distribution and management, interpreter certification, service billing, and sanctioning of the principals. In fact, since cryptographic tracing is a *detection* mechanism, it is useless unless there is a way to sanction cheating sites or the principals responsible for misbehaving agents. Therefore the involved parties must be liable in case of misbehavior or must be subject to some kind of social control. This constraint poses some limitation to the scalability of the proposed mechanism.

An obvious limit comes from the quantity of resources that are needed to enforce the mechanism. The protocols described in sections 4 and 5 make extensive use of public-key cryptography. These cryptographic algorithms are considerably slow when compared to secret-key cryptography. Yet, they are necessary to provide authentication and non-repudiation between untrusted parties. Another issue is posed by the size of the traces collected during execution. In fact, the size of the traces may be large, even if compressed. Several mechanisms can be used in order to reduce the size of the traces. For example, instead of a complete execution trace it could be possible to log just the signature of black statements and the points in execution where control flow is non-deterministic. Another extension to the mechanism could be devised that allows the programmer to define a *range* of statements to be traced. The programmer may require that the values of some critical variables must satisfy a set of constraints before entering that particular group of statements. In a similar way, a mechanism could allow a programmer to specify that a group of statements must *not* be traced and that just the final values of the modified variables must be included in the trace. This mechanism could be useful in search procedures when, during a loop, several values are retrieved from the external environment and only a subset is saved in the agent's state.

Another set of issues stem from the nature of the language adopted for agents. If the language is too low-level, the traces produced during execution would be really large. If the language allows management of very complicated data structures, the modifications to the agent's internal state could be difficult to represent and could require a lot of space. In addition, we have made the assumption that agents cannot share memory and are single threaded. If this is not the case, an extension to the tracing mechanism is required. In order to check the execution of an agent, a user would need the trace of all the agents or threads that shared some memory portion with the agent thread under examination. In addition, traces should be extended with some timing information that allows for determining the order of the statements executed by the different threads. As one can easily understand, this mechanism would be practically infeasible.

7   An Electronic Commerce Agent

In order to give an example of the operations involved in agent execution, tracing, and verification, we introduce a simple mobile code language, called SALTA (*Secure Agent Language with Tracing of Actions*)[7], that implements the tracing mechanism. The language is then used to develop an electronic commerce application.

SALTA is a modified version of the Safe-Tcl language [2, 21]. The Safe-Tcl language has been restricted further, and two new instructions have been added, namely: `request` and `go`.

The `request` command allows an agent to access the services provided by a site. The `request` command takes as arguments the service name and a list of strings representing the service parameters. The `go` command allows an agent to migrate to a remote site specified as the command argument. When an agent executes the `go` command, it is suspended and its code and execution state (values of variables, call stack, and program counter) are packed into a message. The message is delivered to the destination site following the protocol described in Section 5. Upon arrival, the agent is unpacked, its execution state is restored, and its execution is restarted from the command following the `go`. From this point of view this language is similar to Agent-Tcl [13].

We use this minimal language to develop a simple agent application. A user, at site `home.sweet-home.com` wants to buy a home video of Tarantino's *Pulp Fiction* movie. Therefore, he dispatches an agent to a site called `agents.virtualmall.com` dedicated to maintain a directory of electronic shops. Once there, the agent performs a directory query for sites offering home videos. Then, the agent visits the provided sites. At each site the agent contacts the local catalog service to determine the current price of the *Pulp Fiction* home video. When all prices have been collected, the agent identifies the best offer and, if the best price is less then a specified amount—say, twenty dollars—the agent goes to the selected site and buys the home video. The transaction identifier is stored in the variable `result`. Upon completion of its task, the agent terminates and its state is returned to its home site. Figure 1 shows the agent's code.

Now suppose that the directory service at `agents.virtualmall.com` has suggested two sites, namely `agents.brockbuster.com` and `agents.towelrecords.com`. The prices of the *Pulp Fiction* home video are fifteen dollars at `agents.brockbuster.com` and seventeen dollars at `agents.towelrecords.com`. The execution trace will be the one shown in Figure 2.

Let us suppose that the Towel Records site wants to modify Brockbuster's offer so that Towel Record's offer appears to be the most convenient. Before the agent computes the best price, the Towel Records site modifies the home video

---

[7]   "Salta" is also an Italian verb meaning "jump".

```
1     : go agents.virtualmall.com
2     : set shoplist [request directory query homevideo]
3     : foreach shop $shoplist {
3.1   :     go $shop
3.2   :     set price($shop) [request catalog movies "Pulp Fiction"]
      : }
4     : set best_price 20
5     : set best_shop none
6     : foreach p [array names price] {
6.1   :     if {$price($p) < $best_price} {
6.1.1:         set best_price $price($p)
6.1.2:         set best_shop $p
      :     }
      : }
7     : if {$best_price > 20} {
7.1   :     set result "No offers below \$20!"
7.2   :     exit
      : }
8     : go $best_shop
9     : set result [request buymovie "Pulp Fiction" $best_price]
10    : exit
```

Fig. 1. The Pulp Fiction Agent.

home virtualmall		brock	towel
1	2,shoplist = brock towel	3.2,price(brock) = 15	3.2,price(towel) = 17
	3	3	4
	3.1	3.1	5
		9,result = PF11	6
		10	6.1
			6.1.1
			6.1.2
			6
			6.1
			6.1.1
			6.1.2
			7
			8

We made the following substitutions:
```
home       = home.sweet-home.com
virtualmall = agents.virtualmall.com
brock      = agents.brockbuster.com
towel      = agents.towelrecords.com
```

Fig. 2. Pulp Fiction Agent execution traces.

price associated with Brockbuster, raising its value to twenty-two dollars. As a consequence, the agent buys the home video at Towel Records. The trace, in this case will be the one shown in Figure 3.

home virtualmall	brock	towel
1 2,shoplist = brock towel	3.2,price(brock) = 15	3.2,price(towel) = 17
3	3	*price(brock) = 22*
3.1	3.1	4
		5
		6
		6.1
		6
		6.1
		6.1.1
		6.1.2
		7
		8
		9,result = PF11
		10

The illegal tampering with the agent's state is showed in italics.

Fig. 3. Execution traces resulting from tampering.

After having received the agent's final state, the agent owner may decide to verify agent execution. In this case, he/she retrieves the trace produced by the agent at the first site, namely agents.virtualmall.com. Then the owner of the agent simulates the agent's execution following the provided trace, until it comes to the request to migrate to another site, i.e., agents.brockbuster.com. As a consequence, the agent's owner asks Brockbuster's site to provide the agent's trace and the signed checksum of the agent's state received from agents.virtualmall.com. If the checksum computed over the simulator's state does not match the value provided by the Brockbuster site, then Virtuall Mall's site cheated. Otherwise simulation proceeds. When the verification process reaches instruction 8 (see figures 1 and 3) an inconsistency is flagged. In fact, the simulator holds value agents.brockbuster.com for variable best_shop and therefore the go command should have migrated the agent to the corresponding site. Since agents.brockbuster.com sent a signed checksum of the agent state just before the agent left, and agents.towelrecords.com has signed a receipt for that message, A can determine that Towel Records' site cheated. In addition, using the messages produced during the protocol, A can prove to a third party that agents.towelrecords.com tampered with state in an illegal way. The same procedure can be used to flag out tampering with code, inconsistencies in state transmission, computational flow diversion, and service overcharging.

8   Conclusions and Future Work

The interest in code mobility has been raised by the availability of a new breed of technologies featuring the ability to move portions of application code and possibly the corresponding state among the nodes of a wide-area network. Being able to move computations from host to host, mobile code systems raise serious security issues. One of the most difficult problems to solve is the protection of roaming agents from computational environments. We presented a mechanism, based on execution tracing, that allows an agent owner to detect illegal tampering with agent data, code, and execution flow, under certain assumptions. The proposed system does not require dedicated tamper-proof hardware or trust between parties. A language that implements the system concepts has been described, together with a simple electronic commerce example.

Presently, the Software Engineering group at Politecnico di Milano is designing and implementing a first prototype of the SALTA language. The prototype is written in Java, while cryptographic functionalities are implemented using PGP [33]. Aside from the tracing mechanism described in this paper, the SALTA language includes mechanisms to protect sites against malicious agents. We plan to use SALTA to implement electronic commerce applications that require accountability and a high degree of protection against frauds.

References

[1] J.K. Boggs. IBM Remote Job Entry Facility: Generalize Subsystem Remote Job Entry Facility. IBM Technical Disclosure Bulletin 752, IBM, August 1973.

[2] N. Borenstein. EMail With A Mind of Its Own: The Safe-Tcl Language for Enabled Mail. Technical report, First Virtual Holdings, Inc, 1994.

[3] L. Cardelli. A language with distributed scope. *Computing Systems*, 8(1):27–59, 1995.

[4] A. Carzaniga, G.P. Picco, and G. Vigna. Designing Distributed Applications with Mobile Code Paradigms. In R. Taylor, editor, *Proc. of the 19th Int. Conf. on Software Engineering (ICSE'97)*, pages 22–32. ACM Press, 1997.

[5] D.M. Chess, B. Grosof, C.G. Harrison, D. Levine, C. Paris, and G. Tsudik. Itinerant Agents for Mobile Computing. *IEEE Personal Communication*, October 1995. Also available as IBM Technical Report.

[6] G. Cugola, C. Ghezzi, G.P. Picco, and G. Vigna. Analyzing Mobile Code Languages. In J. Vitek and C. Tschudin, editors, *Mobile Object Systems: Towards the Programmable Internet*, volume 1222 of *LNCS*, pages 93–111. Springer, April 1997.

[7] W.M. Farmer, J.D. Guttman, and V. Swarup. Security for Mobile Agents: Authentication and State Appraisal. In Springer, editor, *Proc. of the 4th European Symp. on Research in Computer Security*, volume 1146 of *LNCS*, pages 118–130, Rome, Italy, September 1996.

[8] W.M. Farmer, J.D. Guttman, and V. Swarup. Security for Mobile Agents: Issues and Requirements. In *Proc. of the 19th National Information Systems Security Conf.*, pages 591–597, Baltimore, MD, USA, October 1996.

[9] A. Freier, P. Karlton, and P. Kocher. The SSL Protocol — Version 3.0. Internet Draft, March 1996.

[10] A. Fuggetta, G.P. Picco, and G. Vigna. Understanding Code Mobility. *IEEE Transactions on Software Engineering*, 1998. to appear.

[11] S. Garfinkel and G. Spafford. *Practical UNIX and Internet Security*, chapter Tips on Writing SUID/SGID Programs, pages 716–718. O'Reilly, 1996.

[12] R.S. Gray. Agent Tcl: A transportable agent system. In *Proc. of the CIKM Workshop on Intelligent Information Agents*, Baltimore, Md., December 1995.

[13] R.S. Gray. Agent Tcl: A flexible and secure mobile agent system. In *Proc. of the 4th Annual Tcl/Tk Workshop*, pages 9–23, Monterey, Cal., July 1996.

[14] F. Hohl. An approach to Solve the Problem of Malicious Hosts in Mobile Agent Systems, 1997.

[15] ITU-T. Information Technology - Open Systems Interconnection - The Directory: Authentication Framework. ITU-T Recommendation X.509, November 1993.

[16] D.B. Lange and D.T. Chang. IBM Aglets Workbench—Programming Mobile Agents in Java. IBM Corp. White Paper, September 1996.

[17] S. Lucco, O. Sharp, and R. Wahbe. Omniware: A Universal Substrate for Web Programming. In *Proc. of the 4th Int. World Wide Web Conf.*, Boston, Massachusetts, USA, December 1995.

[18] L.Wall, T. Christiansen, and R. Schwartz. *Programming Perl*. O'Reilly, 2nd edition, 1996.

[19] Sun Microsystems. The Java Language: An Overview. Technical report, Sun Microsystems, 1994.

[20] J. Ordille. When agents roam, who can you trust? In *Proc. of the First Conf. on Emerging Technologies and Applications in Communications*, May 1996.

[21] J. Ousterhout, J. Levy, and B. Welch. The Safe-Tcl Security Model. Technical report, Sun Microsystems, November 1996. Printed in this volume.

[22] R.L. Rivest, A. Shamir, and L. Adleman. A Method for Obtaining Digital Signatures and Public-Key Cryptosystems. *Comm. of the ACM*, 21(2):120–126, February 1978.

[23] T. Sander and C. Tschudin. Towards Mobile Cryptography. In *Proceedings of the 1998 IEEE Symposium on Security and Privacy*, Oakland, CA, May 1998.

[24] B. Schneier. *Applied Cryptography – Protocols, Algorithms, and Source Code in C*. John Wiley & Sons, Inc., 2nd edition, 1996.

[25] K.B. Sriram. Hashjava - A Java Applet Obfuscator. `http://sbketch.org/hash-java.html`, July 1997.

[26] J.W. Stamos and D.K. Gifford. Implementing Remote Evaluation. *IEEE Trans. on Software Engineering*, 16(7):710–722, July 1990.

[27] L.D. Stein. The World Wide Web Security FAQ. `http://www.w3.org/Security/-Faq/`, January 1998.

[28] J. Tardo and L. Valente. Mobile agent security and Telescript. In *Proc. of IEEE COMPCON'96*, February 1996.

[29] C. Tschudin. *An Introduction to the MO Messenger Language*. Univ. of Geneva, Switzerland, 1994.

[30] J.E. White. Telescript Technology: Mobile Agents. In J. Bradshaw, editor, *Software Agents*. AAAI Press/MIT Press, 1996.

[31] U.G. Wilhelm. Cryptographically Protected Objects. Technical report, Ecole Polytechnique Fédérale de Lausanne, Switzerland, 1997.

[32] F. Yellin. Low Level Security in Java. Technical report, Sun Microsystems, 1995.

[33] P. Zimmerman. *PGP User's Guide*, March 1993.

D'Agents: Security in a Multiple-Language, Mobile-Agent System

Robert S. Gray[1], David Kotz[2], George Cybenko[1], and Daniela Rus[2]

[1] Thayer School of Engineering, Dartmouth College
Hanover NH 03755, USA
[2] Department of Computer Science, Dartmouth College
Hanover NH 03755, USA

Abstract. Mobile-agent systems must address three security issues: protecting an individual machine, protecting a group of machines, and protecting an agent. In this chapter, we discuss these three issues in the context of D'Agents, a mobile-agent system whose agents can be written in Tcl, Java and Scheme. (D'Agents was formerly known as Agent Tcl.) First we discuss mechanisms existing in D'Agents for protecting an individual machine: (1) cryptographic authentication of the agent's owner, (2) resource managers that make policy decisions based on the owner's identity, and (3) secure execution environments for each language that enforce the decisions of the resource managers. Then we discuss our planned market-based approach for protecting machine groups. Finally we consider several (partial) solutions for protecting an agent from a malicious machine.

1 Introduction

A mobile agent is a program that moves from machine to machine and executes on each. Neither the agent nor the machines are necessarily trustworthy. The agent might try to access or destroy privileged information or consume more than its share of some resource. The machines might try to pull sensitive information out of the agent or change the behavior of the agent by removing, modifying or adding to its data and code. A mobile-agent system that does not detect and prevent such malicious actions can never be used in real applications. In an open network environment, intentional attacks on both machines and agents will start as soon as the system is deployed, and even in a closed network environment with trusted users, there is still the danger of misprogrammed agents, which can do significant damage accidentally. Security is perhaps the most critical issue in a mobile-agent system. We consider the following four inter-related problems:

- *Protect the machine.* The machine should be able to authenticate the agent's owner, assign resource limits based on this authentication, and prevent any violation of the resource limits. To prevent both the theft or damage of

G. Vigna (Ed.): Mobile Agents and Security
LNCS 1419, pp. 154–187, 1998. © Springer–Verlag Berlin Heidelberg 1998

sensitive information and denial-of-service attacks, the resource limits must include access rights (reading a certain file), maximum consumptions (total CPU time), and maximum consumptions per unit time (total CPU time per unit time).

– *Protect other agents.* An agent should not be able to interfere with another agent or steal that agent's resources. This problem can be viewed as a sub-problem of protecting the machine, since as long as an agent cannot subvert the agent communication mechanisms and cannot consume or hold excessive system resources, it will be unable to affect another agent unless that agent chooses to communicate with it.

– *Protect the agent.* A machine should not be able to tamper with an agent or pull sensitive information out of the agent without the agent's cooperation. Unfortunately, without hardware support, it is impossible to prevent a machine from doing whatever it wants with an agent that is currently executing on that machine. Instead we must try to detect tampering as soon as the agent migrates from a malicious machine back onto an honest machine, and then terminate or fix the agent if tampering has occurred. In addition, we must ensure that (1) sensitive information never passes through an untrusted machine in an unencrypted form, (2) the information is meaningless without cooperation from a trusted site, or (3) that theft of the information is not catastrophic and can be detected via an audit trail.

– *Protect a group of machines.* An agent might consume excessive resources in the network as a whole even if it consumes few resources at each machine. Obvious examples are an agent that roams through the network forever or an agent that creates two child agents on different machines, each of which creates two child agents in turn, and so on. An agent and its children should eventually be unable to obtain any resources anywhere and be terminated. If the network machines are under single administrative control, solutions are relatively straightforward; if the machines are not, solutions are much more complex.

Outline of this paper. Over the past few years we have developed a multi-language mobile-agents system, D'Agents, formerly known as Agent Tcl. A significant component of that effort has been to design and implement security mechanisms and policies to deal the issues described in this section. In this chapter we cover each of the above issues in turn, first describing how D'Agents addresses the first two concerns, and then briefly discussing some possible solutions for the second two concerns. Throughout our discussion we make a careful effort to distinguish between the architectural features of the D'Agents system, particularly its security *mechanisms*, and the security *policies* that are or could be implemented within that framework.

2   Related work

Although all of the problems discussed above have been considered in the mobile-agent literature [18, 4, 28, 22], most mobile-agent systems address only the first two problems, namely, protecting a machine from malicious agents and agents from each other. A growing number of mobile-agent projects, however, are experimenting with techniques for protecting machine groups from malicious agents and protecting agents from malicious machines. Here we consider some representative mobile-agent systems.

Telescript [31, 33, 32, 34], later marketed as part of the Tabriz web-server package and then withdrawn from the market, was the first commercial mobile-agent system. It has two security mechanisms. First, each agent carries cryptographic credentials so that the system could verify the identity of the agent's owner. Second, each agent carries a set of permits that give it the right to use certain Telescript instructions and certain amounts of available resources. Each machine imposes a set of permits on incoming agents to prevent that agent from taking undesired action. Agents that attempt to violate their permits are terminated immediately. Some permits involve resources that are "distributed" across multiple machines (e.g., maximum number of times that an agent can migrate). Since Telescript assumes that all machines are trustworthy, these permits are simply counters that are decremented as the agent travels through the network.

Nearly all mobile-agent systems protect the machine in the same manner as Telescript: (1) cryptographically verify the identity of the agent's owner, (2) assign access restrictions to the agent based on the owner's identity, and (3) execute the agent in a secure execution environment that can enforce these restrictions. The commercial Java-based systems, such as Odyssey [8], Voyager [29], Concordia [35], and IBM Aglets [17], all cryptographically sign the migrating Java code and then enforce access restrictions with the standard Java security mechanisms, i.e., customized class loaders and security managers [6].

Most research systems provide only partial protection for machines, simply because the research focus is often something other than security (or some other aspect of security). Tacoma [13] provides hooks so that a developer can add their own encryption subsystem (and then use this encryption subsystem to sign migrating agents), but does not provide secure execution environments for all of its supported languages. The Tacoma Too project is experimenting with software fault isolation and security automata as a flexible way to enforce access restrictions [26]. (A security automata is a state machine in which each transition corresponds to an *allowed* resource access; software fault isolation instruments the machine or object code with security checks.) Ara enforces restrictions on CPU time and memory usage, but does not yet protect resources such as the filesystem and network [22]; the Ara group is currently implementing a full security model, however, including digital signatures and access restrictions for all system resources. Both Tube [10] and SodaBot [5] provide execute their agents inside secure interpreters that enforce some access restrictions. (SodaBot agents are written in a custom language called SodaBotl, while Tube agents are written in Scheme.)

D'Agents does focus on security issues and provides relatively complete protection for machines. Agents are cryptographically signed using PGP [15], while access restrictions are enforced with Safe Tcl [18], Java security managers [6], and

Scheme 48 modules. Unlike most mobile-agent systems, D'Agents is designed to support multiple languages, and thus focuses on cleanly separating enforcement from policy and on implementing as much of the security mechanisms as possible in a language-independent manner. The D'Agent mechanisms for protecting machines is the focus of most of this chapter.

We plan to use electronic cash to protect groups of machines [2]. Most mobile-agent projects, including Tacoma [13], Ara [22], and Messengers [1], have similar plans. To our knowledge, however, little implementation work has been done by any of these projects.

Finally, there are a range of possible techniques for protecting an agent from malicious machines, most of which were introduced by other mobile-agent projects, and none of which are currently implemented in D'Agents. Since a later section is devoted to describing these techniques, we will present related work in that section.

3   D'Agents

D'Agents is a mobile-agent system whose agents can be written in Tcl Java and Scheme [1] D'Agents has extensive navigation services [23], security mechanisms [9], and debugging and tracking tools [11]. In addition, it is active use at numerous academic and industrial research labs, including labs at Lockheed Martin, Siemens, Cornell, and the University of Bordeaux, and is starting to find its way into production-quality applications.

Like all mobile-agent systems, the main component of D'Agents is a server that runs on each machine. When an agent wants to migrate to a new machine, it calls a single function, agent_jump, which automatically captures the complete state of the agent and sends this state information to the server on the destination machine. The destination server starts up an appropriate execution environment (e.g., a Tcl interpreter for an agent written in Tcl), loads the state information into this execution environment, and restarts the agent from the exact point at which it left off. Now the agent is on the destination machine and can interact with that machine's resources without any further network communication. In addition to reducing migration to a single instruction, D'Agents has a simple, layered architecture that supports multiple languages and transport mechanisms. Adding a new language or transport mechanism is straightforward: the interpreter for the new language must support two state-capture routines, and the "driver" for the new transport mechanism must support asynchronous I/O and a specific interface. The primary language is Tcl, and we are currently adding support for Java and Scheme. The primary transport mechanism is TCP/IP.

Figure 1 shows the D'Agents architecture. The core system, which appears on the left, has four levels. The lowest level is an interface to each available transport mechanism. The next level is the server that runs on each machine. This server has several tasks. It keeps track of the agents running on its machine,

---

[1] See URL http://www.cs.dartmouth.edu/~agent/ for software, documentation, and related papers.

provides the low-level inter-agent communication facilities (message passing and binary streams), receives and authenticates agents that are arriving from another host, and restarts an authenticated agent in an appropriate execution environment. The third level of the architecture consists of the execution environments, one for each supported agent language. All of our languages are interpreted, so our "execution environments" are just interpreters, namely a Tcl interpreter, a Scheme 48 interpreter, and the Java virtual machine. For each incoming agent, the server starts up the appropriate interpreter in which to execute the agent. It is important to note that most of the interface between the interpreters and the servers is implemented in a C/C++ library and shared among all the interpreters. The language-specific portion is just a set of stubs that call into this library.

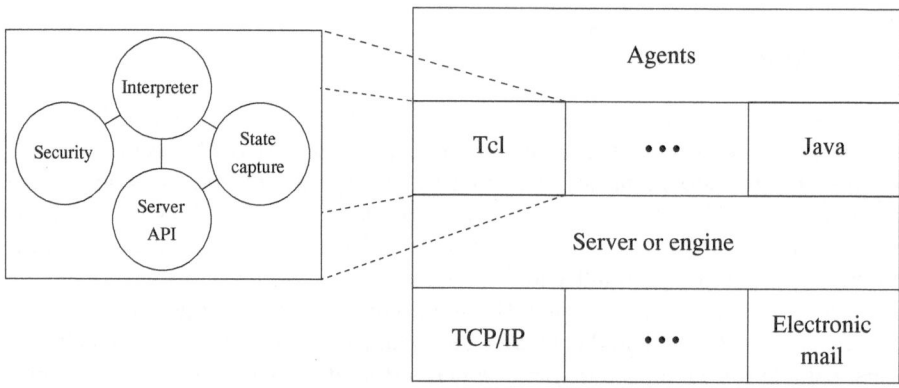

Fig. 1. The architecture of the D'Agents system. The core system, shown at left, has four levels: transport mechanisms, a server that runs on each machine, an interpreter for each supported agent language, and the agents themselves. Support agents (not shown) provide navigation, communication and resource management services to other agents.

The last level of the architecture are the agents themselves, which execute in the interpreters and use the facilities provided by the server to migrate from machine to machine and to communicate with other agents. Agents include both moving agents, which visit different machines to access needed resources, as well as stationary agents, which stay on a single machine and provide a specific service to either the user or other agents. From the system's point of view, there is no difference between these two kinds of agents, except that a stationary agent typically has authority to access more system resources. The agent servers provide low-level functionality. All other services are provided at the agent level by dedicated service agents. Such services include navigation, high-level communication protocols, and resource management.

Figure 2 shows one of the applications in which D'Agents is used. The application's task is to search a distributed collection of technical reports for information relevant to the user's query. The user enters a free-text query into a front-end GUI. The GUI then spawns an agent to actually perform the query. This agent makes two decisions. First, if the connection between the *home* machine (i.e., the user's machine) is reliable and has high bandwidth, the agent stays on the home machine. If the connection is unreliable or has low bandwidth, which is often the case if the home machine is a mobile device, the agent jumps to a proxy site within the network. This initial jump reduces the use of the poor-quality link to just the transmission of the agent and the transmission of the final result, conserving bandwidth and allowing the agent to proceed with its task even if the link goes down. The proxy site is dynamically selected according to the current location of the home machine and the document collections.

Once the agent has migrated to a proxy site, if desired, it must interact with the stationary agents that serve as an interface to the technical report collections. If these stationary agents provide high-level operations, the agent simply makes RPC-style calls across the network (using the inter-agent communication mechanisms). If the stationary agents provide only low-level operations, the agent sends out child agents that travel to the document collections and perform the query there, avoiding the transfer of large amounts of intermediate data. Information about the available search operations is obtained from the same directory services that provide the location of the document collections. Once the agent has the results from each document collection, it merges and filters those results, returns to the home machine, and hands the results off to the front-end GUI for display to the user.

Although the behavior of this agent is relatively complex, it is actually quite easy to implement. Figure 3 shows the Tcl code for a simplified version of the information-retrieval agent. This simplified version always jumps to the proxy site and always spawns child agents, rather than using the network-sensing and directory services. Since using the network-sensing and directory services involves only a few library calls, however, the real agent, including appropriate error-checking and the code to merge and filter the query results, is only about three times as long as the simplified agent.

In addition to excluding error checking, network-sensing and directory lookups, the simplified version of the agent does not explicitly use the D'Agent security services (although it is still subject to the security constraints set by the proxy and collection machines). A version of the agent that does use the security services is presented in the next section.

4   Protecting the machine (and other agents)

Protecting the machine involves two tasks:

- *Authentication.* Verify the identity of an agent's owner.
- *Authorization and enforcement.* Assign resource limits to the agent based on this identity and enforce those resource limits.

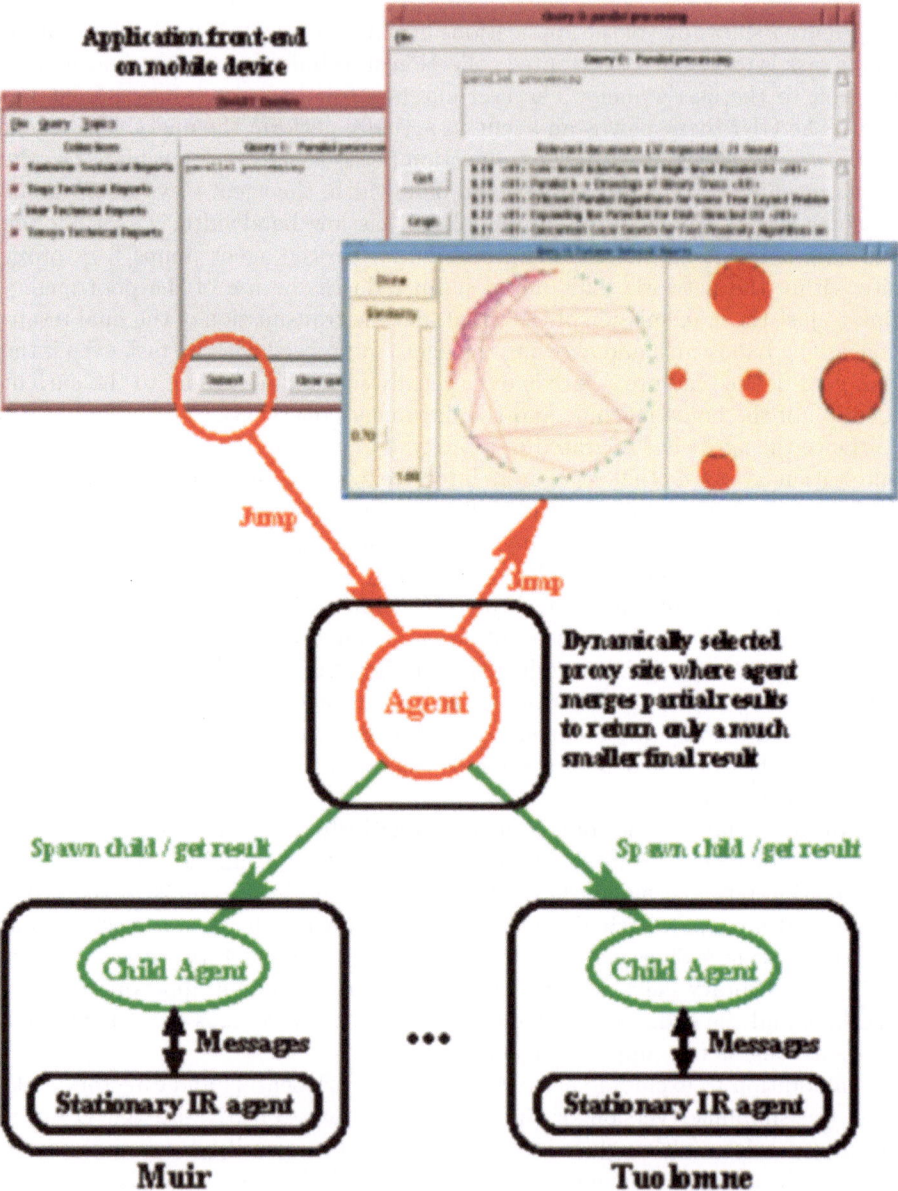

Fig. 2. An information-retrieval application in which D'Agents is used. The user enters a free-text query via a front-end GUI; the GUI then launchs an agent that will search a distributed collection of technical reports for documents relevant to the query. The agent first jumps to a proxy site if the link between the user's machine and the network is unreliable or has low bandwidth. Then, if the query requires multiple operations against each search engine, the agent launches child agents that travel to the search-engine locations and perform the query steps locally to the engine. If the query requires only a single operation, the agent will interact with the search engines remotely.

```
 1    proc runQuery {query expansionWords} {
 2        global agent
 3        # send query to search engine
 4        agent_send "$agent(local-server) search-engine" 0 $query
 5        agent_receive code results
 6        # expand query if we do not have enough results
 7        ...
 8        return $results
 9    }
10
11    # register with the agent system and then migrate to the proxy site
12    agent_begin
13    agent_jump $proxySite
14
15    # send a child agent to each document collection
16    foreach site $collectionSites {
17        agent_submit $site \
18            -vars query expansionWords -procs runQuery \
19            -script {runQuery $query $expansionWords}
20    }
21
22    # receive the query results
23    for {set i 0} {$i < $numSites} {incr i} {
24        set source [agent_receive code results]
25        set queryResults($source) $results
26    }
27
28    # merge and filter the results and then return home
29    ...
30    agent_jump $agent(home-machine)
```

Fig. 3. Tcl code for a simplified version of the information-retrieval agent. First the agent registers with the agent system (line 12). Then the agent jumps to the proxy site (line 13). Once on the proxy site, the agent sends a child agent to the location of each document collection (lines 15–20). The child agents, whose code consists of the runQuery procedure (lines 1–9), communicate with the collection search engines to perform the query, and then return their results to the main agent. Finally, the main agent receives the results from each child agent, merges and filters these results, and jumps back to its point of origin where the results are displayed to the user (lines 22-30). (The variable agent is a global array that is always available to an agent and that contains information about the agent's current location.) The real version of the agent performs several additional actions that are not shown here, namely (1) appropriate error-checking, (2) using the network-sensing services to decide whether or not to jump to a proxy site, (3) using the directory services to identify the proxy site (variable proxySite) and the collection sites (variables collectionSites and numSites) and to decide whether or not to spawn the child agents, and (4) obtaining the query and expansion words (variables query and expansionWords) from the front-end GUI.

D'Agents, like other mobile-agent systems, handles these two tasks with public-key cryptography and secure execution environments that perform authorization checks before each resource access. More specifically, D'Agents has an encryption subsystem, a language-dependent enforcement module, and a language-independent policy module (for each system resource). These three components are shown in Figure 4 and described in the subsections below.

4.1   Authentication

Each D'Agents server distinguishes between two kinds of agents: owned and anonymous. An *owned* agent is an agent whose owner could be authenticated and is on the server's list of authorized users. An *anonymous* agent is an agent whose owner could not be authenticated or is not on the server's list of authorized users. Each server can be configured to either accept or reject anonymous agents. If a server accepts an anonymous agent, it gives the agent an extremely restrictive set of resource limits.

RSA public-key cryptography is used to authenticate an agent's owner. Each owner and machine in D'Agents has a public-private key pair. The server can authenticate the owner if (1) the agent is digitally signed with the owner's public key or (2) the agent is digitally signed with the sending machine's key, the server trusts the sending machine, and the sending machine was able to authenticate the owner itself. In the second case, the sending machine would have authenticated the owner in one of the same two ways: (1) the agent was signed by the owner or (2) the agent was signed by one of the *sending machine's* trusted machines (and that trusted machine was able to authenticate the owner itself). Thus, trust is transitive, and trust relationships must be established carefully. Typically machines under single administrative control would trust each other and no one else.

D'Agents uses Pretty Good Privacy (PGP) for its digital signatures and encryption. PGP is a standalone program that allows the secure transmission of electronic mail and is in widespread use despite controversies over patents and export restrictions [15]. PGP encrypts a file or mail message using the IDEA algorithm and a randomly chosen secret key, encrypts the secret key using the RSA public-key algorithm and the recipient's public key, and then sends the encrypted key and file to the recipient. PGP optionally adds a digital signature by computing an MD5 cryptographic hash of the file or mail message and encrypting the hash value with the sender's private key. Although PGP is oriented towards interactive use, it can be used in an agent system with minimal effort. In the current implementation, D'Agents runs PGP as a separate process, saves the data to be encrypted into a file, asks the PGP process to encrypt the file, and then transfers the encrypted file to the destination server. This approach is much less efficient than tightly integrating PGP with the rest of the system, but is simpler and more flexible, especially since it becomes trivial to create an D'Agents distribution that does not include PGP or that uses different encryption software [30].

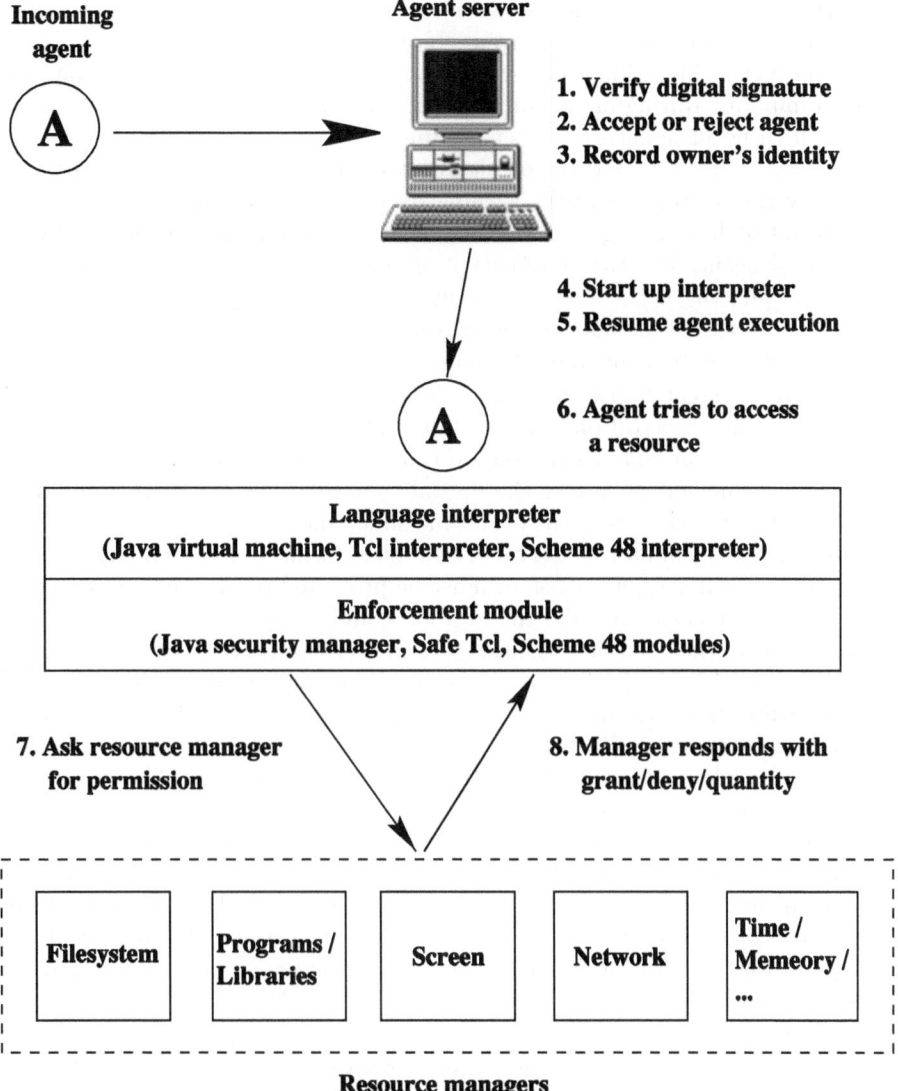

Fig. 4. The components of the D'Agents security architecture. When an agent arrives at an agent server, the server verifies the agent's digital signature if present (step 1), and then either accepts or rejects the agent according to its current access lists (step 2). If the server accepts the agent, it records the identity of the agent's owner for future use (step 3), starts up an execution environment for the agent (step 4), and resumes agent execution (step 5). Once the agent is executing, it might try to access some system resource such as a particular file (step 6). The language-specific enforcement module sends the access request to the appropriate resource manager, which is just a stationary agent that defines the security policy for that resource (step 7). The manager checks the request against its current policy and returns a grant or deny message to the enforcement module (step 8).

An agent chooses whether to use encryption and signatures when it migrates or sends a message to another agent. If the agent is not concerned with interception during migration, it turns off encryption. If the agent is not concerned with tampering during migration and can accomplish its task as an *anonymous* agent, it turns off signatures. When sending a message, the agent makes the same decisions, except that it turns off signatures only if the recipient does not need to verify the sender's identity. Turning off either encryption or signatures is a significant performance gain due to the slowness of public-key cryptography, and thus most agents will turn off encryption and signatures whenever the needed resources and the network environment allow it. In the rest of this section, we assume that the agent does *not* want to be an anonymous agent and does *not* want to send anonymous messages, and thus has digital signatures turned on.

When an agent registers with its home server using the **begin** command (Figure 5), the registration request is digitally signed with the owner's private key, optionally encrypted with the destination server's public key, and sent to the server. The server verifies the digital signature, checks whether the owner is allowed to register an agent on its machine, and then accepts or rejects the request. If the agent and the server are on different machines, all further requests that the agent makes of the server must be protected to prevent tampering and masquerade attacks.[2] Ideally, the system would generate a secret session key, known only to the agent and the server, and then use this session key to encrypt the requests [15]. PGP does not provide direct access to its internal secret-key routines, however, making it impossible to generate and use session keys without modifying PGP. Therefore, the current implementation of D'Agents handles the additional requests in the same manner as the initial registration request, digitally signing them with the owner's private key. Since public-key algorithms are much slower than secret-key algorithms, we will switch to secret session keys once we replace PGP with a more flexible encryption library. When the agent and the server are on the same machine (which is the predominant case), there is no need for a session key, since it is impossible to intercept or tamper with the additional requests or to masquerade as the registered agent.[3] Thus all additional requests are transmitted in the clear.

When an agent migrates for the *first time* with the **jump** command, the state image is digitally signed with the owner's private key, optionally encrypted with the destination server's public key, and sent to the destination server. The server verifies the digital signature, checks whether the owner is allowed to send agents to its machine, and accepts or rejects the incoming agent. This process is shown in Figure 6. Of course, once the agent has migrated, the owner's private key is no longer available. Therefore, for all subsequent migrations, the agent is digitally signed with the private key of the sending server. If the destination server trusts the sending server, and the sending server was able to authenticate the owner itself, the destination server considers the owner authenticated and gives the

---

[2] A masquerade attack here is another agent passing itself off as the registered agent.

[3] The server uses different communication channels for local agents and can tell without cryptography whether a request came from a specific local agent.

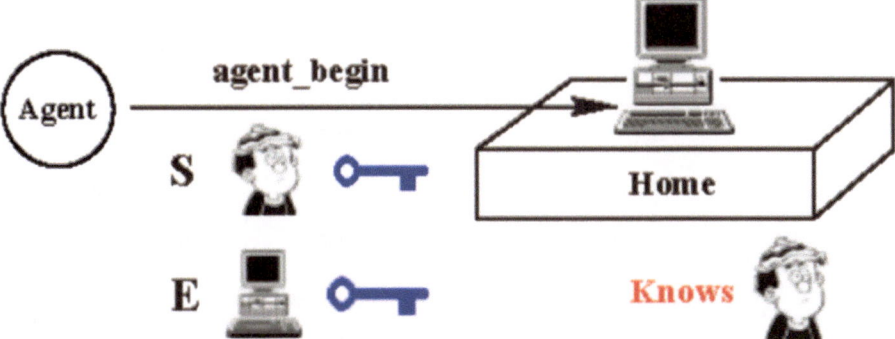

Fig. 5. Encryption for the begin command. When an agent uses the `begin` command to register with the server on its home machine, the registration request is signed with the owner's private key (S) and optionally encrypted with the receiving machine's public key (E).

agent the full set of resource limits for that owner. If the destination server does not trust the sending server, or the sending server could not authenticate the owner itself, the destination server considers the agent to have no owner and will either (1) accept the agent as an anonymous agent or (2) reject the agent if it is not allowed to accept anonymous agents. Typically, D'Agents servers are configured so that machines under single administrative control trust each other but no one else.[4] Thus, if an agent migrates from its home machine into a set of mutually trusting machines (and then stays within that set), each machine will be able to (directly or indirectly) authenticate the owner, and will give the agent the full set of access permissions for that owner. Once the agent leaves the set of machines, however, it becomes anonymous, and remains anonymous even when it comes back, since the nontrusted machines might have modified the agent in a malicious way. While the agent is on a particular machine, it will make requests of that machine's server. As in the case when an agent registers with a server on the same machine, however, no encryption or digital signatures are needed for these requests.

When a new child agent is created on a different machine (with the `fork` or `submit` command), or when a message is sent to an agent on a different machine (with the `send` command), the same strategy is used as with `jump`. The message or child agent is signed with the owner's key if the sending agent is still on its home machine, and with the machine's key if the sending agent has already migrated (Figure 7). The recipient server will believe the owner's identity if it trusts the sending server. When receiving a message, the recipient agent gets both the message and a security vector. The security vector specifies the owner of the sending agent, whether the owner could be authenticated, the sending machine,

---

[4] For example, all the machines in the Computer Science Department at Dartmouth trust each other.

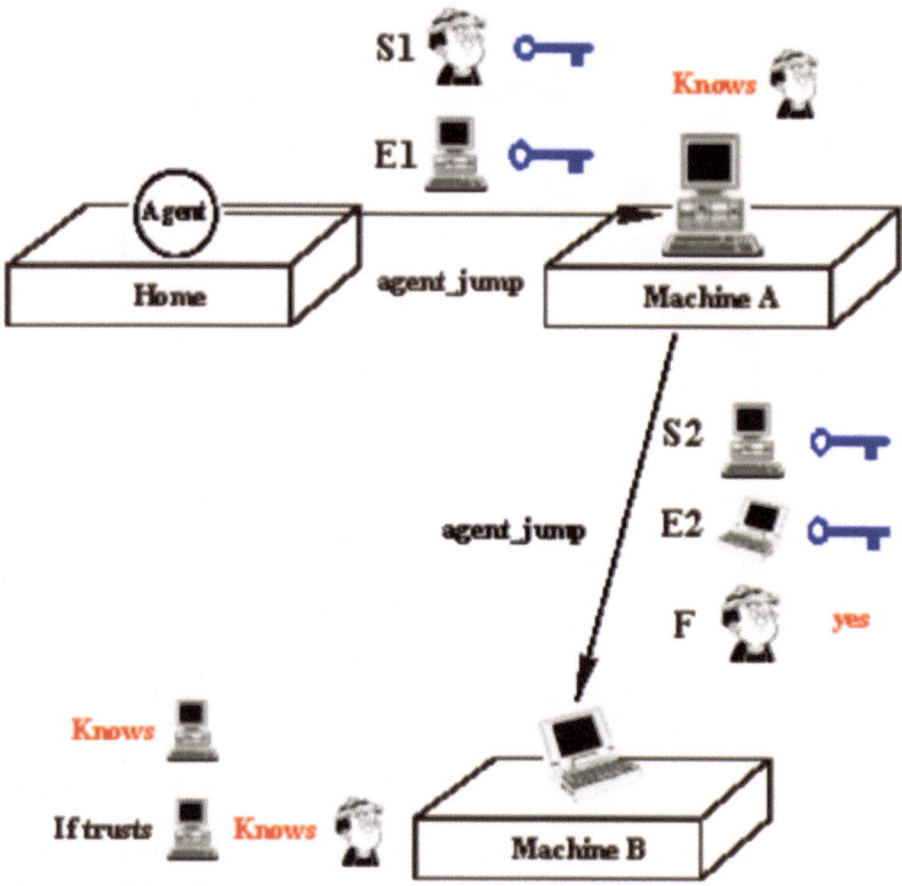

Fig. 6. Encryption for the jump command. On the first jump, the agent is signed with the owner's private key (S1). On the second and later jumps, the agent is signed with the sending machine's private key (S2), and the sending machine sets a flag (F) to indicate whether it was able to authenticate the agent's owner itself; if the target machine trusts the sending machine, and the sending machine reports that it was able to authenticate the agent's owner, the target machine considers the owner authenticated.

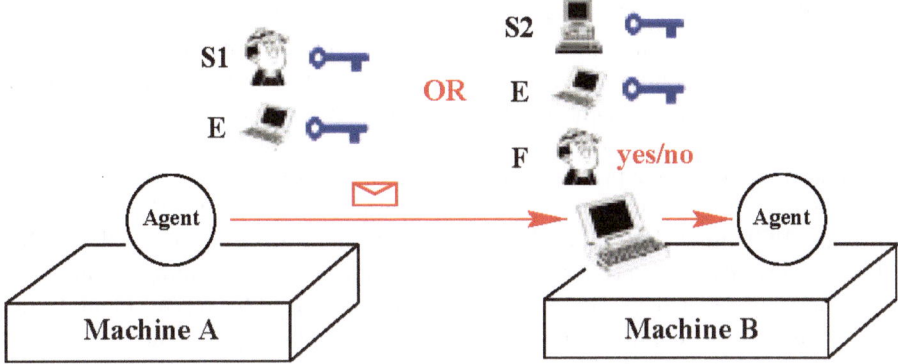

Fig. 7. Encryption for the send command. If the agent has not left its home machine, the message is signed with the owner's private key (S1). If the agent has left its home machine, the message is signed with the sending machine's key (S2), and the sending machine sets a flag (F) to indicate whether it was able to authenticate the agent's owner itself; if the target machine trusts the sending machine, and the sending machine reports that it was able to authenticate the agent's owner, the target machine considers the owner authenticated.

whether the sending machine could be authenticated, whether the message was encrypted, and whether the sending agent is on the same machine. The recipient agent, which might be controlling access to some resource such as a database, bases its own security decisions on this security vector. When a new agent is created on the same machine, or a message is sent to an agent on the same machine, no encryption or digital signatures are required. The new agent inherits the security information of its parent. The recipient of the message gets the same five-element security vector.

This authentication scheme has five weaknesses. First, and most serious, once an agent leaves its home group of trusted machines, it becomes anonymous as soon as it migrates again. Making the agent anonymous is essential in the current system since a malicious machine can modify an agent arbitrarily (or lie about the identity of its owner). Thus, when dealing with machines that do not trust each other, an application that needs the full access rights of its owner to accomplish its task cannot send out a single agent that migrates through the machines, since the agent will become anonymous on the second jump. Instead the application must send an agent to the first machine, wait for the results, send a new agent to the second machine, and so on. Although this problem does not prevent an application from accomplishing its task, it places an additional burden on the programmer, and reintroduces some of the network traffic that mobile agents are meant to avoid. At the same time, it is important to note that many applications operate entirely within a set of trusted machines, and that many others, especially in the Internet, can be accomplished with anonymous agents. Solving the multi-hop authentication problem revolves around detecting malicious modifications to an agent. Then, confident that certain kinds of malicious modifications (such as modifications to the static code) will always be detected, a machine can assign access rights that fall somewhere between those of an anonymous agent and those of the actual owner. Detecting malicious modifications is discussed below.

The remaining four problems are less serious and have clear solutions. First, PGP is extremely slow, especially since D'Agents executes PGP as a separate process. PGP must be replaced with a faster encryption library. Second, PGP does not provide access to its internal encryption routines, making it impossible to generate session keys for ongoing communication. The replacement library must support both public-key and secret-key cryptography. Once the system can generate session keys, it should use session keys rather than public/private keys whenever possible due to the speed advantage of secret-key cryptography, For example, two servers that are communicating extensively might generate a shared session key, even if different agents are responsible for each communication. Third, D'Agents does not include an automatic distribution mechanism for the public keys. Each server must already *know* the public keys of all authorized users so that it can authenticate incoming agents (agents signed with an unknown public key become anonymous). A modest key-distribution or certification mechanism must be added to D'Agents to reduce the burden on the system administrator. Finally, the system is vulnerable to replay attacks in which an attacker replays a migrating agent or a message sent to an agent on a different machine. Here a server could have a distinct series of sequence numbers for each server with which it is in contact.

4.2   Authorization and enforcement

Once the identity of an agent's owner has been determined, the system must assign access restrictions to the agent (*authorization*) and ensure that the agent does not violate these restrictions (*enforcement*). In other words, the system must guard access to all available resources. We divide resources into two types. *Indirect* resources can be accessed only through another agent. *Builtin* resources are directly accessible through language primitives (or libraries) for reasons of efficiency or convenience or simply by definition. Builtin resources include the screen, the file system, memory, real time, CPU time, and the agent servers themselves.[5]

For indirect resources, the agent that controls the resource enforces its own access restrictions, rejecting or allowing requests from other agents based on the security vector attached to the incoming communication. Typically, the resource agent would simply check each request against an access list, although one request could return capabilities for use in later requests. Care must be taken with capabilities, however, since a migrating agent will carry its capabilities along with

---

[5] The agent servers are accessed through the agent commands, such as `begin`, `jump` and `send`. All agent commands use server CPU cycles; several use server memory; and several require network access.

it, possibly through malicious machines. One reasonable solution is to allow an agent to obtain a capability only if it is on the same machine as the resource, and include sufficient identification information in the capability so that it becomes invalid as soon as the agent leaves[6]; this solution makes it impossible for valid capabilities to exist on other machines, preventing theft *and* eliminating severe administrative problems. D'Agents will eventually provide both access-list and capability libraries for use in resource agents; currently each resource agent must provide its own implementation.

For builtin resources, the agent servers enforce several absolute access policies. For example, an agent can *terminate* another agent only if its owner is the system administrator or if it has the same owner as the other agent. The *name* operation reserves certain symbolic names for certain agent owners, preventing an arbitrary agent from masquerading as a service agent (such as a yellow page agent that provides directory services). The *notify* operation requires the server to remember which agent asked for the notification, taking up server memory. Thus, the server has a per-agent limit on the number of outstanding notifications; the limit is small for visiting agents, but large for agents that belong to the machine's owner or administrator, since notifications are the most efficient and convenient way to implement monitoring tools that track which agents are currently on the machine.[7] There are similar access policies for the other agent operations. In particular, most operations can be configured to reject requests from remote machines. In a typical configuration, for example, the *begin* operation rejects any request from a remote machine, allowing only agents on the local machine to register with the server. The *begin* operation also imposes a limit on the total number of agents and the total number of *anonymous* agents executing on the machine at one time. The specific limits and access restrictions are specified in a server configuration file.

For all other builtin resources, security is maintained using the language-specific security (or enforcement) module and a set of language-independent *resource-manager* agents. When an agent requests access to a builtin resource, either implicitly or explicitly, the security module forwards the request to the appropriate resource manager. The resource manager, which is just a stationary agent, implements a security policy that determines whether the access request should be approved or denied. The security module then enforces the decision (and also caches the decision when appropriate to minimize the load on the resource managers). This approach provides a clean separation between security policy and mechanism, with the same resource managers making security decisions for all agents, regardless of their implementation language. A

---

[6] For example, the capability could include the agent's id and the time at which it arrived on the local machine. The agent will get a different timestamp (and usually id) if it leaves and returns, making it impossible to reuse the capability after a migration. In addition, since the ids are locally unique, no other agent can *ever* have the same combination of id and timestamp, making it impossible to transfer the capability to another agent.

[7] Or, more precisely, notifications will be the most convenient way once an agent can request notifications for a wider range of events.

system administrator can easily change the security policy by choosing a different resource-manager implementation.

There are currently six resource managers and three enforcement modules (one for each language)in the D'Agents system. Each of them are described below.

Resource managers

- *Consumables.* This resource manager handles consumable resources, such as CPU time, wall-clock time, number of child agents, maximum depth of the parent-child hierarchy, and number of migrations. Unlike other resources (such as the file system), access control is not an issue, only allocation. Furthermore, although there is an infinite supply of these resources, each agent should be limited to a finite consumption to prevent system overload. Since access to these resources is either implicit (as with CPU time) or takes place through the generic agent core (migration), enforcement actually takes place in the core, with the language-specific security module simply setting the new limits after the manager returns its decision. In addition, in contrast with the other builtin resources, the agent starts with a small allowance and must *explicitly* ask the manager for more.

  Limits on these resources are enforced across *groups* of mutually trusting machines. When making its decision, the consumables manager considers the amount of the resource used by the agent on other machines within the group.[8]

  Notably absent from this set of consumable resources is memory. Our concern is that a visiting agent could mount a denial-of-service attack against other agents by allocating all available virtual memory (or, indirectly, most available physical memory). A coarse-grained solution is trivial for Java and Scheme 48, which use their own memory-allocation routines and already have command-line arguments to specify a maximum heap size. Tcl, on the other hand, calls the standard `malloc` and `free` routines, and we have not yet implemented the necessary wrappers for these routines.

  Also absent from the current set of consumable resources is *CPU seconds per real second,* i.e., the fraction of the CPU cycles available to the agent, and agent operations per real second. Our concern is that a visiting agent could mount a denial-of-service attack against other agents by sitting in a computationally-intensive loop, or flooding the local server with requests. A solution to this problem requires better support from the operating-system scheduler.
- *File system.* This manager controls read and write access to files and directories. It also imposes a maximum size on writable files so that an agent cannot fill up the file system. Thus it has two roles: access control and allocation. Access control, as in most file systems, is determined on a file-by-file,

---

[8] Migrating agents include a vector that specifies how much of each resource they have used so far.

whole-file basis. (If record-based access control is necessary, the data should be accessed through a stationary database-manager agent.) The main weakness of the current file-system manager is that it does not impose a limit on disk accesses per second, making it possible for an agent to thrash the local disk. Again, we would require more support from the operating system.

- *Libraries.* This manager determines which libraries of Tcl functions, Scheme functions, or Java classes each agent can load.
- *Programs.* The *programs* manager determines which external programs each agent can execute. Since an external program is not subject to the same security checks as the agents themselves, policies implemented by this manager tend to be conservative. Typically, visiting agents obtain necessary services through requests to trusted stationary agents that perform sensitive tasks with careful security checks.
- *Network.* This manager decides which agents are allowed to directly access low-level TCP/IP and UDP network services. It either grants complete access to the network, or no access at all. Again, the policies implemented here is usually conservative.

  We plan to expand this manager's capabilities to allow the manager more flexibility, for example, to distinguish between different hosts, domains, ports, or protocols. In particular, one reasonable policy would allow all agents to access certain RPC-based services, especially when they are on a dedicated proxy site. Then, if a resource is not on an agent-enabled machine, an agent can migrate as close as possible to that machine and interact with the resource using standard cross-network calls [19].

  Again, as with the consumable and file-system managers, we do not currently support usage-rate limitations, such as messages per second. Ideally, some operating-system support would allow us to control access to the network bandwidth.
- *Screen.* Our current screen-manager mechanism can, as with the network manager, allow all access or allow no access. Thus, policies tend to be conservative, disallowing visiting agents any access to the screen. Our concern is that malicious agents might, for example, create a window that covered the entire screen and then grab the global focus.

  We are currently expanding the capabilities of the screen manager to allow more detailed control, making decisions about the number, placement, and size of windows, among other things. Our initial policy will be determined by the user: the screen-manager agent itself pops up a GUI window allowing the user to set limits on each agent that arrives.
- *Others.* There are other resources for which we do not currently have resource managers, such as microphones, speakers, cameras, and printers. They would all fit into the same security architecture, which provides two options. The resource may only be available indirectly, through requests sent to a specialized service agent, or it might be directly available (as with resources like the screen and network) after access has been granted by the appropriate resource-manager agent. The choice is determined primarily by performance considerations.

Security policies Most of our resource managers are currently implemented with extremely simple security policies. Each resource manager has a configuration file that specifies the access rights and limits for a particular *owner*. The manager loads this access list on startup and then checks the owner of each requesting agent against the list. Of course, the manager also takes into account whether the owner could be authenticated and whether the requesting agent is on the same machine. Anonymous agents are given limited access rights (mainly read access to certain libraries and initialization files), and remote agents are given no access rights.

We are currently implementing more involved security policies for the network resource, in which the network-resource manager allocates bandwidth to agents according to the outcome of a competition in which agents bid for access.

Enforcement modules Each language (Tcl, Java, and Scheme) needs its own enforcement module, although as we mention above, some of the resource decisions are enforced by the common code in the agent core. We discuss each of the three languages below, but first we discuss features common to all three.

Decision caching. Since the resource managers are implemented as separate agents, and communication between the visiting agent and the resource-manager agent involves passing messages between processes, we need to keep that communication to a minimum. In particular, it would be too inefficient to ask the resource manager for permission to read each character of a file, to display each pixel on the screen, or to send each packet on the network. Thus, our enforcement modules cache the decision of the resource managers in an internal access list.

For example, if an Agent Tcl program issues the Tcl command **exec ls**, the Tcl enforcement module (see below) checks the internal *program* access list. If permission to execute **ls** has already been granted, the command proceeds. If permission to execute **ls** has already been denied, the command throws a security exception. Otherwise the command contacts the *program* resource manager, adds the response to the *program* access list, and then either proceeds or throws the security exception.

Caching of the resource-manager decisions does not preclude dynamic changes to access-control policy. The caches simply must be invalidated whenever the policy is changed. We are currently working on a graphical administrative utility that lets the machine owner or administrator change the current policies of the resource managers. This utility sends the policy changes to the resource managers and cache invalidation messages to all running agents. Open issues involve sending the cache-invalidation message efficiently and *revoking* a resource permission that has already been granted to an agent. In the latter case, an agent might have opened too many windows, and the user wants to not only change the screen security policy, but also force the agent to close some of its existing windows. Such revocation is quite complex if we allow the agent to continue executing. For example, an agent must include significant error-handling code to handle the sudden disappearance of a window or the sudden closure of a file to which it previously had access. Simpler solutions would be to either terminate the agent or to send the agent back to its home machine.

"Require." An agent can also explicitly ask a resource manager for access permissions with the **require** command. The **require** command takes the symbolic name of the resource manager, e.g., *filesystem*, and a list of *(name, quantity)* pairs that specify the desired access permissions, e.g., *(/home/rgray/test.dat, read)*. The **require** command causes the enforcement module to send the list of desired access permissions to the appropriate resource manager. The procedure waits for the response and then adds each access permission to the internal access lists, indicating for each whether the request was granted or denied. Regardless of whether an explicit request is made via the **require** command, or an implicit request is made via the use of a sensitive command, the resource manager will send back the most general access permissions possible, effectively preloading the internal access lists and eliminating future requests. For example, if an agent requests access to a particular file, but is actually allowed to access the entire file system, the manager's response will grant access to the entire file system. In addition, although the current implementation does not prevent an agent from contacting the resource managers directly, such contact accomplishes nothing since the response will not go through the enforcement module and will thus not have any effect on the internal access lists.

"Restrict." An agent can impose access restrictions on *itself* with the **restrict** command. In the case of the *consumable* resources, these access restrictions remain in effect even when the agent migrates to a new machine. For example, the agent can restrict itself to a particular number of children, even if it is migrating and creating the children on different machines. More usefully, perhaps, the agent can restrict itself to a specific amount of CPU or wall time.

Tcl enforcement module. The Tcl enforcement module is implemented with Safe Tcl. Safe Tcl is a Tcl extension that is designed to allow the safe execution of untrusted Tcl scripts [18, 21]. Safe Tcl provides two interpreters. One interpreter is a "trusted" interpreter that has access to the standard Tcl/Tk commands. The other interpreter is an "untrusted" interpreter in which all dangerous commands have been replaced with links to secure versions in the trusted interpreter. The untrusted script executes in the untrusted interpreter. Dangerous commands include obvious things such as opening or writing to a file, creating a network connection, and creating a toplevel window. Dangerous commands also include more subtle things such as ringing the bell, raising and lowering a window, and maximizing a window so that it covers the entire screen. Some of these subtle security risks do not actually involve damage to the machine or access to privileged information, but instead involve serious annoyance for the machine's owner.

Agent Tcl uses the generalization of Safe Tcl that appears in the Tcl 7.5 core [18]. Agent Tcl creates a trusted and untrusted interpreter for each incoming agent. The agent executes in the untrusted interpreter. All dangerous commands have been removed from the untrusted interpreter and replaced with links to secure versions in the trusted interpreter. The secure version contacts the appropriate resource manager and allows or rejects the operation depending on the resource manager's response.

The Safe Tcl security module does not provide safe versions of all dangerous commands. For example, an agent that arrives from another machine cannot use the Tk `send` command, which sends a Tk event to another Tk interpreter.[9] In addition, there are (currently) no safe versions of the network and screen commands, since the resource managers either grant complete access to the screen and network or no access at all. The network and screen commands simply remain "hidden" until the resource managers grant access.

Java enforcement module. The Java enforcement module is implemented as a Java security manager [6]. A Java security manager is a class that provides a set of access-control methods, such as `checkExec`, `checkRead`, and `checkExit`. The Java system classes call these methods to see if the corresponding operation is allowed. For example, the `System.exec` method calls `checkExec` to see if the Java program is allowed to execute the specified external program.[10] Our security manager for agents is exactly equivalent to the Safe Tcl mechanism above: each `checkXXX` method checks its internal access list, and if necessary contacts the appropriate *resource manager*; it then throws a security exception if the resource manager denies access. Implementation of the Java security manager is not yet complete. Since the methods follow the same logic as the corresponding Safe Tcl procedures, however, implementation is proceeding rapidly.

Scheme enforcement module. Scheme 48 has a module system [16]. A *module* is a set of Scheme functions with some of those functions marked as *exported* or *public*; a program can load the module and invoke any of the exported functions. Implementing the Scheme enforcement module is mainly a matter of redefining the system modules so that they no longer export dangerous functions, but instead export secure versions of those functions that perform the same security checks as in Tcl and Java. It appears that the necessary module redefinitions can be accomplished without changing the Scheme 48 virtual machine. Implementation of the Scheme enforcement module is also not complete.

4.3 Status

The mechanisms for protecting the machine are nearly complete. There are a few remaining issues, some of which will be resolved soon, and some are left for future work:

---

[9] It is likely that the Tk `send` command will never be available since it is difficult to make secure and agents should communicate within the agent framework anyway.

[10] The *filename* of the external program is a parameter to `checkExec`.

- The implementation of the Java and Scheme enforcement modules is expected to be complete in Spring 1998.
- The screen manager and network manager are being expanded to allow finergrained control.
- The current implementation requires that a new enforcement module be written for each language. This approach minimizes the changes to the standard interpreters, but is time-consuming and error-prone. Eventually we will move to the Ara model in which the core provides secure versions of all system functions [22]; these core functions would still contact the resource managers to determine access rights.
- An agent can still mount several denial-of-service attacks: (1) it can sit in a tight loop and consume CPU time as fast as possible; (2) it can flood the local agent server with requests; (3) it can flood the local network by sending requests to remote agent servers as fast as possible (or by using some network service such as RPC to which it has been given direct access); (4) it can allocate all available virtual memory; and (5) it can thrash the local disk by randomly reading from any file to which it has been given access (or by allocating a data structure that is too large for main memory and then accessing the data structure in such a way as to cause frequent page faults). Preventing these denial-of-service attacks is not difficult; preventing them without artificially reducing performance is difficult (and impossible using only our current enforcement modules). Efficient allocation of the available resources to the current set of agents requires more support from the underlying operating system, as well as an appropriate allocation policy. The former is an implementation issue; the latter is an open research question.
- The specification of appropriate security policies, whether in the context of our security infrastructure or another, is a critical area for future research. The Aglets project has one preliminary proposal [14].

Finally, we note that other security models exist. D'Agents uses discretionary access control, in which each resource has an associated access list that specifies the allowed actions for each agent owner. Other security models include (1) mandatory access control, in which programs, people and data are assigned classification levels, and information can not flow from higher to lower levels, (2) security automata [25], in which a program's current allowed actions depend on its past resource usage,[11] and (3) computer immunology [7], in which a program is considered malicious if its current pattern of resource usage does not match its normal pattern. It is an open research question to decide which, if any, of these models is most appropriate for mobile-agent systems.

4.4 Examples

Figures 8 through 11 show two sample agents that use the D'Agent security features. One agent is an information-retrieval agent that jumps to a site, interacts

---

[11] For example, an agent might be permitted to communicate with a remote machine as long as it has not read from a sensitive file.

```
1    # turn on digital signatures
2    security signatures on
3
4    # register with the agent system
5    agent_begin
6
7    # migrate to the search engine site
8    agent_jump $engineSite
9
10   # interact with the search engine
11   agent_send "$agent(local-server) search-engine" 0 $query
12   agent_receive code results
13   ...
14
15   # return home
16   agent_jump $agent(home-machine)
```

Fig. 8. Tcl code for a simple information-retrieval agent. The agent registers with the agent system (lines 4–5), migrates to the location of a search engine (lines 7–8), performs a multi-step query (lines 10–13), and then returns home (lines 15–16). (The variable **agent** is a global array that is always available to an agent and that contains information about the agent's current location; initialization of the variables **engineSite** and **query** is not shown.) The only security feature in this agent is line 2, which turns on digital signatures so that the machine **engineSite** can verify the identity of the agent's owner. (Since PGP is slow, the current default is both digital signatures and encryption off; once we replace PGP with a faster encryption subsystem, the default will be digital signatures on and encryption off.) The search-engine agent, which is shown in Figure 9, makes more extensive use of D'Agent security features.

with a search engine to perform some query, and then jumps back to the home machine. The other agent is the search engine itself. Figures 8 and 9 show the agents implemented in Tcl. Figures 10 and 11 show the agents implemented in Java. In general, there is a one-to-one correspondence between the Tcl agents and the corresponding Java agents, except that the Tcl agents access agent services through a set of Tcl commands, while the Java agents access agent services by creating an instance of a class **Agent**.

The retrieval agent only uses one D'Agent security feature. It turns on digital signatures so that the search engine's machine can verify the identity of the agent's owner. The search-engine agent uses more D'Agent security features. First, it requests access to the needed system resources, namely, real time so that it can live for a long time, and the filesystem so that it can access the index to the document collection and the documents themselves. Then, after it receives a query from a retrieval agent, it rejects the query unless the agent is on the same machine and has a verifiable owner. It also rejects the query if the owner

```
1    # turn on digital signatures and register with the agent system
2    security signatures on
3    agent_begin
4    agent_name search-engine
5
6    # ask for a long lifetime and for access to the document collection
7    require wall $lifetimeSeconds
8    require file [list $documentIndex read]
9    require directory [list $documentDirectory read]
10
11   # wait for queries
12   while {1} {
13
14       # wait for a query
15       set id [agent_receive code string -security secVector -blocking]
16
17       # make sure that the querying agent is on the same machine
18       if {[lindex $secVector 3] != "agent-auth"} {
19           agent_send $id 1 ERROR; continue
20       }
21
22       # make sure that the querying agent has an authenticated owner
23       set ownerInformation [lindex $secVector 0]
24       if {[lindex $ownerInformation 1] != "owner-auth"} {
25           agent_send $id 1 ERROR; continue
26       }
27
28       # make sure that the authenticated owner is on our access list
29       set ownerName [lindex $ownerInformation 0]
30       if {[isAllowed $ownerName] != "yes"} {
31           agent_send $id 1 ERROR; continue
32       }
33
34       # handle the query
35       ...
```

Fig. 9. Tcl code for the search-engine agent. The search-engine agent handles queries from the information-retrieval agents. This version of the search-engine agent will only accept queries from agents that are on the same machine and only from agents whose owner is on a collection access list. After registering with the agent system, the agent requests access to the needed system resources (lines 6–9). Then the agent waits for a query (lines 14–15). Once the agent has a query, it verifies that the querying agent is on the same machine (lines 17–20), that the owner of the agent could be authenticated (lines 22–26), and that the owner is on the collection access list (lines 28–32). As with the other code examples, error-checking and some initialization code (and procedure isAllowed) have been omitted for clarity. In addition, note that this search-engine agent must be started by an owner (such as the machine administrator) whose agents are allowed to access the filesystem and to live for a long time. (Also note that the lindex command is simply used to access a particular element of a Tcl list.)

is not on its own access list. Not all search engines will reject queries in these situations. Some search engines that provide a high-level interface might allow remote queries, whereas some search engines will make their service available to anyone. Such search engines would simply exclude the corresponding security checks.

```
1    // create the agent
2    Agent agent = new Agent ();
3
4    // turn on digital signatures
5    agent.setSignatures (true);
6
7    // register with the agent system
8    agent.begin ("localhost", timeout);
9
10   // migrate to the search engine site
11   agent.jump (engineSite, timeout);
12
13   // interact with the search engine
14   Message queryMessage = new Message (0, query);
15   AgentId engineAgent = new AgentId (engineSite, "search-engine");
16   agent.send (engineAgent, queryMessage, timeout);
17   ReceivedMessage resultsMessage = agent.receive (timeout);
18   ...
19
20   // return home
21   String homeMachine = agent.getHomeId().getMachine();
22   agent.jump (homeMachine);
```

Fig. 10. Java implementation of the information-retrieval agent from Figure 8. The Java agent first creates an instance of the class **Agent**, which provides all of the agent operations. After that, the Java agent corresponds exactly to the Tcl agent. It turns on digital signatures (lines 4–5), registers with the agent system (lines 7–8), migrates to the location of the search engine (lines 10–11), performs the multi-step query (lines 13-18), and returns home (lines 20–22). As with the Tcl examples, error-checking and some initialization code have been omitted. In addition, the definition of the enclosing Java class (and method) has been omitted, but this class is a normal Java class.

5   Protecting a group of machines

There are two distinct types of machine groups to protect: (1) all the machines are under single administrative control, as in a departmental LAN, or (2) all the machines are *not* under single administrative control, as in the Internet. The key

```
1    # turn on digital signatures and register with the agent system
2    Agent agent = new Agent ();
3    agent.setSignatures (true);
4    agent.begin ("localhost", timeout);
5    agent.name ("search-engine");
6
7    # ask for a long lifetime and access to the document collection
8    FilePermission indexPermission =
        new FilePermission (documentIndex, FilePermission.c_READ);
9    DirectoryPermission directoryPermission =
        new DirectoryPermission (docDirectory, FilePermission.c_READ);
10   TimePermission timePermission = new TimePermission (lifeSeconds);
11   agent.require (indexPermission);
12   agent.require (directoryPermission);
13   agent.require (timePermission);
14
15   # wait for queries
16   while (1) {
17
18       # wait for a query
19       ReceivedMessage queryMessage = agent.receive (timeout);
20       AgentId senderId = queryMessage.getId();
21       Security securityVector = queryMessage.getSecurity();
22
23       # make sure that the querying agent is on the same machine
24       if (!securityVector.isAgentAuth()) {
25           ...; continue;
26       }
27
28       # make sure that the querying agent has an authenticated owner
29       if (!securityVector.isOwnerAuth()) {
30           ...; continue;
31       }
32
33       # make sure that the authenticated owner is on our access list
34       if (!isAllowed (securityVector.getOwnerKeyname())) {
35           ...; continue;
36       }
37
38       # handle the query
39       ...
```

Fig. 11. Java implementation of the search-engine agent from Figure 9. Aside from the creation of the initial **Agent** instance, the Java code corresponds exactly to the Tcl code. After registering with the agent system, it requests access to the needed system resources (lines 7–13), waits for a query (lines 18–21), and makes sure that the querying agent is on the same machine (line 23–26) and has an allowed, authenticated owner (lines 28–36). As with the Java retrieval agent, error-checking, some initialization code, and the definition of the enclosing class and method have been omitted.

difference is that machines within an administrative domain typically trust each other, but distrust most other machines in the Internet.

5.1 Within an administrative domain

It is straightforward to protect a group of machines that *are* under single administrative control. An agent is assigned a maximum resource allowance when it first enters the machine group. The allowance and the amount that the agent has used so far is propagated along with the agent as it migrates. If the agent exceeds its group allowance, it is terminated.[12]

The current implementation of D'Agents provides this kind of group protection, by including a *usage vector* in migrating agents. The usage vector lists the maximum allowance and the amount used, for each resource. Agents entering an administrative domain have their maximum allowance reduced if it exceeds that permitted to the agent's owner in that domain. The usage is updated and the limits enforced by the enforcement modules and resource managers described above.

Normally, packet tampering is not a serious issue within an administrative domain, so the agents and the agent's usage vector do not need to be encrypted or signed. If the administrative domain does span suspicious network links, however, each machine must digitally sign the agent and its usage vector so that the usage cannot be reduced, or the allowance increased, during transit. Thus, once an agent is inside an administrative domain, its usage vector is securely maintained and enforced.

5.2 The general case

When the machines are not in a single administrative domain, matters become much more complex. The usage vector carried by an agent migrating between mutually distrusting machines must, for all intents and purposes, be ignored, for the destination machine cannot trust the fact that the source machine has properly accounted for the agent's usage or properly retained the maximum allowances.

A more attractive solution, which we are currently exploring and implementing [2], is to use a market-based approach in which agents pay for their resource usage with cryptographically-protected electronic cash (for example, [3, 27]). When an agent is created, it is given a finite currency supply from its owner's own finite currency supply. The currency does not need to be tied to legal currency, but it must be impossible to spend a currency unit more than once, and it must be impossible for a user to quickly accumulate an arbitrarily large supply. The agent pays for its resource usage with its currency and splits its currency

---

[12] Alternatively, the agent could be sent back to its home machine or to a designated proxy site, although the current D'Agents system does not provide such functionality. An agent can inspect its group allowance, however, and can migrate out of the machine group if it sees that it is about to run out of some resource.

with any child agents that it creates. Eventually the agent and all its children run out of currency and are sent back to the home machine, which either provides more currency or terminates the agent. Resource managers accumulate payments on behalf of the machine's owning user, who can then use the cash to pay for his or her own agents' travels.

There are several advantages to a market-based solution. First, all machines need not trust each other; they need only trust a set of banks that manage the currency. Second, by setting prices accordingly, each machine can express its resource-allocation priorities, e.g., some users may raise the cost of their CPU time during the work day, so that most agents stay away, and lower the cost of CPU time when they are away to allow agents to visit. Third, the agents can autonomously decide how to spend their currency to accomplish their task according to their own priorities, e.g., choosing space-efficient algorithms when memory is expensive, and time-efficient algorithms when CPU is expensive.

There are many detailed issues that must be resolved to make the market-based approach work well, most notably the development of policies for resource managers to set prices, and policies for agents to make decisions about prices. We are examining all of these issues in the D'Agents project, and their full exposition is beyond the scope of this paper.

6   Protecting the agent

Protecting an agent from a malicious machine is the most difficult security problem. Unless "trusted (and tamper-resistant) hardware" is available on each agent server [4], something which is extremely unlikely in the near future, there is no way to prevent a malicious machine from examining or modifying any part of the agents that visit it. Thus, the real problem is not to prevent theft and tampering, but instead to prevent the machine from using stolen information in a meaningful way and to detect tampering as soon as possible, ideally as soon as the agent migrates onto the next machine. Unfortunately, there is no single mechanism that can solve this problem, and it is unlikely that there will ever be a complete *technical* solution, due to the unimaginable variety of theft and tampering attacks that can be mounted against a visiting agent. Instead, some part of the solution will always be sociological and legal pressures [4].

There are, however, several partial technical solutions. Hopefully, by choosing from these partial solutions, most agents will be able to protect themselves adequately for their current task, but still move freely throughout the network. Before considering some of these partial solutions, it is worthwhile to consider two broad categories of tampering attacks.

- *Normal routing.* The malicious machine allows the agent to continue with its normal itinerary, but holds the agent longer than necessary, charges the agent extra money, or modifies the agent's code or state. Holding the agent longer than necessary prevents a time-critical agent from accomplishing its task. Modifying the agent's code or state causes the agent to perform some work on behalf of the malicious machine, take some dangerous action, or simply reach an incorrect result. These modification threats are why D'Agents agents currently become *anonymous* as soon as they migrate through an untrusted machine.

— *Rerouting.* The malicious machine reroutes the agent to a machine that it would not have visited under normal circumstances, or prevents the agent from migrating at all and pretends that it is the next machine on the agent's normal itinerary. The latter attack might be used against an agent that is migrating through a sequence of service providers, attempting to find the best price for some service or product. A service provider can hold the agent on its machine, masquerade as the other service providers, and report higher prices than its own price. Although such an attack requires the service provider to recognize what a particular agent is doing and then update the agent's state as if it had actually visited the other machines, many applications will involve pre-packaged agents that users purchase from the application developers. Recognizing and fooling these well-known agents will not be difficult.

Now, with both theft and tampering attacks in mind, we consider the partial solutions.

— *Trusted machines and noncritical agents.* Note that many agents do not need protection at all, either because they are performing some noncritical task (e.g., an anonymous agent interacting with a free search engine), or because they operate entirely on trusted machines (e.g., an agent that is installing new software on a department's machine). Trusted machines can include not only all the machines in your own department, but also machines belonging to large, well-known corporations, such as America Online, Microsoft, Netscape, and United Airlines.

— *Partitioning.* An agent can migrate through trusted machines only, such as a set of general proxy sites under the control of a trusted Internet service provider. Then it either interacts with untrusted resources from across the network using standard RPC, or sends out child agents that contain no sensitive data and will not migrate again, instead just returning their result. More complicated partitioning schemes can be used if needed. In fact, partitioning can achieve as much client protection as in traditional distributed computing, since the sensitive portion of the agent can always be left on the home machine.

— *Replication and voting.* Tacoma uses a replication and voting scheme to handle malicious machines that either terminate an agent outright or provide the agent with incorrect information [20]. Here, if the task requires a single agent to visit n services in sequence, the application instead sends out several agents, each of which visits distinct but supposedly equivalent copies of the n services. The agents exchange results after each stage, each agent keeping the majority result. Although this scheme prevents many kinds of attacks, it also has several drawbacks. First, there must be multiple copies of each service[13]; in addition, since the copies might be functionally equivalent but not identical, the agent must be able to handle different interfaces and different result formats. Second, if the agents are spending money to access the services, the user will spend much more money than if a single agent had migrated through a single copy. Finally, the cryptographic overhead is large. Despite these disadvantages, replication and voting schemes will be used in many agents, since they are the only way to handle services that provide incorrect information (assuming that the incorrectness cannot be easily detected). Tacoma also includes *rear-guard* agents that restart a vanished agent.

- *Components.* Perhaps the most powerful idea is to divide each agent into components [4]. Components can be added to the agent as it migrates, and each component can be encrypted and signed with different keys. The agent's static code and the variables whose values never change would make up one component, and would be signed with the owner's key before the agent left the home machine. If a malicious machine modifies the code or variables, the digital signature becomes invalid and the next machine in the migration sequence will immediately detect the modification. In addition, if an agent obtains critical information from a service, it can put this information into its own component. Then the component is signed with the machine's key to prevent tampering, and can even be encrypted with a trusted machine's key (e.g., the home machine or a proxy site) so that other machines cannot examine it. Of course, the agent must return to that trusted machine before it can use the information again itself. Similarly, any code or data that is not needed until the agent reaches a particular machine can be encrypted with that machine's key. For example, an agent might encrypt the bulk of its electronic cash with a proxy site's key, so that it could migrate through untrusted machines without worrying about theft. The agent would return to the proxy site when it needed to spend the cash. Depending on the migration model, this component approach also allows a machine to place greater trust in an agent that has migrated through untrusted machines. For example, if the code to be executed on the current machine is in its own component, digitally signed with the owner's key, and this code does not depend on any volatile variables, the code can be executed with the owner's permissions, rather than as *anonymous*. Finally, components make it easier for an agent to use the partitioning approach above; an agent can leave a particular component behind on a trusted machine, or can create and send out a child agent that includes only certain components.
- *Self-authentication.* In most agents, certain parts of the agent's state will change as the agent migrates from machine to machine, such as the variable values and the control information on the interpreter's stack. Although it is impossible to detect all malicious modifications to this state information, it is possible to construct an authentication routine that will examine the

---

[13] And the copies cannot be under the control of a single organization. Otherwise all the copies might have the same malicious behavior.

state information for any obvious inconsistencies or impossibilities [22]. The authentication routine could also examine the current set of components. Such an authentication routine would be placed in its own component and digitally signed with the owner's key. Each agent server would execute the authentication routine, terminating the agent (and notifying the home machine) if the routine finds any inconsistencies. The authentication routine would run as *anonymous* and would only have authority to examine the state image. Like the components themselves, such an authentication routine allows a machine to place greater trust in an agent that has migrated through untrusted machines.

- *Migration history.* It is possible to embed a tamper-proof migration history inside a moving agent [20]. This movement history allows the detection of some rerouting attacks, particularly if an agent is following a fixed itinerary, and, in combination with additional digital signatures, makes it impossible for a malicious machine to drop an entire component from the agent. The movement history could also be examined inside the authentication routine above.
- *Audit logs.* Machines should keep logs of important agent events so that an aggrieved agent or owner can request an audit from an authorized third-party [4]. The auditor would seek to identify the machine responsible for a theft or modification and penalize that machine appropriately. The exact contents of the audit logs is largely an open question. It is clear that all electronic-cash transfers must be logged, however, so that a machine cannot steal electronic cash without providing the desired service. Of course, a malicious machine can construct a false log, so the auditor must look for log entries that are inconsistent with log entries from other machines, rather than just log entries that explicitly indicate a malicious action. In addition malicious machines can collude in their logging to make an honest, intervening machine *look* malicious. Thus, in some situations, the auditor can impose serious sanctions only after it has observed an apparent attack happening to *multiple* agents (that are following different migration trajectories).
- *Encrypted algorithms.* Finally, recent work [24, 12] involves encrypting a program and its inputs in such a way that (1) the *encrypted* program is directly executable, (2) the encrypted program performs the same task as the original program, and (3) the output from the encrypted program is also encrypted and can only be decrypted by the program encrypter. Although this work is in its infancy and remains either theoretical or unproven, it has great promise for mobile-agent systems, since it would become much harder for a malicious machine to make a targeted modification, i.e., a modification with a known, useful effect, to an agent or its state.

Even taken together, these techniques cannot provide complete protection. In addition, many of the techniques involve substantial cryptographic and logging overhead, forcing an agent to trade performance for protection. Most agents should be able to realize adequate protection through some combination of these techniques, however, while still maintaining reasonable performance. The overriding issue is how to design a protection interface that allows the agent to easily use the desired combination of techniques.

None of these solutions are currently implemented in the D'Agents system.

7   Conclusion and future work

D'Agents is a simple but powerful mobile-agent system that supports multiple languages, namely, Tcl, Java and Scheme, and protects machines from malicious agents with a straightforward security model. It has been used in numerous distributed applications, particularly information-retrieval applications, both at Dartmouth and in external research labs. Several areas of security-related future work remain, however. We must address several denial-of-service attacks, finish the electronic-cash system and develop the market-based control policies, and extend the screen and network resource managers to provide finer-grained access control. We are also continuing to develop information-retrieval applications so that we can experimentally compare mobile agents with other approaches, to better evaluate the feasibility of our security mechanisms and policies. As part of this work, we hope to formally characterize when an agent should remain stationary and when and how far it should migrate. Finally, we are continuing to develop support services, such as a debugger, a hierarchical service index, a docking system for mobile computers, and several network-sensing and planning modules. As this work progresses, D'Agents will be able to realize its full potential and become a convenient, efficient, and secure platform for general distributed applications.

8   Availability

The Tcl portion of D'Agents version 2.0, which is the version of D'Agents described in this paper, is available now on the D'Agents web page[14]. The Java portion will be available by the time of publication. The Scheme portion, which is farther from completion, may be available at the time of publication. D'Agents runs on most Unix platforms. A port to Windows 95 and Windows NT is planned, but the completion date is uncertain.

9   Acknowledgments

Many thanks to Scott Silver, Jeffrey Steeves and Jonathan Bredin for their work on the encryption and resource-management subsystems; to Eric White, David Gondek, Alik Widge, Bill Bleier and Joshua Mills for their work on the Java and Scheme components; to the Air Force and Navy for their generous financial support (ONR contract N00014-95-1-1204, AFOSR contract F49620-93-1-0266, and Air Force MURI grant F49620-97-1-0382); and to all the graduate and undergraduate students who have contributed to the D'Agents (Agent Tcl) system over the past four years.

---

[14] http://www.cs.dartmouth.edu/~agent/

References

[1] Lubomir F. Bic, Munehiro Fukuda, and Michael B. Dillencourt. Distributed computing using autonomous objects. *IEEE Computer*, 29(8):55–61, August 1996.

[2] Jonathan Bredin, David Kotz, and Daniela Rus. Marked-based resource control for mobile agents. To appear in the conference Autonomous Agents '98, October 1997.

[3] David Chaum and Stefan Brands. "Minting" electronic cash. *IEEE Spectrum*, 34(2):30–34, February 1997. Special issue on Technology and Electronic Economy.

[4] David Chess, Benjamin Grosof, Colin Harrison, David Levine, Colin Parris, and Gene Tsudik. Itinerant agents for mobile computing. *IEEE Personal Communications*, 2(5):34–49, October 1995.

[5] Michael H. Coen. SodaBot: A software agent environment and construction system. In Yannis Labrou and Tim Finin, editors, *Proceedings of the CIKM Workshop on Intelligent Information Agents, Third International Conference on Information and Knowledge Management (CIKM 94)*, Gaithersburg, Maryland, December 1994.

[6] Gary Cornell and Cay S. Horstmann. *Core Java*. Sunsoft Press (Prentice Hall), 1997.

[7] Stephanie Forrest, Steven A. Hofmeyr, and Anil Somayaji. Computer immunology. *Communications of the ACM*, 40(10):88–96, October 1997.

[8] *Odyssey: Beta Release 1.0*, 1997. Available as part of the Odyssey package at `http://www.genmagic.com/agents/`.

[9] Robert S. Gray. Agent Tcl: A flexible and secure mobile-agent system. In *Proceedings of the 1996 Tcl/Tk Workshop*, pages 9–23, July 1996.

[10] David Halls, John Bates, and Jean Bacon. Flexible distributed programming using mobile code. In *Proceedings of the Seventh ACM SIGOPS European Workshop*, pages 225–231, September 1996.

[11] Melissa Hirschl and David Kotz. AGDB: A debugger for Agent Tcl. Technical Report PCS-TR97-306, Dept. of Computer Science, Dartmouth College, Hanover, NH, February 1997.

[12] Fritz Hohl. Protecting mobile agents with blackbox security. In *Proceedings of the 1997 Workshop on Mobile Agents and Security*, University of Maryland, October 1997.

[13] Dag Johansen, Robbert van Renesse, and Fred B. Scheidner. Operating system support for mobile agents. In *Proceedings of the Fifth IEEE Workshop on Hot Topics in Operating Systems (HTOS)*, pages 42–45, May 1995.

[14] Günter Karjoth, Danny B. Lange, and Mitsuru Oshima. A security model for Aglets. *IEEE Internet Computing*, 1(4):68–77, July/August 1997.

[15] Charlie Kaufman, Radia Perlman, and Mike Speciner. *Network Security: Private Communication in a Public World*. Prentice-Hall, New Jersey, 1995.

[16] Richard Kelsey and Jonathan Rees. A tractable Scheme implementation. *Lisp and Symbolic Computation*, 7(4), 1995.

[17] Danny B. Lange and Mitsuru Oshima. *The Aglet cookbook*. 1997. In progress. Selected chapters available at `http://www.trl.ibm.co.jp/aglets/aglet-book/index.html`.

[18] Jacob Y. Levy and John K. Ousterhout. Safe Tcl toolkit for electronic meeting places. In *Proceedings of the First USENIX Workshop on Electronic Commerce*, pages 133–135, July 1995.

[19] Mobile Agent Facility Specification (joint submissions). Technical report, Crystaliz, General Magic, GMD FOKUS, Internal Business Machine Corporation, and The Open Group, 1997. Response to OMG's Common Facility Task Force RFP3. Draft 5 is available at http://www.genmagic.com/agents/MAF/.

[20] Yaron Minsky, Robbert van Renesse, Fred B. Schneider, and Scott D. Stoller. Cryptographic support for fault-tolerant distributed computing. In *Proceedings of the Seventh ACM SIGOPS European Workshop*, pages 109–114, September 1996.

[21] John K. Ousterhout, Jacob Y. Levy, and Brent B. Welch. The Safe-Tcl security model. Technical report, Sun Microsystems Laboratories, 1997. In progress. Draft available at http://www.sunlabs.com/people/john.ousterhout/safeTcl.html.

[22] Holger Peine and Torsten Stolpmann. The architecture of the Ara platform for mobile agents. In *Proceedings of the First International Workshop on Mobile Agents (MA '97)*, volume 1219 of *Lecture Notes in Computer Science*, Berlin, April 1997. Springer-Verlag.

[23] Daniela Rus, Robert Gray, and David Kotz. Transportable information agents. *Journal of Intelligent Information Systems*, May 1997. To appear.

[24] Thomas Sander. On cryptographic protection of mobile agents. In *Proceedings of the 1997 Workshop on Mobile Agents and Security*, University of Maryland, October 1997.

[25] Fred B. Schneider. Security in Tacoma Too. In *Proceedings of the 1997 DAGSTUHL Workshop on Mobile Agents*, September 1997.

[26] Fred B. Schneider. Towards fault-tolerant and secure agentry. In *Proceedings of the 11th International Workshop on Distributed Algortithms*, September 1997.

[27] Marvin Sirbu and J. D.Tygar. NetBill: An Internet commerce system optimized for network delivered services. In *Proceedings of 40th IEEE Computer Society International Conference (COMPCON 95)*. IEEE Computer Society Press, March 1995.

[28] Joseph Tardo and Luis Valente. Mobile agent security and Telescript. In *Proceedings of the 41th International Conference of the IEEE Computer Society (CompCon '96)*, February 1996.

[29] Voyager technical overview. ObjectSpace White Paper, ObjectSpace, 1997.

[30] Peter Wayner. *Agents Unleashed: A public domain look at agent technology*. AP Professional, Chestnut Hill, Massachusetts, 1995.

[31] James E. White. Telescript technology: The foundation for the electronic marketplace. General Magic White Paper, General Magic, Inc., 1994.

[32] James E. White. Telescript technology: An introduction to the language. General Magic White Paper, General Magic, 1995.

[33] James E. White. Telescript technology: Scenes from the electronic marketplace. General Magic White Paper, General Magic, 1995.

[34] James E. White. Telescript technology: Mobile agents. 1996.

[35] D. Wong, N. Paciorek, T. Walsh, J. DiCelie, M. Young, and B. Peet. Concordia: An infrastructure for collaborating mobile agents. In *Proceedings of the First International Workshop on Mobile Agents (MA '97)*, volume 1219 of *Lecture Notes in Computer Science*, Berlin, April 1997. Springer-Verlag.

A Security Model for Aglets*

Günter Karjoth[1], Danny B. Lange[**2], and Mitsuru Oshima[2]

[1] IBM Research Division, Zurich Research Laboratory
gka@zurich.ibm.com
[2] IBM Research Division, Tokyo Research Laboratory
danny@acm.org
moshima@ibm.trl.ibm.co.jp

Abstract. Aglets are Java-based mobile agents developed at IBM's Tokyo Research Laboratory. This article describes a security model for the aglets development environment that supports flexible architectural definition of security policies.

1 Introduction

Mobile agents offer a new paradigm for distributed computation, but their potential benefits must be weighed against the very real security threats they pose. These threats originate not just in malicious agents but in malicious hosts as well [1]. For example, if there is no mechanism to prevent attacks, a host can implant its own tasks into an agent or modify the agent's state. This can lead in turn to theft of the agent's resources if it has to pay for the execution of tasks or to loss of the agent's reputation if its state changes from one host to another in ways that alter its behavior in negative ways.

Moreover, if mobile agents ultimately allow a broad range of users to access services offered by different and frequently competing organizations, then many applications will involve parties that may not trust each other entirely [2]. The operation of a mobile agent system will therefore require security services that implement the agreements made by the involved parties, whether declared or tacit. Thus, they can not be violated, either accidentally or intentionally by the involved parties or by malicious or curious parties not bound by these agreements.

The security frameworks of Java and other script languages for "remote programming" such as Safe Tcl have allowed developers to make some progress toward one issue of mobile agent security—namely, the safe execution of untrusted code—through restricted environments based on sandboxing or a separated execution environment. Some current agent systems offer basic privacy

---

* ©1997 IEEE. Reprinted, with permission, from IEEE INTERNET COMPUTING, Vol. 1, No. 4: JULY-AUGUST 1997, pp. 68-77

** Since collaborating on this article, Danny B. Lange has joined General Magic, Inc.

G. Vigna (Ed.): Mobile Agents and Security
LNCS 1419, pp. 188–205, 1998. © Springer–Verlag Berlin Heidelberg 1998

mechanisms such as a secure channel between machines via encryption of agents and messages on transmission. Some offer means of authentication and integrity via the signing of agents and messages sent between hosts, again using a variety of cryptographic tools. Even fewer agent systems (Agent Tcl [3], Telescript [4]) offer mechanisms to control resource consumption. Finally, the Mobile Agent Facility under development at the Object Management Group will include a security model based on the CORBA security specification. However, no system at present provides a general security model.

In this article, we present our security model for the IBM Aglets Workbench, a Java-based environment for building mobile agent applications. We detail both the reference model and corresponding security architecture that represent a framework for the inclusion of security services in future releases of the AWB. This work therefore represents an additional step toward the comprehensive security model required for widespread commercial adoption of mobile agent systems to occur.

2 Aglets Workbench

The IBM Aglets Workbench lets users create *aglets*, mobile agents based on the Java programming language. The AWB consists of a development kit for aglets and a platform for their execution. It is based on the aglet object model, whose major elements are aglets, contexts, and messages. The Aglet Transfer Protocol (ATP) and the Aglet API (A-API) are further AWB components that define how to transport aglets and how to interface to aglets and contexts.

In this section we briefly describe these elements as far as necessary to understand the security work presented next. For more details on aglets, see Lange and Oshima [5], available as a working draft "cookbook" on the aglets site [1] at the Tokyo Research Laboratory. For tutorials on aglets and AWB, see Sommers [6] and Venners [7,8].

2.1 Aglets Object Model

Aglets are Java objects that visit aglet-enabled hosts in a computer network. An aglet that executes on one host can halt execution, dispatch to a remote host, and resume execution there. When the aglet migrates, it brings along its program code as well as its data. An aglet is autonomous because it runs in its own thread of execution after arriving at a host; it is reactive because it can respond to incoming messages.

A *context* is an aglet's workplace. It is a stationary object that provides a means for maintaining and managing active aglets in a uniform execution environment where the host system is secured against malicious aglets. A *proxy* is a representative of an aglet. It serves as a shield to protect the aglet from direct access to its public methods. The proxy also gives the aglet location transparency; that is, it can hide the aglet's real location.

---

[1] http://www.trl.ibm.co.jp/aglets

A *message* is an object exchanged between aglets. As mobile and autonomous objects, aglets do not exist in statically configured object structures but must instead interact with objects that might originate from unknown sources. Aglets therefore communicate by message passing and not by method invocation. Message passing allows flexible interaction and exchange of knowledge between systems.

Other agent languages, for example Agent Tcl [3] and Telescript [4], focus on process migration, which lets an agent "leave" one machine in the middle of a loop and resume execution in the middle of that loop on another machine. Aglets, by comparison, use an event-based scheme, as in window system programming. They implement several event-handling methods, which can be customized by programmers. These methods cover all important events in an aglet's life cycle (see Table 1). For example, if an aglet is moved, it will be notified upon leaving its host and upon arriving at the new host.

Table 1. Aglet life-cycle events and their methods

Event	Methods	
	As the event takes place	**After the event has taken place**
Creation		`onCreation()`
Cloning	`onCloning()`	`onClone()`
Dispatching	`onDispatching()`	`onArrival()`
Retraction	`onReverting()`	`onArrival()`
Disposal	`onDisposing()`	
Deactivation	`onDeactivating()`	
Activation		`onActivation()`
Messaging	`handleMessage()`	

An aglet is created within a context. The new aglet is assigned an identifier, inserted into the context, and initialized. The aglet starts to execute as soon as it has been initialized. The cloning of an aglet produces an almost identical copy of the original in the same context, except that the clone has a different identifier and restarts execution.

Dispatching an aglet from one context to another will remove it from its current context and insert it into the destination context, where it will restart execution. We say that the aglet has been "pushed" into its new context. The retraction of an aglet will "pull" (remove) it from its current context and insert it into the context from which the retraction was requested.

Deactivation of an aglet removes it temporarily from its current context and holds it in secondary storage. Activation of an aglet restores it into a context. Disposal of an aglet halts its current execution and removes it from its current context. Figure 1 illustrates these events in the life cycle of an aglet.

Aglets communicate via messages. Each aglet can be equipped with a message-handling method that lets it react to incoming message objects sent from an-

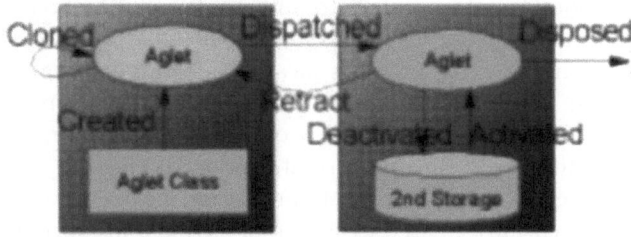

Fig. 1. Life cycle of an Agent

other (possibly remote) aglet. Aglet message handling can be synchronous or asynchronous. A future-reply object returned by the message-sending method allows the aglet either to wait for a reply or to continue processing and get the reply later. An aglet can also multicast a message to all aglets within the same context that have subscribed to that message.

2.2   Aglet API

The Aglet API [9] defines the methods necessary for aglet creation and manipulation. A-API is public and therefore allows the development of platform-independent mobile agents written in the Java programming language. Aglets written to the API will run on any machine that supports it. A-API has two core classes and core interface.

The Aglet class, a subclass of Object, is the abstract base class. It defines final methods for controlling an aglet's own life cycle–namely, methods for cloning, dispatching, deactivating, and disposing of itself. It also defines methods that are supposed to be overridden in its subclasses by the aglet programmer, and provides "hooks" to customize an aglet's behavior. These methods are invoked systematically by the system when certain events take place in the life cycle of an aglet (see Table 1).

The AgletProxy class serves as a shield for aglets, protecting them from direct access to their public methods. Interaction with an aglet takes place only via its proxy. Aglets do not interact with other aglets by invoking their methods. For example, a proxy is returned on any of the following aglet creation requests:

- AgletContext.createAglet(...);
- Aglet.clone();
- AgletProxy.clone();

The context or other aglets might use several of the proxy's methods—such as clone(), dispatch(), dispose(), and deactivate()—to control the aglet. The method sendMessage() is used to send asynchronous messages to the aglet via its proxy.

An aglet uses the AgletContext interface to obtain information about its environment and to send messages to the environment, including to other aglets currently active in it. The interface provides means for maintaining and managing active aglets in an environment where the host system is secure against malicious aglets. If an aglet has access to a given context, it can create new aglets or retract remotely located aglets into the current context. It can also retrieve a list (enumeration) of proxies of its fellow aglets present in the same context.

The aglet context is typically created by a system having a network daemon that listens for aglets. The daemon inserts incoming aglets into the context. Often, a user interface component will provide a graphical or command line interface to the context. In general, any user can set up a context. Thus, an aglet network potentially includes contexts that not all users trust.

3   Threats, Attackers, and Countermeasures

There are four security issues specific to a mobile agent system [3]. They are

1. protection of the host against aglets,
2. protection of other aglets,
3. protection of the aglet from the host, and
4. protection of the underlying network.

Whereas the literature discusses all of these issues (for example, see Chess et al [10] and Farmer et al. [2]), researchers have found serious solutions only for the first two. Our security model for the Aglets Workbench also focuses on these two issues, although the model is flexible enough to accommodate eventual solutions to the latter two as well.

While developing the model, we assumed that an aglet system is subject to the fundamental threats of disclosure, modification, denial of use, misuse, abuse, and repudiation. Aglets are exposed to these threats not only when they travel but also when they are in aglet contexts. We assumed that attackers can perform passive and active attacks utilizing aglets, aglet contexts, or other mechanisms.

Table 2 lists and briefly describes the attacks possible on aglets. A secure aglet system must provide services to counter these threats. However, there is no countermeasure if the attacker exploits systems flaws or security weaknesses such as bypassing controls, exploiting trapdoors, or introducing Trojan horses [11].

A security architecture must therefore confine key security functionality to a trusted core that enforces the essential parts of the security policy. These parts include

- protecting aglet transfer and communication as required by the security policy,
- performing the required access control and auditing of aglet execution,
- preventing (groups of) aglets from interfering with each other or gaining unauthorized access to each other's state, and
- preventing aglets from interfering with their hosting aglet system.

Table 2. Possible attacks on aglets

Eavesdropping	Information is revealed from monitored communications.
Intercept/alter	A communicated data item, such as a Java class file, is changed, deleted, or substituted while in transit. In particular, any context visited on the aglet's itinerary could strip data added by previous contexts.
Replay	A captured copy of a previously sent legitimate aglet is retransmitted for illegitimate purposes.
Masquerade	An entity pretends to be a different entity, for example, one aglet pretends to be another.
Resource exhaustion	A resource is deliberately used so heavily that service to other users is disrupted.
Repudiation	A party to a communication exchange later denies that the exchange took place.

Additional requirements to be met in some systems include

- allowing the use of different cryptographic algorithms,
- keeping the amount of information encrypted for confidentiality to a minimum, and
- being compatible with standard distributed security frameworks such as those of IETF, X/OPEN, and OMG.

However, there are security requirements for agents and hosts that cannot be fulfilled [2,10]. It is impossible, for example,

- to hide anything within an agent without the use of cryptography,
- to communicate secretly with a large, anonymous group of agent platforms,
- to prevent agent tampering unless trusted hardware is available in agent platforms, and
- to distinguish an agent from a clone.

These limitations imply that an agent cannot carry its own key (or other secrets, such as a credit card number) in a form that can be used on untrusted hosts.
     Moreover, it is impossible for an agent to verify whether

- an interpreter is untampered,
- an interpreter will run an agent correctly,
- a host will run an agent to completion, or
- a host will transmit an agent as requested.

Because aglets are Java objects, they have potential access to all Java class files on the host; they also rely on the security of the Java interpreter for their proper execution. Thus, aglet security and Java security go hand in hand. All the security concerns raised about Java also affect the safe execution of aglets (for example, see FAQs at JavaSoft and the Princeton Secure Internet Programming

Team). A small local bug in the implementation of the hosting Java interpreter will affect the security of the Aglet Workbench.

Together, these limitations outline the bounds of possibility achievable by technological means only. Although legal or social controls may offer other means of protecting mobile agents, the scope of our security model is restricted to solutions achievable with standard security technology.

4   Security Model

We have developed a security model that provides an overall framework for aglet security. The model supports the flexible definition of various security policies and describes how and where a secure system enforces security policies.

Security policies are defined in terms of a set of rules by one administrative authority. The policies specify

- the conditions under which aglets may access objects;
- the authentication required of users and other principals, which actions an authenticated entity is allowed to perform, and whether entities can delegate their rights;
- the communications security required between aglets and between contexts, including trust; and
- the degree of accountability required for each security-relevant activity.

An aglet might be unaware of the security policy of the hosting context and how it is enforced. If so, the user can be authenticated prior to creating the aglet; security is then enforced automatically. Some aglets will need to control or influence which policy is enforced by the system on their behalf, but will not enforce it themselves. Others will need to enforce their own security, to control access to their own data, or to audit their own security-relevant activities.

4.1   Principals and Identities

A principal is any entity whose identity can be authenticated by a system that the principal may try to access. A principal can be an individual, a corporation, a daemon thread, or a smart card. An identity consists of a name and possibly other attributes.

Our aglets security model identifies several principals, each having certain responsibilities and interests, which are summarized in Table 3. Aglets and contexts are processes (threads) running on behalf of a user; manufacturers, owners, masters, and authorities are users imposing "roles" on aglets and contexts that reflect their organizational, functional, or social position.

Aglets. Every aglet has an identifier that is unique over its life time and independent of the context it is executing in. Its value, however, is not known before the aglet has been created and thus not easily accessible for authorization purposes. Therefore, the aglet identity includes its class name—a kind of

Table 3. Principals defined in the aglets security model

Aglet	Instantiation of the aglet program itself (thread)
AgletManufacturer	Author of an aglet program (human, company, content rating service, and so on)
AgletOwner	Individual that launched the aglet (human) or principal that has legal responsibility for the aglet's behavior
Context	Interpreter that executes aglets (process, thread, and so on)
ContextManufacturer	Author of a context program/product (human, company, and so on)
ContextMaster	Owner/administrator/operator of the context (human, company, and so on)
Domain	A group of contexts owned by the same authority
DomainAuthority	owner/administrator/operator of the domain (human, company, and so on)

"product" name—for authentication. The identifier might be used in policies that refer to specific instances of aglets; for example, it might indicate that a particular aglet can dispose of any of its offsprings. An aglet's product name might be used when only a certain type of aglet is meant; for example, aglets of class `ibm.aglets.samples.Watcher` might have access to specific HTML files.

The aglet manufacturer produces a well-defined and reliable aglet. It is in the manufacturer's interest that no damage can be claimed to have been caused by a malfunctioning aglet. For its own protection, the manufacturer might define terms of liability.

The aglet owner is concerned mainly about the safety of the launched aglet. Can the returned results be trusted? Did every context execute the aglet properly? For that purpose, the owner may define security preferences, a set of rules that specify who may access/interact with the aglet on its itinerary. However, as the aglet has to rely on the context to carry out compliance, the preferences are no more than a statement of intent. Security preferences also allow the owner to limit the aglet's capabilities, for example to specify some global allowance on the maximum number of hops, CPU-time consumption, and so on.

Contexts. The context manifests the execution platform of the aglet. Its identity is the URL of the host together with a qualifier if there is more than one context. Unlike aglets, contexts are long-lived objects and thus may keep their identity—that is, their address—even after updates or complete replacements of the software and hardware that realize the context. For security-critical applications that associate trust with a specific version of the context, the identity of a context must have an attribute like the serial number of a CPU. Just as a software license can be granted to only one specific computer, identified by the serial number of its CPU, a context's serial number refers to a specific release of its software and hardware.

The context manufacturer produces a reliable context according to the A-API specification. Again, it is in a manufacturer's interest that no damage can be claimed to have been caused by a malfunctioning context. The manufacturer's specification of the context's functionality sets the basis for the context master.

The context master is responsible for the safety and security of the context and its underlying machine. A master defines the security policy for the context under its control, that is, for protecting local resources against aglets. The master is also responsible for guaranteeing that no aglet can interfere with any other aglet active in the same context if not explicitly permitted by the aglet owner.

Domains. Several things make it appealing to organize contexts into groups. For example, a context provides a certain infrastructure—general services for aglet administration (creation, activation, retraction), communication, support of audio and images—as well as specific security services such as authentication, authorization, and accounting. A single context providing all these services might be very expensive, so grouping contexts can be efficient and cost-effective. It might also easily achieve secure communication between contexts of the group if communication is local and thus protected by means of the operating system.

All domain members follow the same security policies as set up by the domain authority. In some cases the DomainAuthority and the ContextMasters of the domain members are the same principal. In other cases the DomainAuthority and the ContextMasters are different principals, as in the case of a mall provider and a set of shop owners.

A domain might correspond with an Internet subdomain, for example the set of all contexts with the address *.trl.ibm.com. It might also be the set of all contexts owned by the same master or defined by a directory or a certificate stating the context's membership in the domain.

4.2 Security Policies

All principals introduced here may define security policies, in particular the aglet owner and the context master. Thus, a secure aglet system should implement the overall effect of all security policies involved. For example, although the aglet owner might have specified that the aglet may consume up to 10 seconds within each context visited, the context master can set a limit of 5 seconds, which will override the owner's limit.

The hierarchy of security policies defined by different principals is

$$\text{AgletManufacturer} < \text{AgletOwner} < \text{ContextMaster} < \text{DomainAuthority}$$

indicating that the domain authority sets the basic policies on the execution of aglets within a given context, which can than be refined but not overwritten by the context master, aglet owner, and aglet manufacturer.

A policy database represents the policy defined by the context master; security preferences represent the policy defined by the aglet owner.

4.3   Aglet Mobility

If the aglet manufacturer, aglet owner, context manufacturer, and context master can be properly identified—for example by their public key and with the help of a suitable certification infrastructure—the following example describes the steps it takes to create an aglet and to let it travel securely.

Before the owner can launch an aglet, the context authenticates the owner as a registered user. Within the creation request the aglet owner defines security preferences to be applied on the aglet. When the context instantiates the aglet from the corresponding Java class, it might include information about the manufacturer, owner, and the aglet's original context—that is, about itself. This information, together with the aglet code and the owner's security preferences, forms the static part of the aglet, and will be signed by the context. Thus, any receiving context can verify the integrity of the static part of the aglet.

Aglets move when they are either dispatched to a remote location or retracted from a remote location. We use the following terminology to describe an aglet's travel:

- origin context —the context in which the aglet has been created.
- destination context —the context that receives an aglet.
- current context —the context that delivers the aglet to the receiving context.

Current and destination contexts establish a secure channel between themselves. The current context protects the integrity of aglet data by computing a secure hash value that allows the destination context to perform after-the-fact detection of tampering during the aglet's transit. Unauthorized parties can be prevented from reading sensitive information held by an aglet while it is in transit between two aglet contexts if the peer contexts agree on the use of cryptography for encryption.

For each context, a security policy describes the proper communication mechanism with any peer context. For example, although an aglet might not require any security protection for its transfer to the destination context, the destination context's security policy may lay down the use of the Secure Socket Layer (SSL) protocol with client authentication.

4.4   Access to Local Resources

When an aglet enters a context, the context receives a reference to it, and the aglet resumes execution in the new context. The aglet can also obtain a reference to the context interface. An aglet uses the context to gain information about its new environment, in particular about other aglets currently active in the context in order to interact with some of them.

Contexts have to protect themselves against aglets and aglets must be precluded from interfering with each other. The aglet context establishes a reference monitor, which gives an aglet access to a resource only if it complies with the access control policy instated by the context master. Thus a context establishes a realm of services wherein a common security policy governs each agent's access rights.

The master of the context configures authorization policies for incoming aglets. In general, there is the following hierarchy of authorization policies:

- general level for an unauthenticated manufacturer,
- organization level for an unauthenticated owner, and
- per-aglet level otherwise.

In addition, authorization may be given with respect to computing power, occupancy level, organizational affiliation, pricing, code certification, or the type of aglet (such as a game or search aglet).

According to a security policy defined using this hierarchy, the reference monitor of an aglet context might give permission to obtain file information; to read, write or delete local files; to connect to a network port on the origin context or to any other context; to load a library; or to create a pop-up window. These resources are taken from the Java model. In an aglet system, there are additional resources for such things as creating new aglets, cloning a specified aglet, and dispatching or disposing of an aglet.

Because an aglet carries the security preferences of its owner, it usually includes rules that govern its consent for cooperation. However, the aglet has to rely on the context for compliance. The aglet's security preferences describe who and under which circumstances the context or another aglet may dispose of, deactivate, clone, dispatch, or retract the aglet. The preferences may further define which other aglets may call which of its methods.

5   Security Architecture

The security architecture implements the security model by providing a set of components and their interfaces. In this section, we introduce two components of the aglets security architecure, the policy database of the context master and the preferences of the aglet owner. Because both context master and aglet owner have their own specific interests concerning what an aglet should be able to do, both may want to restrict its capabilities. Such restrictions might apply to either accessing the local resources of a context or offering services to other aglets. The policy database and security preferences therefore constitute powerful elements in introducing security into the Aglets Workbench.

Any useful mobile agent system must implement general and flexible security policies. Our model simplifies the administration of these policies by introducing the notion of roles, namely, the manufacturer, owner, master, and authority principals. In the following, we describe a language for defining policies using the concepts presented in our security model, and show how a context master and an aglet owner can use it to define their policies. The language provides named groups, composite principals (a set of principals), and a hierarchical resources with associated permissions that allow the definition of high-level authorization policies. To allow fine-grained control, a security policy consists of a set of named privileges and a mapping from principals to privileges. Furthermore, the language allows the definition of black lists that disallow aglets and contexts known not to behave well.

5.1   Authorization Language

For illustration, we define the following principals:

    manufacturer – Hermes, Athena, Cronos
    owner   – Semele, Leda
    master   – Apollo, Hades
    authority   – Zeus
    context   – Olympus, Underworld
    aglet   – Castor, Pollux

We use these names to simplify our discussion, but the real value of Olympus might be something like `atp://www.trl.ibm.co.jp` and its product name might be `ibm.aglets.tahiti.Tahiti`. The product name of aglet Castor might actually be `ibm.aglets.samples.Writer`.

Basic principals address single aglets or groups of aglets. Examples of basic principals are:

`aglet=Pollux`
    – denotes the aglet Pollux.
`owner=Semele`
    – denotes all aglets launched by Semele.
`manufacturer=Hermes`
    – denotes all aglets written by Hermes.
`context=Underworld`
    – denotes all aglets arriving directly from Underworld.
`master=Apollo`
    – denotes all aglets arriving directly from contexts mastered by Apollo.
`authority=Zeus`
    – denotes all aglets arriving directly from contexts controlled by Zeus.

A manufacturer might become authenticated by a signed Java class file. A master might become authenticated by peer authentication. The use of wild cards enables the specification of groups of contexts, for example `www.*.ibm.com` or `*.edu`.

In particular, principals that denote contexts or masters indirectly identify the context from which an aglet has arrived. By convention, when an aglet is launched, the context and master refer to the corresponding principal of the local host.

Composite principals offer a convenient way to combine privileges that must be granted to multiple principals into a single access right. Such a grouping feature considerably simplifies the security administration. Membership in a group supports the combination of various principals that should have the same access rights. For example, the following specifications combine principals of the same type into named groups and use these group names in rule definitions later:

```
GROUP AssociationOfManufacturers=Hermes,Athena
```

This rule indicates that group "Association Of Manufacturers" consists of Hermes and Athena.

```
Cronos IS_MEMBER_OF Titans
```

This rule adds Cronos to group Titans.

Three other constructors denote set difference (EXCEPT), set union (OR), and set intersection (AND). Set difference is useful for handling exceptions, such as a privilege that should be given to a group except a certain user.

The following are examples of these constructions:

```
owner=Leda OR context=Underworld
```
– any aglet owned by Leda or arriving from context Underworld.
```
owner=Semele AND context=Underworld
```
– any aglet owned by Semele and arriving from Underworld.
```
manufacturer=AssociationOfManufacturers EXCEPT manufacturer=
Titans
```
– any aglet written by any member of "Association Of Manufacturers" except those written by members of group Titans.
```
owner=Semele EXCEPT manufacturer=Cronos
```
– any aglet launched by Semele but not written by Cronos.

Privileges Privileges define the capabilities of executing code by setting access restrictions and limits on resource consumption. A privilege is a resource, such as a local file, together with appropriate permissions such as read, write, or execute in the case of the local file. Our security architecture currently considers the following resource types:

```
File     – files in the local file system
Net      – network access
Awt      – the local window system
System   – any kind of system resources, such as memory and CPUs
QoP      – quality of protection
Context  – resources of the context
Aglet    – resources of the aglet
```

Resources are structured hierarchically. Thus, permissions can be given to a set of resources or even to a complete resource type, for example universal file access. An example with a simple hierarchy is the resource type File:

```
File                    – all files
File /tmp/sample.txt    – the file /tmp/sample.txt
```

Net access is a more elaborated resource. Our authorization language lets you distinguish among different protocols (for example, TCP and HTTP) and to select ports or port ranges to build resources:

```
Net                    – any kind of networking
Net TCP                – any kind of TCP connections
Net TCP host           – TCP connections to host
Net TCP host port      – TCP connections to host but only on port
```

Each resource also has a corresponding set of permissions. The permissions for networks are send, receive, any, connect, and accept.

The services provided by the aglet context are also subject to control. The context provides methods to create, retract, and activate aglets; to send or receive messages to/from other aglets; to obtain aglet proxies, the hosting URL, audio clips, and images; and to get or set the properties of the context. The following are example privileges:

```
Context AGLET retract
```
    – the aglet can retract any aglet in the context.
```
Context AGLET owner=Leda retract
```
    – the requester of method retractAglet can retract the specified aglet
      if the owner of the retracted aglet is Leda.
```
Context PROPERTY origin get
```
    – the aglet can retrieve property origin of the context.
```
Context MESSAGE subscribe
```
    – the aglet can subscribe to messages.

Combining resources with permissions, privileges are defined as follows:

```
File /tmp read,write
```
    – the aglet is allowed to read and write from tmp.
```
Net TCP Underworld 930-933 NOT connect
```
    – the aglet cannot connect to context Underworld using TCP on ports
      930-933. (Note that this privilege expresses negative permission.)
```
System LIBRARY ibm.db2.info
```
    – the aglet can load library ibm.db2.info.
```
System MAX_MEMORY 12
```
    – the aglet may not allocate more than 12 Mbytes of memory.
```
System MAX_DISK_SPACE 200
```
    – the aglet may not consume more than 200 Kbytes of disk space.
```
AWT Top_level_windows 1
```
    – the aglet can create one top-level window.

Our authorization language also introduces a special permission called enter, which allows an aglet to enter the context if granted. Used as a negative permission, it can exclude certain aglets from executing in that context (again, the idea of a black list).

5.2   Context Master Policy Database

The context master defines the security policy for aglet contexts under its control. This policy defines the actions an aglet can take. In the policy database, the context master combines principals that denote aglet groups and privileges into rules. The syntactic form of a rule is

$$\langle\text{label}\rangle: \langle\text{principal}\rangle \rightarrow \langle\text{privileges}\rangle$$

When an aglet matches multiple principals, we say that a "consensus voting rule" combines the policies for those principals. In other words, a negative rule rejects the request. The contents of a policy database might then look like this:

```
TRUSTED:
 manufacturer=Athena OR master=Hades  ->
 File /tmp read,write
 Net TCP Underworld accept
 Top_level_windows 3
 Aglet owner=Leda retract
GUEST:
 manufacturer=Hermes ->
 Net message Olympus receive
 Top_level_windows 1
 Aglet Property get,set
REJECT:
 manufacturer=Hermes,Titans  ->
 Context NOT enter
```

Note that none of the aglets mapping into the Reject group will be allowed to enter the context because they do not have the necessary **enter** privilege.

5.3   Aglet Owner Preferences

The aglet owner has the opportunity to establish a set of security preferences that will be honored by the contexts the aglet might visit. Preference combines context groups and privileges into rules. The syntactic form of a rule is

$$\langle\text{label}\rangle: \langle\text{context\_group\_definition}\rangle \rightarrow \langle\text{privileges}\rangle$$

The following list defines the set of methods on aglets that an owner can restrict:

- clone/deactivate/dispatch/retract/dispose
- get AgletClassName / AgletContext / CodeBase / Identifier / Itinerary / MessageManager / Property / PropertyKeys / Text
- send Message
- set Itinerary/Property/Text
- subscribe/unsubscribe (all) messages

These actions can be requested by the aglet itself or by other actions via the AgletProxy. The following are examples of security preferences:

```
context=Olympus EXCEPT master=Apollo -> ITINERARY set
```
    – the aglet's itinerary might be changed at context Olympus but only
    if this context is not mastered by Apollo.

```
master=Hades -> MESSAGE welcome subscribe
```
    – at all contexts mastered by Hades, the aglet might subscribe to mes-
    sages of kind `welcome`.

```
-> aglet=Pollux OR owner=Leda AGLET dispose
```
    – at any context the aglet might only be disposed of by aglet Pollux
    or any other aglet owned by Leda.

Allowances are preferences dealing with the consumption of resources such as CPU time or memory. They can be local, concerning only the current context, or global and thus apply to the set of all hosts visited. A global allowance restraining an aglet's actions over its lifetime has the nice property that it effectively limits the agent owner's liability [12]. Aglets can split up common allowances to be shared in groups. The allowance defines a maximum age or size, and indicates whether new aglets can be created. In the case of aglet creation or cloning, the allowance must be divided.

6   Conclusions

Like any other downloadable and executable code, mobile agents are a potential threat to a system. But they are also exposed to threats by their hosting system, a situation not currently dealt with in traditional security systems. It is our belief that applications based on aglets will be widely accepted only if users are convinced that the security services provided can cope with both kinds of threats.

Our security model for aglets is a first step toward alleviating these threats. The model clearly defines the principals within an aglet system with respect to their responsibilities (liabilities) and interests. The model explains how aglets migrate and depicts their access to local resources. Thus it serves as a reference for a corresponding security architecture. We introduced two elements of the security architecture, the policy database and owner-specified preferences, and demonstrated how security-unaware aglets are controlled by their use.

Our current work adresses the aglet security API that will enable aglet application developers to enforce their own security—so that an aglet can, for example, control access to its own data or audit its own security-relevant activities. Such security-aware aglets could implement, say, the secure KQML, as proposed by Thirunavukkasu et al [13], using the offered API primitives. The API design takes into account the security features added to the Java Developer's Kit Version 1.1 and subsequent versions. In particular, protection domains and a uniform way to access user identities that were established in multiple ways have been proposed [14]. This may ease the implementation of the aglet security API. However, to prevent denial-of-service attacks and thus to implement the observance of allowances, the context must monitor resource consumption. This may not be possible without also changing the Java virtual machine.

Although our authorization language is already quite expressive, we will extend it to support contextual information, such as aglet history and time, in access decisions. For example, a policy that allows network access only if the aglet has not previously accessed the file system certainly allows network permission to be given to a larger group of aglets.

We have not resolved how to protect an aglet's internal state against snooping and tampering, and a generic solution to this problem is still a very challenging research topic. However, there are security mechanisms today for limited mobile agent applications, and more will be developed soon. Proposals for such mechanisms were discussed recently at a DARPA Workshop on Foundations for Secure Mobile Code [15]. Our strategy is to provide a well-defined and rich set of security services within the Aglets Workbench that will enable the implementation of these mechanisms to better protect an aglet from a malicious host.

Acknowledgments

The article was originally puplished in IEEE Internet Computing Vol. 1, No. 4: July/August 1997, pp. 68-77. This latter version contains corrections to a few minor errors in the original publication. Note that the Aglet API described in this paper was adapted to the Java AWT 1.1 event model when AWB Alpha5 was released. However, this change does not invalidate the Aglet security model presented.

References

1. J.J. Ordille. When agents roam, who can you trust?. *Proc. First Conf. on Emerging Technologies and Applications in Communications* (etaCOM), http://etacom.org/, May 1996.
2. W.M. Farmer, J.D. Guttman, and V. Swarup. Security for Mobile Agents: Issues and Requirements. *Proc. 19th National Information Systems Security Conference (NISSC 96)*, 1996, pp. 591-597.
3. R.S. Gray. Agent Tcl: A flexible and secure mobile-agent system. In M. Diekhans and M. Roseman, editors, *Fourth Annual Tcl/Tk Workshop (TCL 96)*, 1996, pp. 9-23.
4. J. Tardo and L. Valente. Mobile Agent Security and Telescript. Proc. IEEE CompCon 96, IEEE Computer Society Press, Los Alamitos, Calif., 1996.
5. D.B. Lange and M. Oshima.   Java Agent API: Programming and Deploying Aglets with Java.   to be published by Addison-Wesley, Fall 1997; a working draft "Programming Mobile Agents in Java" is available at http://www.trl.ibm.co.jp/aglets/aglet-book/index.html.
6. B. Sommers,   Agents: Not Just for Bond Anymore.   *JavaWorld*, http://www.javaworld.com/javaworld/jw-04-1997/jw-04-agents.html, April 1997.
7. B.   Venners.   The   Architecture   of   Aglets   *JavaWorld*, http://www.javaworld.com/javaworld/jw-04-1997/jw-04-hood.html, April 1997.
8. B. Venners. "Solve Real Problems with Aglets, a Type of Mobile Agent. *JavaWorld*, http://www.javaworld.com/javaworld/jw-05-1997/jw-05-hood.html, May 1997.

9. D.B. Lange. Java Aglet Application Programming Interface (J-AAPI). White paper
   - draft no. 2, http://www.trl.ibm.co.jp/aglets/JAAPI-whitepaper.html.
10. D. Chess et al. Itinerant Agents for Mobile Computing. *IEEE Personal Communications*, Vol. 2, No. 5, Oct. 1995, pp. 34-49.
11. D.   Chess.   Things   that   Go   Bump   in   the   Net.
    http://www.research.ibm.com/massive/bump.html, 1995.
12. H. Peine and T. Stolpmann. The Architecture of the Ara Platform for Mobile
    Agents. *Proc. First International Workshop on Mobile Agents (MA'97)*, 1997, Lecture
    Notes in Computer Science No. 1219, Springer, pp. 50-61.
13. C. Thirunavukkarasu, T. Finin, and J. Mayfield. Secret Agents - A Security Architecture for the KQML Agent Communication Lanaguage. *Proc. Intelligent Information Agents Workshop* held in conjunktion with Fourth Int'l Conf. Information and
    Knowledge Management CIKM 95, Baltimore, Dec. 1995.
14. L. Gong. New Security Architectural Directions for Java. *Proc. IEEE CompCon
    97*, IEEE Computer Society Press, Los Alamitos, Calif., 1997, pp. 97-102.
15. DARPA   Workshop   on   Foundations   for   Secure   Mobile   Code.
    http://www.cs.nps.navy.mil/research/languages/wkshp.html,   Monterey,   Calif.,
    26–28 March 1997.

Signing, Sealing, and Guarding Java™ Objects

Li Gong and Roland Schemers

JavaSoft, Sun Microsystems,Inc.
901 San Antonio Road, CA 94303, USA
gong,schemers@eng.sun.com

Abstract. Many secure applications are emerging using the Java™ language and running on the Java platform. In dealing with Java security issues, especially when building secure mobile agents on the Java platform, we inevitably depend on the underlying object orientation, such as data encapsulation and type safety.

In this paper, we describe three new constructs for signing, sealing (encrypting), and guarding Java objects. These constructs enrich the existing Java security APIs so that a wide range of security-aware applications can be significantly easier to build.

1 Introduction

Many interesting applications are being built using the Java [5,6] language on the Java programming platform. The typical application is built using the Java™ Development Kit (JDK, from JavaSoft, Sun Microsystems), which provides not only the Java virtual machine (JVM) and tools such as the compiler `javac`, but also a set of standard libraries or application programming interfaces (APIs) that simplify the development work.

Through the JVM and these APIs, especially the `java.security` package, the base platform provides a consistent security model that supports policy-based, configurable, extensible, and fine-grained access control [4].

On the Java platform, to protect crucial resources such as the file system or network access, we use a protection system that is programmed in the Java language. Therefore, we inevitably depend on the underlying object orientation, such as data encapsulation, object name space partition, and type safety. This dependence is also evident in the protection of the runtime's internal state, which is often represented and maintained as Java objects.

When building distributed Java applications that span across multiple Java virtual machines, for example, using the Java Remote Method Invocation package (RMI), it is sometimes convenient or even necessary to protect the state of an object for integrity and confidentiality. These security requirements exist when concerned objects are inside a runtime system (e.g., in memory), in transit (e.g., stored in IP packets), or stored externally (e.g., saved on disk).

G. Vigna (Ed.): Mobile Agents and Security
LNCS 1419, pp. 206–216, 1998. © Springer–Verlag Berlin Heidelberg 1998

In this paper, we describe a few new constructs for signing, sealing (encrypting), and guarding Java objects. These constructs enrich the existing Java security APIs so that a wide range of security-aware applications can be significantly easier to build.

Classes java.security.SignedObject and java.security.GuardedObject are part of JDK1.2, the forthcoming Java™ Development Kit, while class javax.crypto.SealedObject is included in JCE1.2, the forthcoming Java™ Cryptography Extension.

Note that object signing is different from code signing, a feature in JDK1.1.x, Netscape Navigator 4.x, and Microsoft Internet Explorer 4.x. Code signing facilitates the authentication of static code (bytecode in the case of Java technology, native code in the case of Microsoft's Authenticode), while object signing deals with objects that may represent a complex transaction application complete with active state information.

In the rest of the paper, we describe each of the three new features in more detail. For each feature, we discuss the motivation, the design in terms of APIs, and performance as appropriate. We also give sample code to show how these features can be used. We conclude the paper with a summary and future directions.

2   Signing Java Objects

This class is an essential building block for other security primitives. Potential applications of a SignedObject include the following.

- A SignedObject can be used internally to any Java runtime as an unforgeable authorization token – one that can be passed around without the fear that the token can be maliciously modified without being detected.
- A SignedObject can be transmitted across machines (JVMs) and its authenticity can still be verified, assuming that the underlying digital signature algorithm is not compromised.
- A SignedObject can be used to sign and serialize an object for storage outside the Java runtime (e.g., storing critical access control data on disk). One possible application would be to restart a JVM from a previously saved state, where the authenticity of the state is provided by the SignedObject.
- A series of nested SignedObject can be used to construct a logical sequence of signatures, resembling a chain of authorization and delegation.

A SignedObject contains the signed object, which must be Serializable, and its signature.

Informally speaking, a Serializable object is an object that implements the Serializable interface, so that it supports readObject() and writeObject() method calls that convert an object's in memory representation to and from an "on-the-wire" format that can be transmitted via input and output streams provided on the Java plafform.

SignedObject and SealedObject

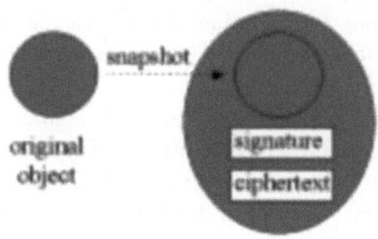

Fig. 1. Signed and Sealed Objects

If the signature is not null, it contains a valid digital signature of the signed object, as illustrated in Figure 1.

The underlying signing algorithm can be, among others, the NIST standard DSA, using DSA and SHA-1. The algorithm is specified using the same convention for signatures, such as "SHA-1/DSA". Sun's JDK always has a built-in implementation of DSA and SHA-1.

The signed object is a "deep copy" (in serialized form) of an original object. Once the copy is made, further manipulation of the original object has no side effect on the copy. In fact, a `SignedObject` is immutable.

2.1 API Design

The signature of the class is as follows. For brevity, we do not list exception declarations.

```
public SignedObject(Serializable object, PrivateKey signingKey,
                    Signature signingEngine)

public final void sign(PrivateKey signingKey,
                       Signature signingEngine);

public final Object getContent();
public final byte[] getSignature();
public final String getAlgorithm();
public final boolean verify(PublicKey verificationKey,
                            Signature verificationEngine);
```

It is intended that this class can be subclassed in the future to allow multiple signatures on the same signed object. In that case, existing method calls in this base class will be fully compatible in semantics. In particular, any get method will return the unique value if there is only one signature, and will return an arbitrary one from the set of signatures if there is more than one signature.

2.2   Performance

As part of development, we measured the performance by running the latest in-house built of JDK1.2beta on a 166MHz Sun Sparc Ultra-1 running Solaris 2.5.1.

The performance of `SignedObject` depends on how fast object serialization can be done, and how fast the underlying signature algorithm runs. We first run 1000 rounds, with 512-bit DSA key. The numbers are record in Table 1, time in milliseconds,

object size	serialization	signing	verification
		512-bit SHA-1/DSA	
10 bytes	0ms	25ms	43ms
100 bytes	0ms	26ms	44ms
10K bytes	1ms	134ms	153ms
100K bytes	9ms	1119ms	1138ms

Table 1. Performance of SignedObject (09/05/97)

Note that as object size increases, the increase in times for signing and verification can be accounted for by the increased input size to the hash algorithm SHA-1. Note that the object size includes both code size and data size, but is dominated by data size in our experiment. The simple timer using `System.currentTimeMillis()` apparently does not have sufficient precision to measure serialization time when the object size is under 1K bytes.

We repeated the measurement with 1024-bit DSA keys, with the result in Table 2 below.

object size	serialization	signing	verification
		1024-bit SHA-1/DSA	
10 bytes	0ms	80ms	151ms
100 bytes	0ms	83ms	157ms
10K bytes	1ms	189ms	260ms
100K bytes	9ms	1168ms	1237ms

Table 2. Performance of SignedObject (09/05/97)

2.3   Application Examples

The underlying signing algorithm is designated by a Signature parameter to the sign and verify method calls. A typical usage for signing is the following:

```
Signature signingEngine =
        Signature.getInstance(algorithm, provider);
SignedObject so = new SignedObject(myobject,
                                   privatekey, signingEngine);
```

A typical usage for verification is the following (having received `SignedObject so`):

```
Signature verificationEngine =
        Signature.getInstance(algorithm, provider);
if (so.verify(publickey, verificationEngine))
   try {
       Object myobj = so.getContent();
   } catch (ClassNotFoundException e) {};
```

Obviously, for verification to succeed, the specified public key must be the public key corresponding to the private key used to generate the signature.

Since `getContent()` in a sense loses typing information by returning an object of the type `Object`, we expect that signed object will be used between collaborating parties, so that the correct casting can be done. For example, the above code can be changed as follows:

```
String myobject = new String(''Greetings.'');
SignedObject so = new SignedObject(myobject);
...
if (so.verify(publickey, verificationEngine))
   try {
       String myobj = (String) so.getContent();
   } catch (ClassNotFoundException e) {};
```

In fact, it is probably more common to subclass `SignedObject` so that the correct casting is performed inside the subclass, so that static typing information is better preserved.

Note that there is no need to initialize the signing or verification engine, as it will be re-initialized inside the `verify` method.

More importantly, for flexibility reasons, `verify` allows customized signature engines, which can implement signature algorithms that are not installed formally as part of a cryptography provider. However, it is crucial that the programmer writing the verifier code be aware what `Signature` engine is being used, as its own implementation of the verify method is invoked to verify a signature. In other words, a malicious Signature may choose to always return true on verification in an attempt to bypass security check. It is for similar reasons that `verify` in the `SignedObject` class is final.

3   Sealing Java Objects

This class enables a programmer to create an object and protect its confidentiality with a cryptographic algorithm.

Given any Serializable object, one can create a `SealedObject` that embeds in its content the original object, in serialized format (i.e., a "deep copy"). Then, a cryptographic algorithm, such as DES, can be applied to the content to protect its confidentiality. The encrypted content can later be decrypted with the corresponding algorithm using the correct decryption key.

After decryption, the original content can be obtained in object form through deserialization. The content, while encrypted, is not available to anyone who does not possess the correct decryption key, assuming that the cryptosystem is secure.

This class is very similar to `SignedObject`, except that the former provides confidentiality while the latter provides integrity only. The two classes can be used together to provide both confidentiality and integrity. (Although the two classes can be combined into one class, keep them separate is desirable as they are subject to different U.S. export rules.) Since blindly signing encrypted data is sometimes dangerous, we recommend that a `SignedObject` is created first and signed, and then is used to create a `SealedObject`.

3.1   API Design

The signature of the class is as follows. Again we leave out exception declarations.

```
public SealedObject(Serializable object, Cipher c);
```

```
public final Object getContent(Cipher c);
```

3.2   Application Examples

A typical usage is illustrated with the following code segments. First we generate a DES key and initialize the DES cipher.

```
KeyGenerator keyGen = KeyGenerator.getInstance("DES");
SecretKey desKey = keyGen.generateKey();
Cipher cipher = Cipher.getInstance("DES");
cipher.init(Cipher.ENCRYPT_MODE, desKey);
```

Now we create a `SealedObject` and encrypt it. Note that the `Cipher` object must be fully initialized with the correct algorithm, key, padding scheme, etc., before being applied to a `SealedObject`.

```
String s = new String("Greetings");
SealedObject so = new SealedObject(s, cipher);
```

Later, we decrypt and retrieve the original object.

```
cipher.init(Cipher.DECRYPT_MODE, desKey);
try {
    String s = (String) so.getContent(cipher);
} catch (ClassNotFoundException e) {};
```

Once more, `SealedObject` can be subclassed to provide better static typing information.

The performance of `SealedObject` is similar to that of `SignedObject` in that it depends on the serialization time and the speed of the underlying cryptographic algorithm. We do not report the speed of DES or triple-DES in this paper.

4   Guarding Java Objects

A `GuardedObject` is an object that is used to protect access to another object. Once an object is encapsulated by a `GuardedObject`, access to that object is controlled by the `getObject` method. The `getObject` method controls access to the object by invoking the `checkGuard` method on the `Guard` object that is guarding access. If access is not allowed, a `SecurityException` will be thrown. This is illustrated in Figure 2, where solid lines represent method calls and dotted lines represent object references.

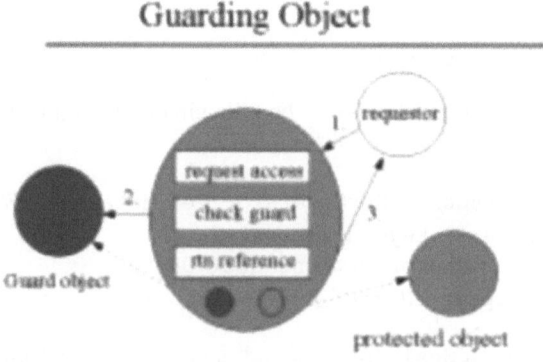

Fig. 2. Guard and GuardedObject

Here, when a requestor asks for a guarded object, the guard object is consulted, and the reference to the object is returned to the requestor if the guard object allows it.

One major motivation for this new class is that there are often application scenarios, where the supplier of a resource is not in the same execution context (such as a thread) as the consumer of that resource. In this case, a security check within the security context of the supplier is often inappropriate, because the check should occur within the security context of the consumer.

For example, when a file server thread responds to a request to open a file for read, and this request comes from a different environment, the decision to supply the file must take into account information of the requestor. However, it is sometimes inconvenient for the consumer to provide with the supplier with such information due to one of the following reasons.

- The consumer program does not always know, a priori, what information should be provided (this is quite possible in a dynamically changing environment), and it is undesirable (e.g., for performance reasons) to engage in a dialog or negotiation for each request.
- The consumer regards information of its execution environment too security sensitive to pass on to another party.
- There is too much information or data to pass on.

To make access control in these situations more uniform and easier to program, the basic idea of `GuardedObject` is that the supplier of the resource can create an object representing the resource, create a `GuardedObject` that embeds the resource object inside, and then provide the `GuardedObject` to the consumer. In creating the `GuardedObject`, the supplier also specifies a `Guard` object such that anyone (including the consumer) can only obtain the resource object if certain (e.g., security) checks inside the `Guard` are satisfied. `Guard` is an interface so any object can choose to become a `Guard`.

There are several ways to view the benefits of using `GuardedObject`.

- One can correctly embed the protection mechanism together with the protected object so that access to the object is guaranteed to occur in a context where the protection mechanism would allow it.
- One can delay access control decision from time of request to time of actual access, thus simplifying server programs.
- One can replace often used access control lists with object stores and simply store a set of `GuardedObject`.
- A guarded object class itself does not need to know its own protection semantics, as long as it is protected within a `GuardedObject` and the `Guard` implements the correct security checks.
- The same programming pattern can be used to encapsulate protection mechanisms for an object, which can differ for its different method invocations, all inside a `Guard`.

Note that, because the built-in base class `java.security.Permission` implements the `Guard` interface, all permissions of this type, including all permissions (on file, network, runtime, and other resources) defined in JDK, are instantly usable as `Guard`.

4.1 API Design

The interface `Guard` contains only one method.

```
public abstract void checkGuard(Object object);
```

The signature of the `GuardedObject` class is the following.

```
public GuardedObject(Object object, Guard guard);
```

```
public Object getObject();
```

4.2 Application Examples

Let us start by showing how to use `GuardedObject` to encapsulate an object's protection semantics completely inside an appropriate `Guard`. We use the class `java.io.FileInputStream` as an example, and suppose we create such a stream giving a file name, as in the following code.

```
FileInputStream fis = new FileInputStream("/a/b/c");
```

The implementation of this constructor must be aware that a security check needs to be done, must understand what sort of check is appropriate, and also must sprinkle all constructors with the same (or similar) checks.

We can rewrite this class as follows. First, we note that we have made class `java.security.Permission` a `Guard` by adding a new method that is defined as follows.

```
public abstract Permission implements Guard {
    ...
    public void checkGuard() {
        AccessController.checkPermission(this);
    }
}
```

The above implementation ensures that a proper access control check takes place within the consumer context, when access to the stream is first requested.

Now, the provider side of the code can be simply as follows:

```
FileInputStream fis = new FileInputStream("/a/b/c");
FilePermission p = new FilePermission("/a/b/c", "read");
GuardedObject g = new GuardedObject(fis, p);
```

After object g is passed to the consumer, the following code will recover the `FileInputStream`, but only if the consumer is permitted to obtain read access to file "/a/b/c".

```
FileInputStream fis = (FileInputStream) g.getObject();
```

Note that the implementation of `FileInputStream` itself need not be security aware (as long as it is always protected by a `GuardedObject`). The above design does not further perform security checks once a `FileInputStream` is returned to the consumer, and this is the same behavior implemented in the `FileInputStream` class today. Note that this is just an example. There is no plan to massively change such classes in JDK to use `GuardedObject`.

Another potential application is in the implementation of deferred object requests in Java IDL or a similar product. The obvious implementation of this CORBA-style API is to spin a separate thread in the ORB implementation to actually make the (deferred) request. This new thread is created by the ORB implementation and so any information about which code originated the request is lost, making security check difficult if not impossible. With this new feature, the new thread can simply return a properly guarded object, forcing a security check to happen when the requestor attempts to retrieve the object.

It is worth emphasizing that `Guard` and `GuardedObject` can be extended (subclassed) to implement arbitrary guarding semantics. For example, the guard can check for signature information on class files, resulting in a design that is similar to the Gate pattern and the Permit class in the Java Electronic Commerce Framework [2].

As another example, we can radically rewrite the `FileInputStream` class as follows. For every constructor, if it does not take a `Guard` object g as parameter, a suitable `Guard` is automatically generated. For every access method (such as `read(bytes)`), the uniform security check in the form of `g.checkGuard()` is invoked first.

As with the case of `SignedObject`, subclassing `GuardedObject` can better preserve static typing information, where the base classes are intended to be used between cooperating parties so that the receiving party should know what type of object to expect.

5   Related Work

As we mentioned earlier, the concept of object signing described in this paper differs that of code signing (in Authenticode and signed applet) in that the latter signs and authenticates static code while the former signs and authenticates objects with states.

Earlier work on secure network object using Modula-3 and Oblique [7] is related to `SignedObject` and `SealedObject` in that there was the high-level abstraction of secure remote object invocation. However, this abstraction was implemented by establishing a secure communication channel between the two end points and using this channel to send plain object and data. In other words, there was no explicit concept of signing and sealing objects directly.

The `Guard` concept in `GuardedObject` is similar to the well-known guard concept in programming language research, and has been used elsewhere, albeit mostly in specialized forms (e.g., in the Gated Object model [2]) or as a pattern

[1]. Its combination with `java.security.Permission` is a novel feature that makes `Guard` very powerful for access control on the Java platform.

6 Summary and Conclusion

In this paper, we have described three new constructs for signing, sealing (encrypting), and guarding Java objects. Given the object orientation in the Java language, these constructs enrich the existing Java security APIs so that security-aware applications can be much easier to build. Our testing and performance show that the constructs are practical and usable in commercial products.

For future direction of Java security, we are investigating user authentication, secure communication, and other distributed security features [3]. We expect to report those findings later.

References

1. E. Gamma, R. Helm, R. Johnson, and J. Vlissides. *Design Patterns*. Addison-Wesley, Menlo Park, California, 1995.
2. T.C. Goldstein. The Gateway Security Model in the Java Electronic Commerce Framework. In *Proceedings of Financial Cryptography 97*, pages 291–304, Anguilla, British Virgin Island, February 1997. To be published by Springer Verlag.
3. L. Gong. Java Security: Present and Near Future. *IEEE Micro*, 17(3):14–19, May/June 1997.
4. L. Gong, M. Mueller, H. Prafullchandra, and R. Schemers. Going Beyond the Sandbox: An Overview of the New Security Architecture in the Java™ Development Kit 1.2. In *Proceedings of the USENIX Symposium on Internet Technologies and Systems*, pages 103–112, Monterey, California, December 1997.
5. J. Gosling, Bill Joy, and Guy Steele. *The Java Language Specification*. Addison-Wesley, Menlo Park, California, August 1996.
6. T. Lindholm and F. Yellin. *The Java Virtual Machine Specification*. Addison-Wesley, Menlo Park, California, 1997.
7. L. van Doorn, M. Abadi, M. Burrows, and E. Wobber. Secure Network Objects. In *Proceedings of the IEEE Symposium in Security and Privacy*, pages 211–221, Oakland, California, May 1996.

The Safe-Tcl Security Model

John K. Ousterhout, Jacob Y. Levy, and Brent B. Welch

Sun Microsystems Laboratories
2550 Garcia Avenue, MS UMTV-29-232
Mountain View, CA 94043-1100

Abstract. Safe-Tcl is a mechanism for controlling the execution of programs written in the Tcl scripting language. It allows untrusted scripts (applets) to be executed while preventing damage to the environment or leakage of private information. Safe-Tcl uses a padded cell approach: each applet is isolated in a safe interpreter where it cannot interact directly with the rest of the application. The execution environment of the safe interpreter is controlled by trusted scripts running in a master interpreter. Safe-Tcl provides an alias mechanism that allows applets to request services from the master interpreter in a controlled fashion. Safe-Tcl allows a variety of security policies to be implemented within a single application, and it supports both policies that authenticate incoming scripts and those that do not.

1 Introduction

Security issues arise whenever one person invokes a program written by another person. A program usually executes with all the privileges of the user who invoked it, so the program can read and write the user's files, send electronic mail on behalf of the user, open network connections, and run other programs. If a program is malicious, it can harm the user in many ways, such as by modifying the user's files, leaking sensitive information, or crashing the user's computer.

The traditional "solution" to the security problem has been for people to avoid programs written by people they don't trust. Unfortunately, two trends are making this approach less and less practical. The first trend is an increase in information sharing between people, for example via the World Wide Web; in many cases, the creator of the information is unknown to the recipient of the information. The second trend is a blurring of the distinction between programs and data, so that the act of retrieving and viewing information can cause a program associated with the data to be executed. For example, many systems allow a floppy disk to contain a start-up program that is run silently whenever the disk is inserted into a drive. Another example is the Java[TM] [1] language [1], which allows programs to be associated with Web pages: when such a page is viewed, the program is executed to provide special interactive effects such as animations. As a result of these trends, it is becoming more and more difficult for users to tell when they are running a program or who wrote the program.

---

1. Sun, Sun Microsystems, Java, and the Sun logo are trademarks or registered trademarks of Sun Microsystems Inc. in the United States and other countries.

Safe-Tcl makes it safe for people to run programs written in the Tcl scripting language [8][11] without knowing their origin or trustworthiness. Safe-Tcl avoids potential security problems by restricting the behavior of programs so that they have fewer capabilities than the users who invoke them. The privileges granted to a program can be adjusted to match the program's trustworthiness. Programs of unknown origin should not be trusted at all, so they run with very few privileges. If the author of a program can be authenticated, and if that author is partially or fully trusted, the program can execute with greater privileges. The mechanisms for authentication and granting of privilege are automated, so applications such as Web browsers can use Safe-Tcl without involving the user.

Safe-Tcl is based on an approach we call *padded cells*. In this approach, untrusted scripts (applets) are executed in separate environments that are isolated from the trusted portions of the application in which the applets execute. The features available to the applet can be controlled by the trusted portions of the application. The implementation of Safe-Tcl is based on two basic facilities: *safe interpreters*, which provide restricted virtual machines for executing applets, and *aliases*, which are used by applets to request services from the trusted portions of the application in a controlled fashion. The alias mechanism makes it possible to provide restricted access to features that are essentially unsafe, such as file or socket access. Different security policies may be implemented by providing different sets of aliases in a safe interpreter.

Safe interpreters and aliases function much like the kernel space/user space mechanism that has been used for protection in operating systems for several decades. Safe interpreters correspond to the address spaces for user-level programs, and aliases correspond to kernel calls.

The Safe-Tcl security model has two particular strengths:

- It separates untrusted code from trusted code, with clear and simple boundaries between environments having different security properties.
- Safe-Tcl does not prescribe any particular security policy, but rather provides mechanisms for implementing a variety of security policies. Different organizations can implement different security policies depending on their needs, and a single application can use different policies for different applets. In particular, it is possible to implement highly restrictive security policies for scripts of unknown origin, as well as less restrictive policies for scripts whose authors are known and trusted.

The rest of this paper is organized as follows. Section 2 provides background information on the Tcl scripting language. Section 3 introduces the security issues associated with executing applets. Section 4 describes the basic mechanisms of the Safe-Tcl security model, including safe interpreters and aliases. Section 5 discusses the issues in writing security policies and describes a few sample policies. Section 6 shows how authentication mechanisms can be used in Safe-Tcl, and Section 7 describes how Safe-Tcl allows a single application to support multiple applets at the same time. Section 8 describes how Safe-Tcl deals with denial-of-service attacks. Section 9 discusses the implementation status of Safe-Tcl, and Section 10 compares Safe-Tcl with other security models.

2   Overview of Tcl

Tcl is an interpreted scripting language [8][11]. Its simple syntax is based on commands made up of words, much like Unix shell programs such as sh . For example, the command

    set a 45

contains three words. The first word of each command, such as set in the example, selects a C command procedure that will carry out the command, and the other words are passed to the command procedure as arguments. The Tcl language syntax consists only of a few simple substitution and quoting rules used to parse commands. Most of the behavior of Tcl is defined by the command procedures, which are free to interpret their arguments however they like.

Tcl is embeddable and extensible. The Tcl interpreter is a C library package that can be incorporated in a variety of applications, as shown in Figure 1. Several dozen basic commands are implemented in C as part of the Tcl interpreter. Each application can define additional Tcl commands in C or C++ to augment the basic facilities provided by Tcl. Typically, an application will implement just a few Tcl commands that provide primitive access to its facilities; more complex features are created by writing Tcl scripts that combine the application's primitive features with the built-in commands.

It is also possible to create packages containing useful sets of Tcl commands implemented in C or C++ and then load these packages into any Tcl application on the fly. Tk is one such extension; it provides a collection of commands for creating graphical user interfaces.

Tcl has four properties that make it attractive as a vehicle for executing untrusted scripts:

- The language is interpreted. Since every action is already mediated, there is a natural place to add security controls.

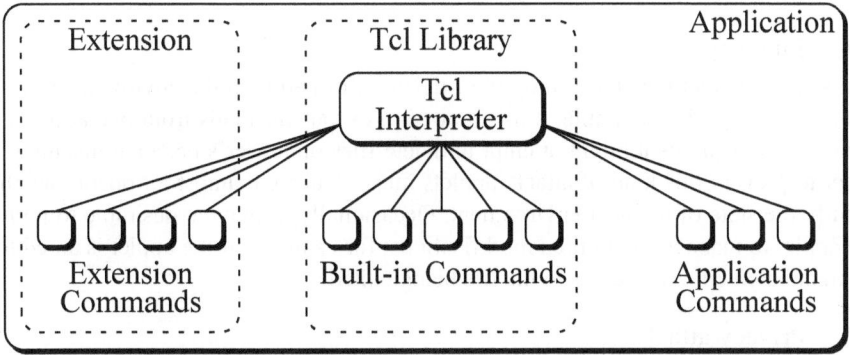

Figure 1. When an application uses Tcl it incorporates application-specific functionality into the Tcl interpreter as additional Tcl commands. The application can also load extensions dynamically to provide yet more Tcl commands.

- The language is safe with respect to memory usage: it has no pointers, array references are bounds-checked, and storage is managed automatically by the Tcl interpreter. This prevents scripts from making wild references to storage.
- Interpreters are first-class objects. An interpreter consists of a set of Tcl commands, a set of variable values, and an execution stack; it completely encapsulates the execution of a Tcl script. A single application can contain multiple interpreters that are totally disjoint from each other. This makes it possible to isolate scripts with different security properties.
- The language is command-oriented, in that the facilities available to a Tcl script are determined by the set of commands defined in its interpreter. Different interpreters can have different command sets with different security properties.

Although we will show in the remainder of this paper how to manage untrusted Tcl scripts, our work does not address security issues in C. Thus we assume that all of the C and C++ code associated with a Tcl application is trustworthy (e.g., that users have properly authenticated it and/or analyzed its security properties).

3   Security Issues

This paper envisions a security environment based on applications and applets. In this environment an untrusted program does not execute by itself; instead, it executes in conjunction with some trusted application. We use the term applet to refer to the untrusted program, and application to refer to the trusted environment in which it runs. The application provides a security model that restricts the execution of the applet. For example, the application might be a Web browser and the applet might be a program that animates the content of a Web page. Or, an application might consist of only a security model with no other functionality, and it might be used to run large "applets" that implement major applications such as spreadsheets or word processors.

The security issues associated with applets fall into three major groups: integrity attacks, privacy attacks, and denial of service attacks. These are discussed individually in the subsections below, followed by a discussion of risk management in general.

3.1   Integrity attacks

A malicious applet may try to modify or delete information in the environment in unauthorized ways. For example, it might attempt to transfer funds from one account to another in a bank, or it might attempt to delete files on a user's personal machine. In order to prevent this kind of attack, applets must be denied almost all operations that modify the state of the host environment. Occasionally, it may be desirable to permit the applet to make a few limited modifications; for example, if the applet is an editor, it might be given write access to the file being edited.

3.2   Privacy attacks

The second form of attack consists of information theft or leakage: a malicious applet may try to read private information from the host environment and transmit it to a conspirator outside the environment. Information disclosed in this way may have direct value to the recipient, such as business information that could affect the price of a company's stock, or its disclosure could damage the party from which it was taken, for example, if it describes an individual's treatment for substance abuse.

One approach to the privacy problem is to prevent applets from accessing sensitive information at all. However, this approach would also prevent applets from performing many useful functions. For example, this approach would prevent applets from helping to display, analyze, and edit sensitive information.

A more desirable approach is to give applets access to sensitive information but prevent them from transmitting the information outside the host environment. This approach is called flow control. In principle, it might seem possible for the security model to analyze the flow of information through the applet and prevent information read from sensitive sources from being written to insecure I/O ports. This might be done by analyzing the application statically to detect illegal flows. Or, it might be done using a technique called data tainting [7], in which data is tagged with information about its sensitivity. Data read from a sensitive source is tagged with a high sensitivity level, and attempts to write that data to an insecure I/O port are denied. Unfortunately, these forms of flow control are hard to implement and use. Static analysis shares many of the difficulties of program verification. Data tainting has difficulties when data from different sources are combined arithmetically or when data is used to control conditional operations. Under these conditions it is difficult to determine whether information has really flowed from one variable to another, so the result must be tainted with the highest sensitivity level of the inputs; this can lead to overclassification, where all of an application's data ends up with a high sensitivity level [3].

Safe-Tcl's approach to flow control is to implement it via access control; rather than allowing access to all objects and restricting flow, Safe-Tcl disallows combinations of accesses that could result in unsafe flow. This means that either an applet can read sensitive information or it can open external I/O ports, but not both. A given applet must choose in advance which kind of access it wishes to have, and the other form will be totally denied to it.

Privacy is often defined in terms of a firewall. For example, many companies have special firewall machines that separate their internal networks from the Internet. Information inside the firewall is considered private, and the company's security policies are designed to prevent private information from leaking outside the firewall. In the rest of this paper we will assume the existence of a firewall; an environment with no firewall can be treated as if each computer is the only computer in a private Intranet.

3.3   Denial of service

The third form of attack consists of denial of service, where the applet attempts to interfere with the normal operation of the host system. For example, it might consume all the available file space, cover the screen with windows so that the user cannot interact with any other applications, or exercise a bug to crash its application.

Denial-of-service attacks are less severe from a security standpoint than integrity or privacy attacks, yet they are harder to prevent. They are less severe because they don't do lasting damage; in the worst case, the effects can be eliminated by killing the application and freeing any extraneous resources that it allocated. In contrast, the effects of an integrity or privacy attack may be difficult to undo (e.g., if sensitive information has been leaked to a large audience its privacy can never be restored). On the other hand, it is difficult to distinguish a denial-of-service attack from acceptable behavior. For example, a perfectly legitimate attempt to write a file could consume most or all of the available file space. Or, a legitimate applet might attempt to create windows that exceed the space available on the screen (e.g., the applet may have been designed for a large screen yet be executing on a laptop with a much smaller screen). If such applets are treated as hostile then many useful forms of behavior may be prohibited.

3.4   Managing risk

It is unlikely that any security policy can completely eliminate all security threats. For example, any bug in an application gives a malicious applet the opportunity to deny service by crashing the application. In addition, there exist subtle techniques for signaling information that make it nearly impossible to implement perfect flow control for privacy [4]. Attempts to completely eliminate the risks would restrict applets to such a degree that they would not be able to perform any useful functions.

Thus, security models like Safe-Tcl do not try to eliminate security risks entirely. Instead, they attempt to reduce the risks to a manageable level, so that the benefits provided by applets are greater than the costs incurred by security attacks. For example, Safe-Tcl makes it possible to reduce the rate at which sensitive information can be transmitted outside a firewall, even though it cannot completely eliminate the threat.

4   Safe Interpreters, Aliases, and Hidden Commands

Safe-Tcl uses a padded cell approach to security: applets are executed in isolated environments where their capabilities can be restricted. Padded cells are implemented using three mechanisms. First, Safe-Tcl uses safe interpreters to isolate applets and prevent them from using any of the unsafe features of the language. Then it restores access to a restricted subset of the unsafe features using aliases and hidden commands. The rest of this section describes these three techniques in more detail.

Tcl applications that don't need to execute applets use a single Tcl interpreter that has complete access to all the capabilities of Tcl, the application, and its user. All scripts running in this interpreter must be trusted. If a Tcl application wishes to execute an applet, it uses two interpreters: a master interpreter and a safe interpreter (see Figure 2). The master interpreter retains full functionality, so only trusted scripts such as those written by the user or the application designer may execute there. The safe interpreter is used for executing the applet. All of the unsafe commands (those that could result in security compromises if misused) are made inaccessible in the safe interpreter. The disabled commands include those for accessing the file system, executing subprocesses, opening sockets, and many more (see Table 1). We refer to the commands that are left as the safe base; these commands will be available to virtually all applets in all applications.

The master interpreter in a Safe-Tcl application is much like kernel space in an operating system: it has complete access to all of the system's facilities. The safe interpret-

Commands	Functionality
open, socket	Open files and network connections.
file, glob	Create, copy, rename, and delete files and directories; query file attributes and file name space.
exec	Invoke subprocesses.
cd, pwd	Manipulate current working directory.
load	Load shared library binary into application from file.
exit	Terminate application.
source	Evaluate Tcl script file.
toplevel	Create top-level window.
send	Invoke Tcl script in another application on the same display.
clipboard, selection	Read and write selection/clipboard information.

Table 1. The Tcl and Tk commands that are not available to scripts executing in safe interpreters.

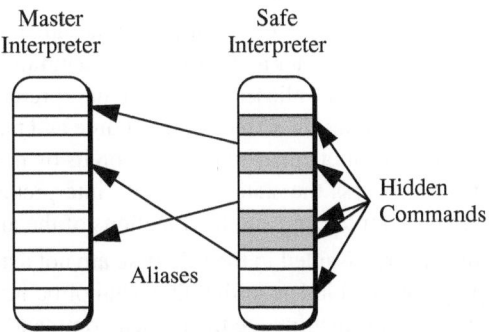

Figure 2. The basic Safe-Tcl mechanisms. Trusted scripts execute in the master interpreter while untrusted applets execute in the safe interpreter. All unsafe commands in the safe interpreter are hidden so that they cannot be invoked from the safe interpreter. Aliases provide a mechanism for the applet to request protected operations from the master. The master interpreter can invoke the hidden commands in the safe interpreter.

er in a Safe-Tcl application is similar to user space in an operating system. From user space it is not possible to access the kernel's memory, manipulate I/O devices, or have any direct communication with the outside world. Similarly, a safe interpreter is isolated from its master and cannot communicate directly with the rest of the application.

The safe base produces an interpreter that is indeed safe for executing applets, but in this state the interpreter is not very interesting because scripts running in it are completely isolated. If a script cannot access files, open sockets, or communicate with other processes, then there aren't many useful things that it can do. In fact, most of the useful things that programs do involve activities that are unsafe in the general case. In order for applets to carry out useful activities, they must have restricted access to unsafe functions. For example, it is not safe to let an applet write arbitrary files, but it probably is safe to let an applet create a single new file of limited size containing the results of its computation.

A similar situation exists in operating systems. By itself a process executing in user space cannot do anything interesting; for example, it cannot write to disk or communicate with the user. To solve this problem operating systems provide system calls, which give user processes restricted access to unsafe features. For example, a user process cannot directly write the disk, but it can invoke a system call that will write the portions of disk containing files owned by the process's user.

The alias mechanism in Safe-Tcl is analogous to system calls in operating systems. An alias is an association between a command in the safe interpreter, called the *source command* for the alias, and a command in the master interpreter, called the *target*. Whenever the source command is invoked by a script in the safe interpreter, the target command is invoked instead. The target command is typically a Tcl procedure. It receives all of the arguments from the source command and its result is returned to the safe interpreter as the result of the source command.

The master interpreter has complete control over the safe interpreter. It can read and write variables in the safe interpreter and initiate the execution of scripts in the safe interpreter. The master manages the aliases for the safe interpreter; it can create and delete aliases at any time and it defines the names of the source and target commands for each alias. The safe interpreter cannot create new aliases on its own. During the execution of an alias, the master can access the state of the safe interpreter and invoke additional scripts in the safe interpreter to carry out the functions of the alias.

The commands that are disabled in the safe base are not actually removed from the safe interpreter; they are just hidden so that they cannot be invoked by the safe interpreter. However, the master may invoke the hidden commands of the safe interpreter. This allows the master to use the commands in restricted ways. For example, Figure 3 shows an alias that allows sockets to be opened only to a pre-specified list of hosts and ports. The socket command, which is used to create network connections, is unsafe so it is hidden in the safe interpreter; the code in the figure creates a new socket command that is an alias. The alias validates the host and port, then invokes the hidden socket command in the safe interpreter. To the applet the socket command appears to work in the normal fashion except that only certain network addresses may be used. Note that two versions of socket exist in the safe interpreter: the hidden command and the alias.

```
# Create an array in which the names of elements are host
# names and the values are lists of acceptable port numbers.

set safeSockets(sage.eng) 1024
set safeSockets(sunlabs.eng) 80
set safeSockets(www.sun.com) {80 8015}
set safeSockets(bisque.eng) {3000 4000 5000}

# Create an alias that causes the AliasSocket command to be
# invoked in the master whenever socket is invoked in the safe
# interpreter.

interp alias $safe socket {} AliasSocket $safe

# Define the procedure that implements the alias.

proc AliasSocket {safe host port} {
    global safeSockets
    if {![info exists safeSockets($host)]} {
        error "Unknown host: $host"
    }
    if {[lsearch -exact $safeSockets($host) $port] < 0} {
        error "Bad port: $port"
    }
    return [interp invokehidden $safe socket $host $port]
}
```

Figure 3. When this code is executed in a master interpreter, it creates an alias that allows a safe interpreter to open sockets to a restricted set of addresses. Whenever the socket command is invoked in interpreter $safe the AliasSocket command will be invoked in the master interpreter with the name of the safe interpreter as its first argument. Thus, if the value of $safe is child, and the command "socket bisque.eng 4000" is invoked in the safe interpreter, then the command "AliasSocket child bisque.eng 4000" will be invoked in the master. The AliasSocket procedure checks to see if the host and port are among those that are allowed. If so, it invokes the hidden socket command in the safe interpreter to actually open the network connection.

Hidden commands are needed because many Tcl commands implicitly modify the interpreter in which they are invoked. For example, the socket command creates a new I/O channel object for use in transferring data over the socket. The channel is created in the interpreter where the socket command executes, so if the alias invoked socket in its own interpreter (the master) then the safe interpreter wouldn't be able to use the resulting channel. The hidden command mechanism allows the master to invoke unsafe commands in the context of the safe interpreter, so that their side effects will occur there.

5   Security Policies

A security policy in Safe-Tcl consists of the commands available in safe interpreters using the policy, including both the safe base and any aliases. One of the strengths of Safe-Tcl is that it permits a variety of security policies. The simplest security policy consists of just the safe base with no aliases at all. Most security policies will probably have a small fixed set of aliases. In an extreme case where the applet is trusted, it might be given a security policy that restores the full set of (unsafe) Tcl/Tk commands. At the other extreme, highly sensitive environments might use security policies that hide some of the commands in the safe base (such as those that provide information about the platform on which the application is running).

Why is it important to allow multiple security policies? Wouldn't it be better to have just one policy that includes all of the features that are safe for applets? Multiple security policies are needed because safe features do not compose: if feature A is safe and feature B is safe, the combination of A and B is not necessarily safe. For example, it is safe for an applet to open network connections outside the firewall as long as the applet cannot communicate with hosts inside the firewall. It is also safe for an applet to read local files, as long as this is the only communication the applet makes outside its interpreter. However, if an applet has access to both of these features then it can transmit local files outside the firewall, which is a breach of privacy.

Since safe features do not compose, no single security policy can include all of the features that are safe in isolation. Safe-Tcl encourages the development of many security policies, each tailored to support a different class of applets. For example, many policies fall into categories we refer to as Outside and Inside. An Outside policy gives an applet access to information outside the firewall, e.g., by fetching Web pages or opening sockets. However, an Outside policy must prohibit all access to sensitive information inside the firewall; otherwise, the script could leak that information outside the firewall. An Inside policy is roughly the opposite of Outside; it allows the applet to access sensitive information inside the firewall, but it must make sure that the applet cannot communicate outside the firewall. Inside policies must also limit access to read-only, so that the applet cannot corrupt data. Each one of these policies is fairly restrictive, yet each supports an interesting class of applets: Outside enables an applet to navigate the Internet on behalf of the user, while Inside allows an applet to search and analyze information inside a corporate firewall.

For example, one of the security policies we have built is called SafeSockets. It allows an applet to open two kinds of network connections. First, SafeSockets allows an applet to connect to hosts and port numbers from a fixed list of network addresses. This list includes well-known Internet sites such as popular search engines and corporate sites, and is managed by the site administrator. Second, SafeSockets allows an applet to connect back to the host from which it was downloaded. SafeSockets is a superset of the standard Java security policy, which only allows connections back to the download host. If the applet was loaded from outside the firewall, SafeSockets is an Outside policy; if the applet was loaded from inside the firewall, the policy is a combination of Inside and Outside (but in this case the applet should be trusted, otherwise it should not have been imported inside the firewall).

Another advantage of having more restrictive security policies is simplicity. If a security policy includes a large number of features, it will be difficult to analyze all of the interactions between its features to uncover security loopholes. If a policy includes only a small number of features, it will be easier to determine whether it is truly secure. Designing security policies is likely to be complicated in any case but simpler, more restrictive policies are likely to be easier to manage than larger, more feature-rich policies.

Safe-Tcl security policies are intended to be independent from applications. Each security policy is packaged as a collection of Tcl scripts that implement the policy's aliases. Policies can be distributed independently of applications and it should be possible to create policies that are useful in a variety of applications. Of course, some policies may take advantage of application-specific features that limit their use to a particular application, but it should also be possible to design application-independent policies. This makes it possible for applets to be used in a variety of applications; if security policies were associated with particular applications, then an applet would have to be coded for the security policy of a particular application and the applet would not be usable with other applications.

When an applet starts execution, its interpreter contains only the safe base plus an alias for loading security policies. The applet requests a specific security policy using the Tcl package mechanism, which invokes the alias. The master interpreter decides whether or not to permit that policy for the applet and, if the policy is permitted, creates the aliases associated with the policy. If the security policy is denied then an error is returned to the applet, which will cause it to abort in most cases. However, if the applet chooses, it can catch the error and request alternate policies or even attempt to execute with no security policy, using only the commands in the safe base.

An applet may use only a single security policy over its lifetime. Once it has successfully loaded one policy it may not load any other policy, even if it gives up the aliases of the first policy. Changing the security policy for an applet would effectively compose the features of the security policies, which is not safe.

6   Using Authentication

If the author of an applet is unknown, the receiving application must assume the worst and restrict what the applet can do. However, if the application can deduce something about the author of an applet then it may be able to grant more privileges to the applet. For example, a company might produce an officially approved set of applets for internal functions such as travel authorization and salary adjustments. If an application can determine that an applet is one of the approved ones, it can make additional security policies available to the applet. The additional policies might provide access to corporate databases associated with travel expenses and salaries, which could not be permitted to applets of unknown origin.

One of the security policies we have written is called Trusted. In this policy, the complete set of Tcl and Tk commands is reenabled, including the unsafe commands that would normally be hidden. This security policy gives applets great power, but it can only be used for applets that have been authenticated and are completely trusted.

There exist a variety of authentication mechanisms for verifying the origin of a particular piece of information (e.g., see [5]). Most techniques involve encryption of some sort. For example, one approach using public key encryption is for the creator of an applet to encrypt the applet with his or her private key and distribute the encrypted applet along with the name of the author. Before executing the applet, an application can retrieve the public key of the author whose name was attached to the applet. If the applet can be decrypted with the public key then it must have been written by the owner of the private key.

Another approach is for an organization to compute a cryptographic checksum for each of its authorized applets. This can be done using algorithms such as MD5 [9], which produce a unique identifier for a string of text. Before an application executes an applet it can recompute the checksum for the applet and compare it against a database of trusted checksums. If it matches, then the applet can be given additional privileges.

The current version of Safe-Tcl does not have built-in support for authentication, but it can be added as an extension and we plan to provide built-in support in a future release.

Authentication mechanisms can also be used to distribute new security policies. For example, the following mechanism allows an untrusted applet to carry a trusted security policy with it; when an application executes the applet, it can safely load the security policy even though it doesn't trust the applet:

1. When the security policy is created, its creator generates a cryptographic certificate for the security policy. For example, an MD5 checksum can be computed for the policy's Tcl script and encrypted with the creator's private key; the encrypted checksum plus the name of the creator form a certificate.

2. The security policy can then be distributed freely along with the certificate.

3. If an applet wishes to use that security policy, it includes the Tcl script and certificate for the policy.

4. When the applet starts executing in an application, it invokes an alias, passing it the Tcl script for the security policy and the certificate.

5. The alias verifies the authenticity of the policy by decrypting the certificate's checksum with the creator's public key, then recomputing the checksum of the Tcl script and verifying that it matches the checksum from the certificate. If the policy has been authenticated, and if the application trusts the policy's creator, the application can safely load the policy even though it doesn't trust the applet that delivered the policy.

The advantage of using authentication for security policies is that it makes it easier to distribute new security policies. For example, a corporate security authority can create new policies, generate certificates for them, and distribute the policies to applet developers. Applet developers can then use those policies and incorporate them with the applets as described above. Any application that trusts the corporate authority can immediately run applets containing the new security policies, even though it doesn't trust the applets. No changes need to be made to applications, and individual users need not install or even understand the new policies.

Even under the best of conditions, security policies are likely to be difficult to write and analyze. New policies are likely to be developed only by experts with special skills. At the same time, it is important to have a rich and constantly improving set of security policies available for use by applets. Authentication makes it possible for a variety of applets and applications to take advantage of new policies developed by experts.

7   Multiple Applets

The Safe-Tcl model permits more than one safe interpreter in a single application, each with its own security policy. A single master interpreter can provide different sets of aliases for each safe interpreter, and it can use the alias mechanism to implement communication between the safe interpreters. This mechanism could be used to provide meeting places for applets, where many independent applets exist simultaneously and communicate with each other. One possible example is an electronic marketplace, where individuals send agents (in the form of applets) to buy and sell goods.

Special care is required when implementing communication between applets, since this effectively composes their security policies. For example, if one applet is using an Inside security policy and another is using an Outside security policy, it is not safe to allow them to communicate. If they could communicate, the Inside applet could read internal information and pass it to the Outside applet, which could then leak the information outside the firewall. Even communication among applets with the same security policy may not be safe. For example, consider a security policy that allows an applet to open a single socket connection anywhere. This policy produces either an Inside applet or an Outside applet, depending on whether the socket's target is inside the firewall or outside the firewall, but in either case information cannot flow from inside the firewall to outside as long as only one socket is open. However, if two different applets using this policy are allowed to communicate, they can collude to pass information through the firewall.

8   Denial-of-Service Attacks

Although Safe-Tcl was designed primarily to address issues of integrity and privacy, its mechanisms can also be used to prevent denial-of-service attacks. For example, an applet can be prevented from consuming all the disk space by hiding the puts command, which writes data to files. In its place an alias can be created to count the bytes that are output and enforce a limit.

However, many denial-of-service attacks, particularly those associated with graphical user interfaces, are hard to prevent. For example, suppose that an applet attempts to create a window that covers the whole screen and prevent the user from interacting with any other applications. Aliases and hidden commands could be used to restrict the sizes of windows, but the applet could then create several smaller windows that together cover the whole area of the screen. Furthermore, in some situations (such as laptop computers with small screens) it may be desirable to let an applet use the entire screen. Another example is grabs, which force the user to interact with a single window before doing anything else. Grabs are a key part of the look and feel of most windowing systems, yet they can result in system lockup if misused.

We plan to handle many of the denial-of-service attacks, particularly those related to GUIs, with a "kill key" that the user can press at any time to destroy the applet under the mouse. With this approach an application need not worry about many denial-of-service attacks; if they occur, the user will notice and kill the offending applet. The kill-key approach is relatively simple to implement and also accommodates a large range of legitimate applet behavior.

The kill-key approach only works if there is a user present and if denial-of-service attacks will be noticed by the user. These conditions are met for most of the attacks that can occur in interactive applications, such as consuming too much CPU time, misusing windows, etc. However, the kill-key approach will not work in non-interactive applications such as an electronic marketplace, since there is no user to notice the problem.

We also plan to implement mechanisms to monitor CPU usage in Safe-Tcl. Otherwise an applet can hang up its application by entering an infinite loop. Safe-Tcl's approach to CPU controls is to invoke a scheduling function in the master interpreter once the safe interpreter has executed a predefined number of commands. The scheduling function can either abort the applet or give it a new "time slice," after which the scheduling function will be invoked again. For interactive applets the scheduling function can check to see if the kill key has been pressed; for non-interactive applets the scheduling function can implement an upper limit on CPU usage.

9   Status

Safe-Tcl has been available in public Tcl releases since the Tcl 7.5 release in April 1996. Safe-Tcl integration with Tk is implemented as part of a Tcl/Tk plugin module for Netscape Navigator, which was released in July 1996 [6]. The plugin allows Tcl/Tk scripts to be included in Web pages; when the pages are viewed, the scripts run in a safe interpreter to display custom GUIs. As of this writing (February 1997) Safe-Tcl is in its 2.0a1 (alpha-1) release, which supports safe interpreters, aliases, mechanisms for creating and installing security policies, and a few simple security policies such as SafeSockets. Safe-Tcl does not yet support a kill key, CPU usage limits, or authentication.

10 Related Work

10.1 The Borenstein/Rose prototype

Nathaniel Borenstein and Marshall Rose implemented a prototype of Safe-Tcl in 1992 that pioneered most of the ideas, including safe interpreters and aliases [2]. The Borenstein/Rose prototype was used for active email messages and later as part of the First Virtual Holdings Internet payment system. The main contribution of our implementation is to generalize the ideas in the Borenstein/Rose prototype. For example, the Borenstein/Rose prototype allowed only a single safe interpreter per application and did not separate specific security policies from the overall security model. In addition, it did not provide hidden commands so several of the security controls had to be hard-wired

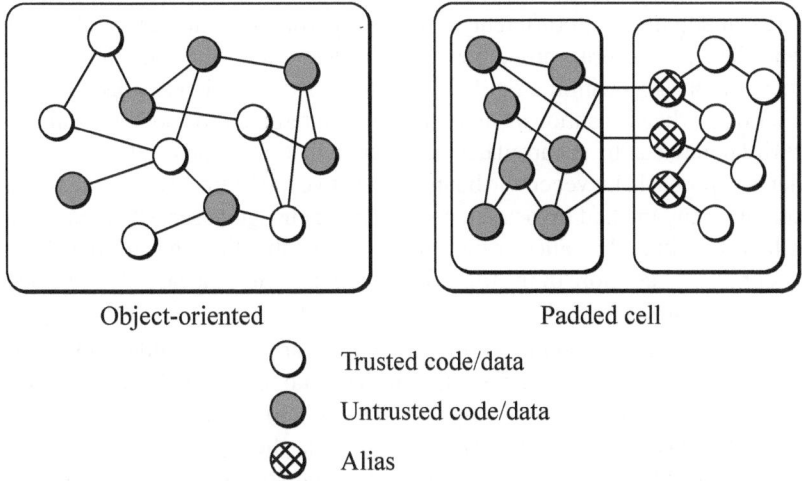

Object-oriented   Padded cell

◯ Trusted code/data

⬤ Untrusted code/data

⊗ Alias

Figure 4. With an object-oriented approach to security (left) trusted and untrusted classes intermingle in a single virtual machine, which results in complex security interactions. With the padded cell approach (right) untrusted code is isolated in a separate virtual machine; interactions between untrusted and trusted code occur only through well-defined aliases, which reduces the complexity of the security issues.

in the C code of Tcl and Tk; our approach allows them to be implemented as Tcl scripts that are part of a security policy.

10.2 Object-oriented approaches

Most other security models for executing untrusted code, such as Java [13] and Tele-script [12], are based on object systems. These models are similar to Safe-Tcl in that they use safe languages that control pointers and memory allocation. However, they differ from Safe-Tcl in that they provide only a single virtual machine that contains all of the objects and classes (see Figure 4). Security properties are associated with individual objects or classes; for example, one class may be marked as coming from an untrusted source while another may be marked as trusted. This information is used when deciding whether or not to allow a particular operation. For example, before allowing a file to be opened, Java checks to see if there are any untrusted classes on the current call stack; if so, the open operation is denied. In contrast, Safe-Tcl's padded cell approach uses multiple virtual machines (interpreters) and the security properties are associated with the virtual machine, not individual pieces of data or code. Security decisions are made based on the virtual machine that is currently executing; for example, while executing in a safe interpreter it is not possible to open a file, but it is possible to open a file if control is first transferred to a trusted interpreter using an alias.

The object-oriented and padded cell approaches are equivalent in that either one can be used to emulate the other. However, the padded cell approach is substantially less complicated in the common case; because of this it makes security problems easier to manage. The reason for Safe-Tcl's simplicity is that it has more clearly defined boundaries between domains with different security properties. In Safe-Tcl, all the data and code with the same security properties are colocated within the same interpreter. As long as execution stays within a single interpreter, no security issues arise. Security issues occur only when execution switches from one interpreter to another via aliases, so the security policy can be encapsulated in the code that implements aliases. In the object-oriented approach, however, the boundaries between different security domains are more complex: any method invocation could cause a change in security domain, and it may be hard for either the caller or the callee to know that there has been a change in security domain. Thus, more of the trusted code will have to be aware of security issues in the object-oriented approach.

Said another way, the complexity of security issues in the padded cell approach grows with the number of virtual machines, which is no more than the number of principals. In most applications this is only two: the user, who is trusted, an an incoming applet, which is not. In the object-oriented approach, the security complexity grows with the number of classes, which is related to the functionality of the system.

Fortunately, object-oriented systems can emulate the padded cell approach by grouping objects and classes according to their security properties and controlling invocations between these groups to simulate multiple virtual machines. We think that such an approach will simplify the security issues in object-oriented systems.

10.3   Pure authentication: ActiveX

Another approach to security is to require authentication of all applets, so that untrusted programs are never executed. In this approach no security mechanisms need to be built into the execution environment since all applets are assumed to be trusted; all that is needed is the initial authentication. The best example of this approach is Microsoft's ActiveX, which is based on pre-existing technology where it is not possible to restrict the execution of applets. It is difficult for ActiveX to implement a security model like Safe-Tcl, so total authentication is the only option.

The problem with the ActiveX approach is that trust involves more than just authentication. Authentication identifies the principal (person or organization) who wrote something, but it doesn't indicate whether the principal is trustworthy. Trust can really only be placed in principals you are familiar with. The authentication approach works well for applets written by large companies that are known to be trustworthy (or that can be sued if their software is defective). However, authentication doesn't help when applets are written by individuals and smaller companies that are not well known. One of the reasons for the popularity of the World Wide Web is that it enables communication among large numbers of individuals and small organizations that have no prior knowledge of each other. If programs are to be attached to the information exchanged on the Web, it is important to allow the programs to be executed without requiring trust.

ActiveX also has the disadvantage of supporting only two levels of trust: complete trust and complete distrust. In practice, trust is often incomplete. Safe-Tcl allows different security policies to be tailored to different levels of trust.

10.4 Software-based fault isolation

Software-based fault isolation (SFI) is a technique whereby untrusted programs written in unsafe languages such as C can be executed safely [10]. SFI modifies the binary output of the compiler to insert additional instructions that check all loads, stores, and jumps and ensure that the program lives within a restricted region of memory. It also provides protected jumps into the environment, which are analogous to aliases. SFI is sometimes referred to as "sandboxing" because it forces a program to "play only in its sandbox."

SFI provides safety and multiple virtual machines for languages like C that do not provide these features inherently. This represents the lowest-level set of facilities required for padded cells. One could build a security model like Safe-Tcl on top of these basic facilities.

11 Conclusions

There is no silver bullet that will make security trivial. Creating safe environments for executing applets will always be difficult, and no security model will ever be totally safe, since even a small bug in programming can open a huge security hole. However, we think it is possible to create environments where applets with varying degrees of trust can be executed with an acceptable level of risk. Safe-Tcl has several properties that simplify the creation of such environments:

- The padded cell model is simple. It generalizes the user space-kernel space model that has been used successfully in operating systems for several decades.
- Safe-Tcl groups data and code with similar security properties together, which reduces the amount of code that must be aware of security issues.
- Safe-Tcl separates security policies into well-defined modules that are distinct from both the host applications and the untrusted applets. This makes it easier to analyze the properties of a security policy and to reuse policies.

Our experiences with Safe-Tcl have taught us two important lessons about security. The first is that safe features do not necessarily compose. This makes it difficult to provide a single security policy with a large variety of features; instead, it encourages a large number of smaller, specialized security policies. The second lesson is that it is important to take advantage of authentication mechanisms yet not require them. If programs are to be intimately tied to information, and if information is to be freely distributed among strangers, then it is important to support the execution of totally untrusted programs. At the same time, authentication can be used to boost the power of applets when they come from known sources. In addition, authentication provides a powerful way to distribute security policies, even as part of unauthenticated applets.

Acknowledgments

This work would never have come about without the pioneering efforts of Nathaniel Borenstein and Marshall Rose, who designed and built the Safe-Tcl prototype. Nathaniel Borenstein, Wan-Teh Chang, Robert Drost, Clif Flynt, Li Gong, Mark Harrison, Ray Johnson, Anand Palaniswamy, Marshall Rose, Rich Salz, Juergen Schoenwaelder, and

Glenn Vanderburg provided useful comments that improved the presentation of this paper.

References

[1]   K. Arnold and J. Gosling, The Java Programming Language , Addison-Wesley, ISBN 0-201-63455-4, 1996.

[2]   N. Borenstein, "EMail With A Mind of Its Own: The Safe-Tcl Language for Enabled Mail," IFIP WG 6.5 Conference, Barcelona, May, 1994, North Holland, Amsterdam, 1994.

[3]   D. Denning and P. Denning, "Data Security," Computing Surveys Vol. 11, No. 3, September 1979, pp. 227-249.

[4]   B. Lampson, "A Note on the Confinement Problem," Communications of the ACM Vol. 16, No. 10, October 1973, pp. 613-615.

[5]   B. Lampson, M. Abadi, M. Burrows, and E. Wobber, "Authentication in Distributed Systems: Theory and Practice," ACM Transactions on Computer Systems Vol. 10, No. 4, November 1992, pp. 265-310.

[6]   J. Levy, Welcome to the Tcl Plugin, http://www.sunlabs.com/research/tcl/plugin/.

[7]   Netscape Inc., "JavaScript in Navigator 3.0," http://home.netscape.com/eng/mozilla/3.0/handbook/javascript/atlas.html#taint_dg   .

[8]   J. Ousterhout, Tcl and the Tk Toolkit Addison-Wesley, ISBN 0-201-63337-X, 1994.

[9]   R. Rivest, The MD5 Message Digest Algorithm RFC 1321, April 1992.

[10] R. Wahbe, S. Lucco, T. Anderson, and S. Graham, "Efficient Software-Based Fault Isolation," Proc. 14th Symposium on Operating Systems Principles, Operating Systems Review, Vol. 27, No. 5, December, 1993, pp. 203-216.

[11] B. Welch, Practical Programming in Tcl and Tk , Prentice-Hall, ISBN 0-13-182007-9, 1995.

[12] J. White, Telescript Technology: The Foundation for the Electronic Marketplace, white paper, General Magic, Inc., 1994.

[13] F. Yellin, "Low Level Security in Java," World-Wide Web Conference Boston MA, December 1995. Also available as http://www.javasoft.com/sfaq/verifier.html.

Web Browsers and Security*

Flavio De Paoli, Andre L. Dos Santos, and Richard A. Kemmerer

Reliable Software Group
Computer Science Department
University of California
Santa Barbara, CA 93106
depaoli@dsi.unimi.it, andre,kemm@cs.ucsb.edu

Abstract. Today the World Wide Web is considered to be a platform
for building distributed applications. This evolution is made possible
by browsers with processing capabilities and by programming languages
that allow web designers to embed real programs into HTML documents.
Downloading and executing code from anywhere on the Internet brings
security problems along with it. A systematic and thorough analysis of
security flaws in the browsers and related technology is necessary to reach
a sufficient level of confidence. This paper presents some preliminary
results of ongoing research that has the final goal of developing properties
for secure browsers and procedures for secure browsing. The research
started by investigating features provided by the standard environment.
The paper describes some experimental attacks that have been carried
out by exploiting features of Java and JavaScript executed by Netscape
Navigator and Microsoft Explorer browsers.

1   Introduction

The growth of the Internet and the World Wide Web (WWW) during the past
few years has been phenomenal. The Internet is currently serving tens of millions
of people connected through millions of computers. Most every business and
government institution has a web page, and the web and web browsing are fast
becoming the primary source of information for people of all ages.

Languages like Java and JavaScript have been developed to embed programs
into HyperText Markup Language (HTML) documents (pages). Java applets,
which are designed to be downloaded from the web and run directly by the
Java virtual machine within a browser, are also increasingly being included in
web pages to provide more sophisticated animation and other desirable features.
Downloading and executing code from anywhere on the Internet brings security
problems along with it. That is, the host computer is open to a variety of attacks,

---

* This is a revised and extended version of [2].
  This research was partially supported by PulsePoint Communications and the University of California through a Micro Grant.

G. Vigna (Ed.): Mobile Agents and Security
LNCS 1419, pp. 235–256, 1998. © Springer–Verlag Berlin Heidelberg 1998

ranging from attacks that simply monitor the environment to export information, to attacks that change the configuration or the behavior of the host (changing files, consuming resources), and finally to attacks that open a back door to let intruders get into the host.

Attacks succeed either because the implementation of the browser is weak (from flaws in the specification and/or from poor implementation) or because the environment in which the browser is executed has flaws. Weaknesses in the environment are mainly due to the new open nature of software. Conventional computing paradigms assume that programs are installed and configured once on any and every machine and that these programs only exchange data. This means that a user can make all possible checks over a new program before running it. This assumption, however, is no longer valid for open and mobile environments, such as Java and the web.

Many security holes in web browsers have been discovered and brought to the attention of the public [1]. Although most of these holes have been patched, a systematic analysis of the features of both the Java and JavaScript languages and the web environment is needed to identify possible design weaknesses in order to avoid similar problems.

Many of the attacks carried out so far require the attacker to have substantial capabilities, such as taking over a web server or a domain name server or assuming that the user will navigate only through hyperlinks. These assumptions, therefore, often limit the likelihood of the attacks due to the low probability that the assumptions could be satisfied or because they require so much knowledge that only highly-skilled programmers could implement the attacks.

This paper describes some experimental attacks that have been carried out by the Reliable Software Group at UCSB. What sets these attacks apart from most of the others is that the attacks presented in this paper can be realized without assuming that the attacker has any capabilities beyond those granted to every user on the net and without assuming that the attackers are highly skilled programmers with complex programs for carrying out the attacks.

This paper reports on two attacks and how they were modified to contend with browser improvements that negated the original versions of the attacks. The first attack deals with the violation of privacy; it requires only that the victim downloads a honey-pot page that includes an attacker applet, which collects and sends information back to the attacker's server. The second attack is as powerful as a "man-in-the-middle" attack, but it too requires only that the victim downloads a honey-pot page, which in this case includes an applet that can detect when the victim visits a certain site and displays an imposter page for that site in order to steal sensitive information, such as credit card numbers or personal identification numbers.

The web is constantly changing, and the browsers that are used for navigating the web are constantly being updated and improved. Most of the experiments described in the literature can no longer be reproduced using the latest versions of the web browsers. In fact, at the time this paper is published this will likely be true for the attacks that are described here. Therefore, the main purpose of this paper is to provide a historical view of the web browser security issues and to give samples of the kinds of problems that can result from inaccurate or security-unaware designs or from poor implementations.

The paper is structured in the following way. Section 2 summarizes the browser and language features that have been used. Section 3 briefly reviews some previously known attacks. Section 4 gives more details on applet capabilities and features to establish the background for the attacks. Section 5 describes the new attacks. Finally, future work and conclusions are presented.

2   Browsers and Languages

The World Wide Web is a hypertext of network-accessible information. It was designed to support static links to display static multimedia documents. The rapid growth of the web and the related technology has changed this initial view. Today the web is considered to be a platform for building distributed applications. This evolution is made possible by browsers with processing capabilities and by programming languages that allow web designers to embed real programs into HTML documents.

This section outlines the characteristics of Java and JavaScript, which are the most popular languages for programming the web, and of Netscape Navigator and Microsoft Explorer, which are the most popular browsers.

2.1   Java

The Java language is a general-purpose object-oriented language that was introduced by Sun Microsystems in 1995 [5]. One of the major design goals for Java was portability. The result is that not only the Java source code, but also the binary code is executable on all processors. This is accomplished by compiling the source code into platform independent bytecode, which is then run by the Java virtual machine.

Some of the features of the Java language that make it simpler and supposedly more secure are that it is strongly typed, there are no preprocessor statements (like C's #define and #include), there are no pointers, no global variables, and no global functions. By keeping the language simple and without many of the error prone features, such as multiple inheritance, it is expected that Java will be more secure.

A Java program is a collection of classes and instances of classes. Each class is compiled into bytecode, which is then interpreted to execute the program. Java supports *object references*, rather than pointers. It also supports dynamic creation of instances and bindings. When a class instance (an object) is needed, it is created explicitly and a reference to it is returned; when a method is invoked on an object, the interpreter selects the method to be executed according to the class hierarchy and method overloading. Object destruction is automatically handled by a *garbage collector*, so that memory management is completely in the control of the interpreter.

Another feature of Java is the support for concurrent programming via *threads*. Threads allow programmers to associate an independent execution flow with each class. A class with a thread can be started, stopped, and suspended independently from the execution of the rest of the system of which it is a part. Synchronization among thread executions can be accomplished by class *monitors*.

As mentioned above, Java code was designed to run on any client; therefore, compiled Java programs are network and platform independent. The absence of physical pointers and automatic memory management help achieve this independence. Moreover, the bytecode has been designed to fully support the typing mechanism of Java so that dynamic code verification can be performed. This is a safety and a security feature designed to prevent one from executing corrupted or malicious code.

The *Java Virtual Machine* is emulated in software and can run on numerous platforms [7]. It could also be compiled or implemented directly in microcode or hardware [11], but currently it is mostly emulated in software. The virtual machine deals with class files, which contain Java virtual machine instructions, a symbol table, and a few other necessary items. Java virtual machine instructions are all one byte long, and that is why they are called bytecodes. Bytecode can also be generated from other high level languages, such as Ada or C, or it could be generated manually.

When Java classes are downloaded from the network it is necessary to use a class loader. Java supplies an abstract `ClassLoader` class for this purpose. Because abstract classes cannot be used directly, each browser needs to declare a subclass of this class to be used by the browser for downloading classes. Each subclass must include a customized implementation of the `loadClass()` method to retrieve and download a class from the net. A class is downloaded as an array of bytes that must be converted to an instance of class `Class`. The `ClassLoader` method that actually does the conversion is `defineClass()`. Every class object contains a reference to the class loader that defined it, so related classes can be downloaded by the same class loader. These features make Java suitable for writing programs in a distributed, heterogeneous environment such as the web.

Besides supporting the design of complete applications, Java supports the implementation of small applications, called *applets*, which can be embedded in HTML pages. A special tag in a downloaded HTML file tells the web server to download the bytecode for a Java applet. The most popular web browsers, such as Netscape Navigator and Microsoft Explorer, include support for the execution of applets. Applets can be used for implementing small stand-alone applications, as well as for implementing clients of client/server applications.

A page may have more than one applet embedded in it. In this case, all of the applets are downloaded together. Because a thread is associated with each applet, more than one applet can run concurrently within the same web-page context. The class `Applet` defines a set of methods to control applet behavior. These methods can be overridden by programmers to get the desired behavior from their applets. The most important methods are `init`, `start` and `stop`.

When an applet is downloaded it is automatically created, initiated and started: the methods `init` and `start` are invoked and the applet is labeled *active*. When the page that embeds an applet is not displayed (the browser is iconified or shows another page), the execution of that applet is suspended (i.e., the `stop` method is invoked and the applet is labeled *inactive*). If the page is shown again, the applet execution is resumed (i.e., the `start` method is invoked again and the applet is again labeled *active*). It is possible to keep an applet running even when it is inactive, however. This is accomplished by overriding the `stop` method so that it never returns. One of the experiments described in this paper exploits this feature.

2.2   JavaScript

JavaScript is an object-based scripting language that has been specifically designed by Netscape. JavaScript resembles Java, but without Java's static typing and strong type checking. Scripts are embedded directly in an HTML page and interpreted by the browser. By invoking JavaScript functions, it is possible to perform actions (such as playing an audio file, executing an applet, or sending an e-mail message) in response to a user opening or exiting a page. In the experiments described in this paper, the JavaScript support for forms and the capability to open and use browser windows has been exploited.

The use of forms enables the browser to send information back to the server. A form is an HTML tag that includes an `ACTION` field, an `INPUT` field, and other fields, which are not relevant to this discussion. The `ACTION` field must be filled out with a URL, which usually refers to a Common Gateway Interface (CGI) program. CGI technology is a standard for interfacing external applications with Web servers, and it allows users to start an application on the server. An example of a valid URL for the `ACTION` field is `"mailto:any_e-mail_address"`, which causes an e-mail message to be sent by the browser to the specified address. The `INPUT` field is composed of a set of subfields like `NAME`, `VALUE` (to store the input string) and `TYPE`. One example of type is `"submit"`, which specifies a *pushbutton* that causes the current form to be packaged up into a query URL and sent to a remote server.

JavaScript implements a set of objects to handle different types of forms. Of particular interest is the *submit object*, which has a pre-defined method `click()` that simulates a click on the submit button. By writing a JavaScript statement that invokes that method, it is possible to submit a form automatically, without obtaining the user's acknowledgment. If the specified `ACTION` is `"mailto:..."` the effect is to send an e-mail message from the user without the user knowing it [3]. In Netscape Navigator 3.01 the user was provided with an option to be notified whenever an email was sent.

JavaScript also enables a script to open and use a new browser window. The script can access any method or object of the new browser, except those that access or return privileged information. For example, if the object `URL` is accessed, a null string is obtained, instead of the URL of the currently displayed page. Similarly, the `location` object will return the URL of the page that was requested by the script when the new browser was opened, or the literal string "[object Location]" if the user has downloaded another page. This implementation at first appears to be secure; however, in Section 5 it will be shown that this is not the case.

2.3 Browser Technology

Browser technology is evolving very quickly; new browser versions are released every few months or even weeks. These new releases are intended to enhance the quality of the software and to introduce new features. Quality improvement comes in the form of bug fixes (either functional or security bugs), better performance, or improved user interfaces. These new features often aim at allowing browsers to cover new and different aspects of computing on the net. However, they often introduce new security flaws along with the new features.

2.3.1 Cookies

A technology, which was developed to make up for the stateless nature of web communications, was named "cookies". The specification of this technology was introduced with Netscape Navigator 2.0 and was soon also implemented by Microsoft in Internet Explorer. A cookie is a small piece of text information in the form of a name/value pair. It can either be stored on the user's computer, providing persistence, or on the browser, in which case it will be lost at the end of a browsing session. It can be sent to the server that set it at any time. The first time a server receives a request for a page it sets the cookie(s), which will be sent back to the server at its request. Cookies are useful for maintaining related information during a browsing session or across multiple browsing sessions. Shopping baskets are an example where cookies can be useful in a single browsing session, and configuration preferences is an example where cookies can be useful across browsing sessions. Although cookies have been introduced to improve the quality of the service provided by the web, they can also be exploited to invade the privacy of a user. An example where this happens is described in the next section.

2.3.2 LiveConnect

In version 3.0 of its Navigator Netscape developed a technology called "Live-Connect," which enables communication between Java applets, JavaScript and Plug-ins [8]. This technology was in response to web page developers who asked for interapplication communication at the client side [6]. Applets can now work together with JavaScript and Plug-ins, to give developers all of the features available in all three technologies. Live Connect supports the following communications:

- A JavaScript script may call methods from Java applets or Java builtin methods;

- A JavaScript script may call Plug-in functions;
- A Java applet may call both builtin and user defined JavaScript functions;
- A Java applet may call Plug-in functions;
- A Plug-in may define Java classes;
- A Plug-in may call Java and JavaScript functions.

Security restrictions have been introduced that only allow communication between an applet and a script contained in the same page and Plug-ins that were loaded by this page. Moreover, since one of the Java, JavaScript, and Plug-in applications can access builtin functions of the other, they are not supposed to be able to subvert the security features in place at the accessed technology.

As a consequence of adding LiveConnect features, concerns that were nonexistent before are now real threats. For example, a JavaScript script can communicate with a Java applet and ask it to open a socket connection on its behalf. This connection could then be used to send the server information that previously was only able to leave the client as a form submission.

2.3.3   Browser Security Options

The current versions of both browsers give the user options to increase security. These options are:

1. Both support the options to turn the execution of Java and/or JavaScript on/off. This enables users to trade the convenience of these languages for the security of not running any outside programs in their machine.
2. Both support the option of alerting users before accepting a cookie, and both let the user choose if he/she wants to continue this operation or not. Netscape Navigator 4.03 also enables the user to totally disable the cookie feature.
3. Both support site certificates, which are digitally signed public keys used for digital signature verification. These are widely used by secure servers in conjunction with the secure socket layer.
4. Netscape Navigator 4.03 has an option to alert the user before sending forms by e-mail.
5. Explorer 4.0 divides sites into zones. It provides the user with four different zones that can be configured with the sites that the user wishes to include. These zones are Local Intranet Zone, Trusted Sites Zone, Internet Zone and Restricted Sites Zone. The user then sets one of four levels of security against active contents for each zone. These levels are high, medium, low and custom. Although this at first seems like a good feature, Explorer fails to explain in an understandable way what the difference between the levels is. The difference, which is very complex, controls whether or not to accept the downloading of software that can be executed by the browser (such as ActiveX), if files can be downloaded or not, what level of security is implemented for Java applets, etc..

6. Both support the secure socket layer (SSL) implementation for communication with a secure server. The SSL is a socket implementation that uses a session key to encrypt all messages passed from the client to the server and vice-versa. One weakness of this implementation is that the client is only guaranteed to communicate with a server in an encrypted way. There is no guarantee that the client is communicating with the server that it thinks it is. When using Netscape Navigator 4.03 there is a small lock on the lower left corner that indicates if the communication is through a SSL(closed) or not (open). If the user clicks on this lock another window pops up with details of the page being shown, including the server that sent it and the certificates if there are any. When using Microsoft Internet Explorer 4.0 a lock appears on the right lower corner when the communication is through SSL.

7. Netscape Navigator 4.03 supports automatic updates. This feature enables a user to receive automatic updates and the installation of the browser and Plug-ins from the network. The user has a chance to look at the certificate for this software before the update or installation is completed. This is a very useful feature for the expert user, but it can be very dangerous for the novice.

8. Netscape Navigator 4.03 supports signed objects. Signed objects are Java applets, JavaScript scripts, or Plug-ins that were signed and that can request capabilities that are not normally available. This enables these objects to read or write to the disk or open network communications. In the case of Java applets, Netscape has developed classes, called capabilities classes, that have methods to request the desired capabilities. JavaScript has a similar model. Microsoft Internet Explorer 4.0 also supports signed programs, which in this case are programs that were signed using Microsoft's support for certificates, which is called *Authenticode* technology.

In carrying out the experiments reported in this paper it was necessary to constantly be aware of the differences between Netscape Navigator and Microsoft Explorer. For instance, with Netscape Navigator, one instance of the Netscape Navigator program can show many windows. Microsoft Explorer (prior to version 4.0) was able to show only one window for each instance of the program. The importance of this is that different program instances are isolated from each other by the features of the operating system that isolate two programs. As a result, these different instances do not share any environment or context. In the remainder of this paper the word browser is used to refer to the browser's windows that are spawned by the same instance of a browser program.

3   A Brief Review of Some Already Known Attacks

There are many known security vulnerabilities in web browsers. The attacks that exercise these weaknesses vary in sophistication and in the amount of resources that the attacker is required to possess in order to carry out the attack.

In this section a few representative attacks are presented. First two very simple though effective attack types, which require only a browser and use standard language features, are presented. Next, an attack that requires the attacker to control a Domain Name Server that advertises wrong addresses is described. This is followed by the discussion of an attack that relies on common assumptions for firewalls to force a connection to a protected port. Finally, the attack known as "web spoofing" is presented to show how an attack may require strong assumptions and a high level of sophistication.

One of the simplest forms of browser attacks and also one of the hardest to stop is a denial of service attack. The attacks reported here use Java features to exhaust resources of the host system or prevent the use of some feature. Two obvious examples of this attack are busy-waiting to consume cpu cycles and repeatedly allocating memory until all of the available memory is exhausted. Another attack in this category is locking a class to prevent access to particular resources (e.g., locking the `InetAddress` class in Netscape Navigator blocks host name lookups). The reason that the denial of service attacks are difficult to stop is that there is no regulation of how much of a resource an applet can consume. That is, an applet is either given as much as it wants or it is given nothing. More of the technical details, which help to understand this attack are given in the next section. Further information on this type of attack can be found in [1].

Another simple attack deals with the use of cookies to keep track of a user's activities, which is a privacy violation. This attack is described in [12] and reports a real situation that has been set up by DoubleClick Corporation. DoubleClick has a network of affiliated sites each of which agrees to having a space in their HTML pages for advertisements that point to the DoubleClick site instead of showing a local graphic file. The first time DoubleClick receives a request for an advertisement by a browser, it selects an advertisement from a list and sends it back along with a request for setting a cookie with a unique identification number. That number will be sent to DoubleClick whenever any DoubleClick affiliated page is visited. This enables them to build a user profile reporting every DoubleClick page and site that is visited. Even though the profile does not report any information about the user identity (only computer names are recorded), it allows DoubleClick to understand a user's tastes and interests. This information can be exploited for marketing purposes, such as sending each user (or computer) personalized advertisements and rating the effectiveness of the advertisements. To prevent this privacy violation, a user should first check the presence of a DoubleClick cookie in his/her computer (its name is `ad.doubleclick.net`) and delete it if necessary. Next, the user should turn on the browser option that alerts the user whenever a cookie is to be placed, and the user should refuse DoubleClick cookies.

The Domain Name Server (DNS) attack assumes that the attacker has control of a DNS, which a trusting host (or even a firewall) uses to validate a server address. In this attack the applet requests a connection to the server by providing the name of the server. The malicious DNS returns the address of a machine other than the one requested by the applet (e.g., the attacker's machine). The result is that the applet can then connect to an arbitrary host. Netscape fixed this problem in Navigator 2.01 by looking up the IP address for each site they process and refusing to listen to (possibly false) updates to that address [10].

The next attack relies on the common assumptions that a firewall trusts all requests originating behind it and that only the first packet of a connection is checked. To start the attack the applet sends the originating server a connection request including a protected port number (e.g., the port for telnet connections). The firewall trusts the request, since it originates from behind the firewall. Subsequent messages from the server are also trusted, since they are related to an already approved connection. The effect is that the attacker can open any connection even though there are firewall controls. This attack highlights security flaws that are the result of assumptions that are not valid for web-based computation. A simple though partial solution is to design browsers that prevent one from issuing requests related to well-known ports (e.g., port numbers below 1024). More sophisticated firewalls already implement more complex filtering rules to ensure better control. A complete description of the firewall attack can be found in [9].

Another interesting attack is the net spoofing attack, which assumes that the attacker has a way to make the user connect to the attacker machine, which delivers rewritten pages in such a way that each URL refers to the attacker machine. The attacker machine works as a "man-in-the-middle." This requires the attacker to have control of the network such that everything that the browser thinks it is sending to the web actually goes to the attacker machine. The attacker may then forward the request to the real machine and relay the results back to the victim, while making copies of the interesting parts before passing them on. This attack is fully described in [4].

4   Applet Security

Java applets are designed to be downloaded from the web and to be run directly by a Java virtual machine within a browser. Since applets are automatically run by the browser just by accessing a web page that contains a reference to the applet, security measures, which protect against security, privacy, and denial of service threats, should be taken before users can be expected to accept the concept of running applets from untrusted sources. To alleviate these security concerns the browser, which contains the Java virtual machine, limits the capabilities of the downloaded applets. These limitations are not normally placed on applets loaded from the local file system, however, because the local host is trusted.

This section examines some privacy and security features related to applets. The goal is to understand what interaction is normally allowed between an applet and its environment (i.e., between an applet and the host machine, the host browser, or other applets running in the same browser). Section 4.1 illustrates what system properties an applet can access, Section 4.2 describes what the *context* of an applet is, and Section 4.3 deals with thread-related features, which enabled the original versions of the attacks introduced in this paper.

4.1 System Properties

Since applets are programs to be executed in the host environment, the Java designers posed some restrictions on the interaction between an applet and its environment. The intent is to prevent safety, security and privacy violations. The restrictions that apply to applets are:

- An applet is prevented from reading or writing files on the host that is executing it.
- An applet can make network connections only to the host that it came from.
- An applet cannot start any program on the host that is executing it.
- An applet is prevented from loading libraries or defining native methods.
- An applet can read only a restricted set of system properties. In particular, it can read the file separator (e.g., '/'), the path separator (e.g., ':'), the line separator, the Java class version number, the Java vendor-specific string and URL, the Java version number, and finally the operating system name and architecture.

The idea is that by placing these limitations on downloaded applets the applets are effectively placed in a "sand-box". The applet may do whatever it wants inside the sand-box, but it is limited as to what it can do on the outside.

These restrictions are enforced by the *class loader* and the *security manager*. The class loader implements the downloading rules for classes. Due to the above restriction, this means that an applet cannot download classes other than from the host it came from.

The Java virtual machine also limits the name space of downloaded applets. When a Java virtual machine tries to load a class from a source other than the local host machine a class loader, which cannot be overridden by the downloaded applet, is invoked. The class loader sets up a separate naming environment to accommodate the source. This will assure that name clashes don't occur between the names in this source and the names in classes loaded from other sources. Bytecode loaded from the local file system is set up in the system name space, which is shared by all other name spaces, and the system name space is always searched first to prevent system classes from being overridden.

After the name space is set up, the class loader calls a *bytecode verifier* to assure that the bytecode has proper structure. This is necessary because the bytecode could have been generated by an incorrect Java compiler, by a compiler altered to skip the compile time checks, or by a non-Java compiler. The bytecode also could have been altered after it was produced. The bytecode is verified in four passes and is claimed to satisfy the following conditions if it passes the verification.

- The downloaded bytecode has the proper format for a class file
- All "final" classes are not subclassed, and all "final" methods are not overridden.
- Every class except Object has a superclass.
- All variable and method references have legal names and types.

- Methods are called with the appropriate arguments.
- Variables are assigned values of the appropriate type.
- There are no stack overflows or underflows.
- All objects on the stack are of the appropriate type.

Java provides an abstract `SecurityManager` class to enforce the browsers' security policy. Because `SecurityManager` is an abstract class it cannot be used directly; therefore, each browser must declare a subclass of class `SecurityManager`, which acts as a reference monitor. The security manager is installed when the Java virtual machine within the browser starts up, and it cannot be overridden. The security manager is automatically consulted before any operation related to the environment is performed. In this way it can deny the authorization for any possibly insecure operation. It is important to note that the security policy is defined by the web browser and it is implemented in the browser's security manager. Therefore, the above restrictions are only advice and might not be followed by some browsers. In fact, Microsoft Explorer allows different configuration levels. One of these levels allows applets to download classes from anywhere. In contrast, Netscape Navigator strictly implements all of the restrictions.

The restrictions above cover many of the protection concerns, but there are additional concerns about security. The following subsections discuss some of these.

4.2 The Context of an Applet

A single HTML page may embed more than one applet. In both Netscape Navigator and Microsoft Explorer all applets in the same page define a single *context*. An applet can get a reference to its *context* by the `getAppletContext()` method of the `Applet` class. The context gives an applet access to a set of methods to collect references to other applets in the same page and to interact with the browser. These features could be exploited to make applets collaborate and communicate; for example, they could synchronize their behavior. Two methods of interest are `getApplets()` and `getApplet()`. `GetApplets()` returns a list of all applets *in the same context* (i.e., in the same page), and `getApplet()` returns a reference to an applet when given the applet's name. Each applet has a string name. Once an applet has a reference to another applet, it can invoke any of the methods available for the `Applet` class on the referenced applet.

An applet can interact with the browser to show (download) a new document in a window and to show a message in the status line of the current window. The methods of interest are `showDocument()` and `showStatus()`. `ShowDocument()` shows a new document in a window given its URL, and `showStatus()` shows a string in the status line of the browser.

The `showDocument` method can be asked to open a document in the current window, in a frame of the current window, or in a new window. Both Netscape Navigator and Microsoft Explorer define "window" as "browser window". So the two methods above refer to the browser itself. When `showDocument` opens a new window, it actually opens a new browser and downloads the requested HTML document in that browser.

In Netscape Navigator the new browser can be identified by a unique name that must be supplied to showDocument as a parameter. After being created, that browser can be accessed by name by *any active* applet, regardless of its context. This means that any applet that knows the name of that browser can make it download a document even without user acknowledgment and awareness.

In contrast, Microsoft Explorer (prior to version 4.0) creates an anonymous browser, even if a name is supplied when showDocument is invoked. This means that even the same applet that opened the browser cannot show another document in that browser.

This is an example of different implementations of the same language feature. Both implementations can be criticized. Netscape Navigator can be criticized because a name can be used in a different context as a reference to the same window. This could be a security (or a safety) flaw, since the behavior of two applets in two different contexts could interfere with each other (intentionally or not). Microsoft Explorer can also be criticized because one browser is prevented from opening another browser and then showing a sequence of documents in it.

The showStatus() method allows an applet to display any message on the status line of the browser showing the document. This method could be used to display misleading information to the user.

4.3   Playing with Threads

Since every applet is implicitly associated with a thread, an applet can access another applet by using an instance of the Thread class. The thread class defines the getThreadGroup method, which returns a ThreadGroup object. Using this object one can retrieve a list of references to all threads (i.e., applets) that belong to the *same group or subgroup of this thread group.* For all browser versions prior to 4.0 both Netscape Navigator and Microsoft Explorer define a single thread group that contains all threads associated with all active applets in all of the browsers. The getParent method can be recursively called to get this thread group. This means that an applet can get a reference to, as well as access to, any applet that is embedded in any displayed document through its thread object.

This feature allows the design of applets that continuously monitor the browser to get access to applets embedded in downloaded pages. Once the applet has this information, it can interfere with the execution of other applets in several ways. Denial of service attacks can be based on this feature. For example, an attacker applet may affect performance by delaying, suspending and resuming threads, or by hanging their priority. It is also sometimes possible to kill a thread (and therefore the associated applet).

Every thread has a name associated with it, which is the name of the class that defines the applet. Names in combination with thread references can be exploited to understand what the user is doing. The attacks described in the next section are based on this feature.

5   The Experiments

In this section some experiments that were carried out by the Reliable Software Group at UCSB are described. These experiments led to the definition of two new attacks. One attack results in a privacy violation; its goal is to build dossiers on Internet users. The second is a breach of confidentiality; its goal is to steal access information (e.g., a user's pin).

What is interesting is that both attacks are based on combining features of the browser or of the language exploited. This demonstrates that even a correct implementation of a feature that appears to be secure in isolation can lead to an insecure environment if it is possible to combine "features" that have been designed independently of each other.

For example, in the original attack the JavaScript capability of sending e-mail from within a script, the Java capability of opening a new window and downloading a new HTML page in it, and the object-oriented nature of Java that associates every applet with a thread have been exploited.

As already mentioned, some of the experiments described here no longer work with the latest versions of the Netscape and Microsoft Explorer browsers, and it is likely that others will not work in the near future. However, many Internet users are still using and will continue to use old browsers in which these attacks will work. The following descriptions concentrate more on the architecture of the experiment than on the implementation details. An evolution of the experiments over a few releases of the involved browsers is also discussed to provide a historical view of the issues.

5.1   Privacy Violation: Building User Dossiers

The goal of this attack is to collect and send information about the user back to the server. This is accomplished by JavaScript statements and a spy applet embedded in a honey-pot page.

The attack starts with the victim downloading the honey-pot page. The attack itself is carried out in two steps. First, when the victim downloads the honey-pot page from the attacker server, JavaScript silently fills out a form and sends it from the unsuspecting user back to an address on the server. In this way the server can uniquely identify the victim by his/her e-mail address. Next, the spy applet monitors the victim's activity by collecting information on the victim's running threads. The stop method has also been redefined to keep the spy applet alive even when the document that embeds it is not being shown. This allows the spy applet to monitor all the open browsers at any time. When the spy applet detects that a new thread is running, it retrieves the thread's name and sends it back to the server using a UDP/IP message.

The blueprint of the original attack is:

1. Build a honey-pot HTML document that embeds JavaScript statements to send the e-mail message and that also contains a spy applet with the stop method overridden.

2. When the honey-pot page is downloaded from the attacker server, an e-mail message is sent back to the server to identify the victim, and the spy applet starts monitoring the victim's activity.

3. The spy applet sends the attacker server any information about threads that are embedded in the documents downloaded by the victim. Since the `stop` method of the spy applet has been overridden, it continuously runs even if the victim closes the honey-pot document.

On the server side there is a daemon that receives and collects the information and builds a dossier on the victim. The daemon knows the identity of the victim and a list of names of threads run by the victim. These thread names are searchable by any web search engine. The web is searched to get references to the pages that include the thread executed by the victim's browser. The result of the attack is a user profile with a reasonable degree of accuracy.

There are two technical problems with this attack. The first is that only pages including threads can be monitored. This is considered to be a minor problem, since the number of pages that embed applets is increasing every day. The second problem is that it may happen that the same applet can be embedded in more than one page. Thus, when searching on a thread name the thread name query may result in several HTML pages. In this case, more sophisticated techniques may be required to correlate the collected information.

The attack presented here is likely to succeed since it does not require any special preparation. To be more affective it could be focused on a specific target. For example, the honey-pot page could be a collection of links and information about a particular subject, such as sports. It is likely that web surfers who like sports will go to that page and then follow links to look for information interesting to them. The user profiles that can be built may be used for commercial and marketing studies. For example manufacturers might be interested in deducing what items are more appealing, advertising companies might use this information to better focus their advertisements, or commercial organizations might better understand the interests of customers from different geographic areas, allowing them to offer different items in different stores.

The first version of the experiment was designed and implemented in Netscape Navigator 3.0. In version 3.01 of Netscape Navigator the calls necessary to get the threads no longer worked if called from anywhere on the applet code. However, it was discovered that if the calls originated from the `paint` method it could still get the thread names. This was used to implement a variation of the attack against the 3.01 version of the browser. However, with version 4.0, Netscape changed the implementation of the Java environment preventing an applet from getting information on the thread names of applets running in other pages. The result is that the attack, as described above, could no longer be accomplished. The paragraphs below describe how the same attack could be implemented using flaws that were discovered in LiveConnect and JavaScript, although they are only effective in some versions of the browsers. The advantage of this new version of the attack is that it enables an attacker to monitor *all* pages that a user visits, not only those that have embedded applets.

Starting with Netscape Navigator 3.01 (it was actually introduced in 3.0, but did not work properly) the user was given the option to have the browser request an explicit approval from the user before sending a form by email. This may require some changes to the attack. That is, to identify the user the dossier attack could still stay with the automatic send of an e-mail message relying on the user accepting, or not understanding and accepting, the submission of a form by e-mail. This assumes the user has set the option in Netscape Navigator to be warned by this. If the user did not set the option or he/she is just used to clicking yes for every warning message, then this is the best solution. An alternate solution is to use social engineering to convince the user to submit a form or to have a username/password to access the attacker's page. Depending on what information is available on the attacker's server this can easily be achieved, requiring only that a form requests the user to "register" with the server providing his/her name and e-mail address.

To overcome the impossibility of tracking the thread names in Netscape version 4.0, it was necessary to change the approach. As described in Section 2.3, the LiveConnect technology allows a Java applet to call JavaScript functions. This feature was used to track the URL of the pages downloaded by the user. LiveConnect technology allows an applet to communicate with JavaScript through an object called JSObject. If an applet calls any method of JavaScript using JSObject, a JSException exception is thrown. This exception can be translated to the string: "netscape.javascript.JSException: access disallowed from scripts at http://www.<location>/ to documents at the URL address", where the URL address refers to the URL of the page being shown. To achieve the attack an applet with the stop method overridden was used to call a JavaScript method and get back the URL of the displayed page when an exception was thrown. Unfortunately, a side effect of LiveConnect throwing this exception is that it kills the applet. This occurs because the prototypes of the JSObject methods do not specify that they throw any exceptions. The solution to this problem was to hand-edit the JSObject.class class library to specify that the methods throw a JSException exception. This was possible because the specification of a class file is publicly available [7]. With this change, the spy applet was able to catch the exception, which stopped it from being killed. Using this implementation it was possible to complete the attack as in the first version.

With version 4.01a of Netscape Navigator Netscape fixed this problem by replacing the URL address with the generic string "another domain". Thus, even this variation of the attack would no longer work. Therefore, it was necessary to again redesign the attack with a new honey-pot page that included a spy applet and a JavaScript script that opened a new browser window with a page from the attacker's server. As described in Section 2.2, for security purposes the location object will return the literal string "[object location]" if the user has downloaded a page into the newly opened browser. During the experiments, however, it was discovered that if the location object is requested for the URL after the popped up browser has been closed, then the URL of the page that was last displayed is returned. To exploit this flaw the JavaScript script also defined a function that closed the new browser, got the location of the shown page, opened a new browser with that location, and finally returned the location. By using the `JSObject` object the spy applet could call that function and get the location of the shown page. This information was then sent to the attacker server as in the previous version of the experiment. This implementation bug was fixed in Netscape Navigator 4.02.

The key point of this attack is the frequency of the calls performed by the spy applet. If the interval between two calls is too small, then the user will notice a frequent flicker of the browser. If it is too long the URL of some pages will not be collected.

This last attack requires that there are two open browsers: one with the honey-pot page, and one to be used by the victim. The question is how can one convince the victim to keep the first browser open and use the second for further downloading? For the experiments a second browser, which overlaps the first, is opened. Having the second browser overlap the first is something that most users are willing to accept, especially when browsing new pages. Furthermore, for users that use full-screen browsers the new browser completely overlaps the existing one and will not be noticed.

5.2 "Man-in-the-middle" Attack: Stealing Account and Password Information

The goal of this attack is to monitor a victim's activities to understand when he/she visits a target site (e.g., a bank site) and then to replace the original pages with fake pages in order to retrieve sensitive information. The original version of this attack was written in Java and JavaScript. However, as was the case for the dossier attack, this attack was ineffective for Netscape Navigator version 4.0. This was overcome by designing variations of the original attack similarly to what was described for the dossier attack. Like the dossier attack, this attack also starts with the victim downloading a honey-pot page that includes the spy applet or the spy script. When the victim asks for the honey-pot page, he/she gets a first document on the open browser and a second document on another, new browser. This second browser is to be used by the victim.

In the original version, this second browser is opened by the spy applet embedded in the first document. The purpose of the second browser is to keep the first one displaying the document including the spy applet, so that it never gets suspended. This is required because the attack is based on the `showDocument` method and only *active* applets can execute it. The spy applet can then monitor the activities carried out by the victim and have access to the second browser through the `showDocument` method.

The same technique of monitoring thread names, which directly translate to applet names, is used to discover when the user is looking at the target page. When the victim has downloaded the target page, the spy applet substitutes a fake page from the spy applet's server with the same appearance as the real page. At this point the spy applet is the man-in-the-middle. Now, the attacker has complete control of the victim's interaction with hyperlinks and forms. The fake page has forged links to make the victim interact with the attacker server instead of with the real server for the target site. For the experiment a bank whose home page contained an applet was used as the target site, and the bank's home page was the target page. When the victim chooses the log-on page for the bank he/she actually downloads a pseudo log-on page from the attacking server. Thus, the filled out form, which contains the victim's account number and pin, is sent to the attacker server instead of to the bank. After collecting the wanted information, a bad connection message is displayed and the real page is downloaded, so that the victim can continue his/her activity without understanding what was going on. For the experiment this was accomplished by first downloading a page with an error message "Connection refused, please try again" and then downloading the real log-on page for the bank.

The blueprint of the original attack is:

1. Build a honey-pot page that includes the spy applet.
2. When downloaded, the spy applet spawns a new named browser with the same or a possibly different page.
3. It is assumed that the user uses the new browser so that the spy applet is never stopped and it can monitor the documents downloaded by the victim.
4. When the user retrieves a page that embeds an applet that signals that he/she is looking at the target page that the attacker is interested in (e.g., the bank page), the spy applet calls the `showDocument` method to replace the real page with a forged page downloaded from the attacker server.
5. The forged page sends information back to the attacker server by means of JavaScript support for forms. This causes a CGI script to run on the attacker server.
6. The CGI script stores the information and answers with a page that shows an error message and embeds an applet that downloads the real page to conclude the attack.

A weakness of this attack is that the victim may notice that something is wrong by checking out the URL displayed by the status line and the location line. The former problem was easily overcome by embedding JavaScript statements to overwrite the status line. When the victim points the mouse to a link with a forged URL, the status line still shows the original URL. The JavaScript statement used is `onMouseOver="self.status='faked link';return true"`. This is added to the tag that has the hyperlink for which the status line is to display the desired link instead of the real link whenever the mouse is over it. The latter problem is more subtle. If the victim carefully reads the location address, he/she will surely understand that the contacted server is not the right one. A partial solution is to build up URLs that are similar to the real ones, except for a small detail. It is likely that the victim will only look carefully at the last part of the URL, skipping the first part. One possibility, which was suggested in [4], is to register a domain name with the DNS that is close to the name of the site where the page is to be replaced. For instance, one could replace the letter "b" in bank with the letter "d" in the attacker site.

6   Conclusions

In this paper several versions of two powerful attacks have been presented. The first versions can be accomplished by monitoring thread names, which translates to applet and page names. In the dossier attack the use of applets with distinct names in web pages, makes it possible to identify the site the user is browsing. The man-in-the-middle attack assumes that the target page has an applet, which will be identified at the time the user requests the targeted page. The current trend on the Internet is towards increasing the number of pages with embedded applets and the number of applets on a page is also increasing. As a result, the set of applets in a page is more likely to uniquely identify the page. Thus, as Java applets become more widely used the two attacks become even more of a threat.

In later versions, interaction between Java applets and JavaScript functions is exploited to deliver even more powerful attacks, since the attacks are no longer limited to pages with embedded applets. This time a flaw in JavaScript is used by the spy applet to identify the pages visited by the user.

The two attacks are very easy to implement, and they do not require special resources. The dossier attack only needs a place that serves the World Wide Web, and the man-in-the-middle attack needs the same plus it needs to be able to set a CGI for collecting the form information.

The original dossier attack is similar to the DoubleClick cookie scenario in that they both can only build partial dossiers. The original version of the dossier attack reported in this paper is only able to identify and log pages if they have embedded applets with meaningful names. Similarly, the DoubleClick cookie attack only logs pages of sites that are affiliated with DoubleClick; that is, it logs only pre-marked pages. Thus, the cookie attack has a specific target and each of the target pages need to be marked, which is more difficult to implement. In contrast, the dossier attack is general purpose and requires no changes to the pages that our logged. The dossier attack is also more personalized, since the user is identified by his/her e-mail address, rather than by only an identification number. Moreover, the final version of the dossier attack is able to identify and log all pages that are visited.

The man-in-the-middle attack is much easier to implement than the web spoofing attack [4], since it is not as intrusive as the web spoofing attack. Also, it does not require a special server to understand and dynamically process the requested URLs. Network spoofing is a very powerful technique, but one of the goals for the experiments reported in this paper were that the attacks would be, although very threatening, very easy to implement so that a programmer could implement them without the need for sophisticated tools or special resources.

The two attacks described in this paper and other experiments that the Reliable Software Group has run lead to the conclusion that although much has been done to improve the security of browsers, much more has to be done to reach a sufficient level of confidence. Java is a reasonable starting point, since it has overcome many of the basic security flaws of other conventional languages. At the same time the experiments reported in this paper have demonstrated that even a "secure" language cannot suffice to solve all security problems. Every component of the environment has to be designed to address security. More importantly, each component needs to be aware of the features of the other components in the environment. In this paper it has been shown that the combined use of not-so-bad features of different tools can support the design of very dangerous attacks.

In addition to Java, these experiments have examined JavaScript and cookie technologies by Netscape. JavaScript was designed to give an easy to program environment for Internet developers both to the client side embedded in HTML language and to the server side, where it is called LiveWire, which is used like a CGI. This requirement of being flexible and easy to program subjects JavaScript to many security flaws as per [3]. LiveConnect technology is another example of opening the way to security problems, since the functionality of each of the involved technologies (Java, JavaScript and Plug-ins) is extended. The experiments reported here show how Java in combination with JavaScript support the design of threatening attacks. Cookies were introduced to store and retrieve information on the client side. As discussed in [12] it is possible to use this information to cross reference HTML pages and build dossiers that violate user privacy. The lesson learned is that adding even small features without thorough analysis can open serious security flaws in the whole environment.

For these experiments several versions of the two most popular browsers: Netscape Navigator and Microsoft Explorer were used. Both are aware of the security problems, and both have many optional features that provide better security. However, because these options result in not enabling Java and JavaScript at all or in popping up many annoying warning windows, it is believed that most users are likely to disable the security options. This is a typical example of the trade off between ease of use and security. If the security features are not user friendly, they will not be used.

7   Future Work

This paper has presented the preliminary results of ongoing research that has the final goal of developing properties for secure browsers and procedures for secure browsing.

Other experiments are currently being designed and run. Some are addressing new areas and others are improving on the experiments described in this paper. The man-in-the-middle attack could be improved by taking over the browser. This improved attack exploits the ability of JavaScript to open a new browser without any menu, toolbar, status bar, etc. This is accomplished by using the method `window.open()` with the option `toolbar=no`. The blueprint of the attack is similar to the one described in Section 5.2, except that the second browser is opened as an empty window that shows a page that includes an applet that paints the entire browser window to simulate the browser that is being used. Thus, for Netscape browsers the applet will paint a menu, a location field and toolbars on the top of the window, a scroll bar if necessary, and status bar and security key, broken or not, on the bottom of the window. The result is that the user will see this new window as a new complete browser. From that time on, any interaction between the user and the faked browser will be processed locally by the spy applet and any information will be forwarded to the attacker server through a socket connection. This represents a bigger threat since the victim is completely in the control of the attacker. The attacker applet can act on behalf of the user to perform any transaction. Of course this attack requires much more work on the part of the spy applet to follow the mouse, to respond appropriately to slider moves, etc.

Future plans are to continue collecting information on known attacks and on countermeasures for these attacks and to continue with the preliminary experiments and develop new attacks. The objective is to categorize the browser attacks to determine information such as what resources are needed to exercise the attack, what browsers it works on and why, and what countermeasures could detect and possibly thwart the attack. The process of determining what classification schemes to use when categorizing the attacks is a critical part of the research, for it is only by working with the actual attack scenarios that the appropriate classification schemes become evident. In carrying out some of the preliminary experiments it was discovered that some attacks that were possible when using the Netscape Navigator browser were not possible when using the Microsoft Explorer browser. This is not very surprising, but on further examination it was discovered that the reason that the attack was not successful was due to an implementation error in the Microsoft Explorer browser. Thus, interesting results are sometimes revealed when classifying the attacks.

Finally, based on the understanding gained by analyzing and categorizing the browser attacks and countermeasures, it is expected that properties for secure browsers and procedures for secure browsing will be developed. These two work together, for sometimes by following secure procedures one can work as securely with a less secure browser as with one with a higher level of security assurance. That is, there may be many tradeoffs between implementing secure features or enforcing the user to follow secure browsing procedures. The authors of [4] present a procedural approach that users can use to detect that they are browsing a pseudo page. They suggest that "when the mouse is held over a Web link [on the page], the status line displays the URL the link points to. Thus, the victim might notice that a URL has been rewritten." However, in that same paper they also mention that this function can be blocked. In fact, the second experiment reported in this paper demonstrates this. That is, the spy applet can display anything in the status line, including the name of the desired link in place of the false link that actually exists. This example demonstrates a procedural approach that is not sufficient. In addition, the property that placing the mouse over an applet always displays the link for that applet, which was overridden in the experiment, is an example of a property that should always be preserved in a secure browser.

References

1. Drew Dean, Edward W. Felten, and Dan S. Wallach, Java Security: From HotJava to Netscape and Beyond, Proc. of 1996 IEEE Symposium on Security and Privacy, (http://www.cs.princeton.edu/sip/pub/secure96.html).
2. Flavio De Paoli, Andre L. Dos Santos, and Richard A. Kemmerer, Vulnerability of "Secure" Web Browsers, Proceedings of the 20th National Information Systems Security Conference, Baltimore, MD, USA, October 6-10, 1997.
3. Digicrime, Online Security Experiments, Digicrime, Inc., (http://www.digicrime.com).
4. Edward W. Felten, Dirk Balfanz, Drew Dean, and Dan S. Wallach, Web Spoofing: An Internet Con Game, Proceedings of the 20th National Information Systems Security Conference, Baltimore, MD, USA, October 6-10, 1997, (http://www.cs.princeton.edu/sip/pub/spoofing.html).
5. James Gosling, Bill Joy, and Guy Steele, The Java Language Specification, ISBN 0-201-63451-1, The Java Series, Addison Wesley, 1996, (http://www.nge.com/home/java/spec10/index.html).
6. Jason Levitt, Internetview: An Application Infrastructure, Information Week, June 1996, (http://techweb.cmp.com/iw/582/82iojl.html).
7. Tim Lindholm and Frank Yellin, The Java Virtual Machine Specification, ISBN 0-201-63452-X, The Java Series, Addison Wesley, 1996.
8. Netscape, "LiveConnect," Netscape web site, 1997, http://home.netscape.com/comprod/products/navigator   /version_3.0/   building_blocks/liveconnect/index.html.
9. D. Martin, S. Rajagopalan and A. Rubin, "Blocking Java Applets at the Firewall," in Proceedings of the InternetSociety Symposium on Network and Distributed System Security, February 10-11, 1997.
10. Jim Roskind, Navigator 2.02 Security-Related FAQ, May 1996, (http://home.netscape.com/newsref/std/java_security_faq.html).
11. Siemens, "Embedding Java into smart card ICs", SPECTRUM, Siemens Components Magazine, April 1997, (http://w2.siemens.de/components/com9704/04spect.htm#VIER).
12. Lincoln D. Stein, WWW Security Faq, version 1.3.7, March 30, 1997, (http://www.genome.wi.mit.edu/WWW/faqs/www-security-faq.html).

Author Index